Classroom Lessons

Classroom Lessons: Integrating Cognitive Theory and Classroom Practice

edited by Kate McGilly

A Bradford Book
The MIT Press
Cambridge, Massachusetts
London, England

First MIT Press paperback edition, 1996

This book was printed and bound in the United States of America.

Library of Congress Cataloging-in-Publication Data

Classroom lessons : integrating cognitive theory and classroom
  practice / edited by Kate McGilly.
    p. cm.
  A Bradford book.
  Includes bibliographical references and index.
  ISBN 0-262-13300-8 (HB), 0-262-63168-7 (PB)
  1. Learning, Psychology of. 2. Cognitive learning theory.
3. Education—Experimental methods. I. McGilly, Kate.
LB1060.C52 1994
370.15′2—dc20   93-43187
                                                                            CIP

Contents

Contributors

Carl Bereiter
Ontario Institute for Studies in Education

John Bransford and members of the Learning Technology Center
Vanderbilt University

Ann L. Brown
University of California at Berkeley

John T. Bruer
James S. McDonnell Foundation

Joseph C. Campione
University of California at Berkeley

Robbie Case
Stanford University

Howard Gardner
Harvard University

Irene W. Gaskins
Benchmark School

Sharon Griffin
Clark University

Earl Hunt
University of Washington

Mara Krechevsky
Harvard University

Mary Lamon
University of Western Ontario

Jill H. Larkin
Carnegie Mellon University

Kate McGilly
Saint Louis Science Center

Jim Minstrell
Mercer Island High School

Lynn Okagaki
Cornell University

Marlene Scardamalia
Ontario Institute for Studies in Education

Kathryn T. Spoehr
Brown University

Robert J. Sternberg
Yale University

Foreword

Jill H. Larkin

Since the early 1980s, John Bruer (now president of the James S. McDonnell Foundation) and I have shared a vision of serendipity between the new discipline of cognitive science and the pressing problems of practical education. When John assumed his current position in 1986, we planned a program of research support that would: (1) build on advances in cognitive science to improve our ability to offer high-quality and cost-effective education; and (2) enrich the science of cognition through theory-grounded experimental studies of the nature of effective instruction. In 1987 the foundation initiated the Program in Cognitive Studies for Educational Practice, of which I became director. The chapters of this volume report the work of scientists, supported by that program, who have applied the techniques and theories of cognitive science to the complex world of the classroom. I describe here central principles, viewpoints, and techniques that are (largely) shared by the authors of the following chapters who are contributing to this reality.

Cognitive science, a discipline recognized about two decades ago, seeks to describe mechanisms of mind, that is, mechanisms of memory, reasoning, problem solving, and interacting with the environment. Cognitive scientists come from several domains concerned with mechanisms of mind. These include cognitive psychology, artificial intelligence, cultural anthropology, and education. Learning is fundamental to all processes of mind—people acquire new capabilities and get better at them. They learn by practice, by interacting with others and by reading books, as well as by direct experience. Cognitive scientists often separate the "architecture"—the (hypothesized) basic structure of the mind—from the knowledge it contains. A large amount of that knowledge is learned. Thus the mechanisms of learning are possibly the most central mechanisms of mind. In learning, new knowledge must be constructed by each learner, using innate or developed abilities, prior knowledge, and stimuli from the world (including interaction with people, objects, and instructional materials).

The centrality of learning has made for a natural alliance between some researchers in education and in cognitive science.

Our view in 1987 was that cognitive science was an area of research that could have profound benefits for education. However, two major problems prevented cognitive science from having a much more significant impact on education. First, only a limited group of bright, well-trained scientists was working with such problems, and there was a very low influx of new talent. Second, there was a separation of basic research (located in the laboratory) from practical education (located most often in the classroom). Because the field of cognitive science applied to education was extremely small, and because there are potential, immediate applications of existing research, we felt that the resources of the James S. McDonnell Foundation could have considerable impact by initiating a new wave of interest in the important and intellectually fascinating problems of providing quality education. To maximize impact of these resources, the Program in Cognitive Studies for Educational Practice has focused on just two goals. First, it has supported research that either applies results of cognitive science to improve current education, or clarifies the mechanisms of a problem of recognized and demonstrated importance in practical settings. Second, through its postdoctoral fellowships, the Program has sought to attract high-quality new talent to this field.

This emphasis on mechanisms of learning and knowing is reflected often by explicit models of knowledge with corresponding instruction designed to enable learners to build that knowledge. For example, Spoehr (chapter 4) has designed a hypertext system organized by the "conceptual neighborhoods" she feels reflects the structure of relevant historical and literary knowledge. Hunt and Minstrell (chapter 3) characterize physics knowledge in terms of "facets"—small assertions about the physical world. Gardner, Krechevsky, Sternberg, and Okagaki (chapter 5) have developed theories of the practical intelligence needed to survive and thrive in a school (or life) setting.

The instruction described here systematically aims to facilitate acquisition of such well-specified knowledge. For example, Griffin, Case, and Siegler (chapter 2) describe a structure of primitive mathematical knowledge that, they argue, must be present to allow students to learn primary-level mathematics. They have developed a set of games and activities that systematically address all parts of their hypothesized structure.

The explicit characterization of knowledge and learning (the aim of cognitive science) has been extended here to explicit characterization of mechanisms of classroom practice. This work moves beyond the cognitive-science study of knowledge domains (mathematics, physics, language) and learning in constrained laboratory contexts. It begins to address the details of how knowledge can be made learnable in practical instruction. In most cases, the hypothesized mechanisms of practical instruction and learning are tested in school classrooms by teachers in the schools. For example, Griffin, Case, and Siegler develop appealing games to allow young children to build knowledge structures that underlie arithmetic. Spoehr studies mechanisms of navigation and search in her rich hypertext system. These beginning characterizations of the detailed mechanisms of classroom instruction have been tested in classrooms of ordinary size, and with teachers not originally part of the research project.

The nature of the knowledge addressed arises from analysis of what knowledge is likely to be useful, and often differs profoundly from more traditional curricula. For example, Hunt and Minstrell aim to let students develop the ability to make sense of phenomena and of the physics principles that describe them. There is less emphasis on quantitative problem solving. Many projects explicitly seek to teach knowledge and skills for better learning. Brown and Campione (chapter 9) and Scardamalia, Bereiter, and Lamon (chapter 8) interweave the teaching of science with the teaching of skills for learning and communicating. Gardner and Sternberg address practical intelligence for interacting with people and with knowledge sources in schools. Gaskins (chapter 6) has exploited a similar approach systematically to enable both teachers and learners to focus on learning strategies across a range of topics, from using a set of base words as analogies for learning new words, to developing the habit of writing down homework assignments and keeping an orderly set of school materials.

This work thus makes a break with much educational practice in which knowledge goals may be loosely defined ("Appreciates . . .", "Understands . . .") or described as a list of small objectives without the links that might coalesce them into a coherent and usable knowledge structure.

The premise that learners each construct new knowledge using cues from the environment highlights the fact that other students are a large and knowledge-rich part of the school environment. Scardamalia, Bereiter, and Lamon place this collaborative development of joint knowledge at the center of their instructional methods. Brown and Campione use students as a major source of instruction, and demonstrate how interaction between students comes to be the dominant form of interaction in their classrooms. Hunt and Minstrell formulate their instruction as a set of questions and experiments, with the teacher guiding students in formulating theories that are self-consistent and account for observations.

Despite the emphasis on students constructing their own knowledge, this instruction is very far from free-wheeling discovery learning (a distinction discussed clearly by Brown and Campione). There is no assumption that children will create for themselves the entire store of human knowledge. Instead the premise is that knowledge is incorporated into the mind through action—through posing questions and developing answers and through interacting with and interpreting the environment. Passive reading or listening may develop reading or listening knowledge, but it is unlikely to foster useful knowledge of mathematics or history.

If new knowledge is constructed using preexisting knowledge, then it is crucial that instructional materials and activities be well matched to the learners' existing knowledge. For example, Griffin, Case, and Siegler describe a structure of primitive mathematical knowledge that they argue must be present to allow students to learn primary-level mathematics. The goal is to begin with the existing knowledge of many low-SES preschoolers, and to enable them to build knowledge that will allow them to learn from primary-level mathematics instruction. Hunt and Minstrell base their physics instruction on research explicating common "misconceptions," widely held beliefs about the physical world that do not correspond to the parsimonious and general theories that characterize physics. Typically these misconceptions contain grains of truth. Hunt and Minstrell encourage students to start with their own ideas, and through careful observation and hard thinking, to see how those ideas can become more accurate and self-consistent.

Technology is not a central focus of this book, although several of the projects involve computers. The focus is on tuning the learning environment to the knowledge to be conveyed as well as to the learning capabilities of the students. Thus the heart of this work is the content and nature of instruction, and not its presentation. Where computers are used in these projects, they are used in ways that flow from this emphasis. For example, Spoehr organizes a hypertext environment to reflect her theoretical concept of conceptual neighborhoods. In Brown and Campione's work, students use computers to develop instructional materials. These materials are a vehicle through which each student thinks concretely about new knowledge; they are an external representation of this knowledge, which makes them available for comment by others—thus making the knowledge structure itself a topic of study and reflection. Hunt and Minstrell have developed an interactive computer program based on the "facets" that make up their knowledge structure. On the basis of students' responses to questions posed by the system, it can "diagnose" what facets of knowledge seem to correspond to the students' knowledge. As this knowledge becomes explicit, it can be examined both by the student and the instructor. Scardamalia, Bereiter, and Lamon use a computer system as database for storing knowledge as it is developed by the student community.

The work reported in this volume has begun to make real the dream of mutually beneficial interaction between cognitive science and education that John Bruer and I had envisioned.

Preface

I was a graduate student in a developmental psychology program that specialized in information processing approaches to the study of cognitive processes. When writing research papers and journal articles or preparing presentations, my colleagues and I would usually include references to the educational implications of our research. These references tended to be brief and often vague, on the order of "Understanding of X will have an educational impact because X is involved in many of the learning activities in which children are engaged in school." X might have referred to how children choose problem-solving strategies or learn to debug LOGO programs, or how high school students scan a diagram in a mechanics textbook or learn algebra using a computer tutor. Because our graduate program emphasized cognitive science and not educational applications, we did not usually test these claims formally. Nonetheless, common sense told us that cognitive science ought to inform education to some extent.

The research in this volume represents formal tests of the common-sense claim that cognitive theory has much to contribute to educational practice. Moreover, these applications of cognitive theory to improving instruction and student outcomes in the classroom in turn further the development of cognitive theories of learning.

One reviewer of the original proposal for this volume inquired whether the focus of the book was to inform theory or to influence practice. The answer is both.

Acknowledgments

Several people deserve my thanks and my gratitude for providing the many and various kinds of support this project required. In particular I thank John Bruer, who encouraged me to pursue this project in the first place, provided continuous support and counsel throughout all phases of development of this book, and provided very helpful feedback that helped shape the introductory chapter. Elizabeth Stanton and Teri Mendelsohn were patient and considerate editors, and were very responsive to my many and various requests for assistance. Four anonymous reviewers provided frank and thoughtful reactions that helped improve the book. Donna Boyer patiently tackled the laborious process of checking references for me. Lastly, I am especially grateful to John Long, whose confidence in me never flagged, and who provided the day-to-day support that often mattered the most.

INTRODUCTION

Chapter 1

Cognitive Science and Educational Practice: An Introduction

Kate McGilly

Psychological theory and research have been influential forces in educational practice for decades. Cognitive science is a relatively new branch of psychology. Its inception dates back to the 1950s, and its formal inauguration as a science is often associated with the 1972 publication of Newell and Simon's classic work, *Human Problem Solving*. Cognitive science, the science of mind, explores the mechanisms by which people acquire, process, and use knowledge. A science that focuses on knowledge acquisition and use, by definition, has implications for education. This volume illustrates how the educational implications of cognitive science are now being pursued rigorously in attempts to restructure classrooms and schools.

Students do not appear to learn to their full potential. National Assessments of Educational Progress show little or no improvement in performance from year to year, and reveal students' inabilities to cope with tasks that require skills beyond rote execution of procedures or memorization of facts (NAEP 1983, 1988). According to employers and college teachers, whatever students do learn in school does not prepare them well for the workplace or for higher education. Society is demanding more from high school graduates and more from the school experience. Students must know more than how to repeat historical facts and execute rote mathematical procedures. Students need to acquire learning skills that apply across the curriculum, and beyond school as well. This can be accomplished if educational practice is based on what is known about how people learn and reason. Cognitive science provides this base for educational practice (Bruer 1993).

Proponents of educational change argue that changing the educational system for the better will require everything from revamping school and school district management systems, to revising teacher-training standards, to reconsidering the policies and methods by which learning goals are established and evaluated. The contributors to this volume represent researchers who believe effective educational reform requires new educational approaches that incorporate what cognitive scientists know about learning and instruction. The findings of cognitive science can, and should, serve as the foundation for instructional innovations, and as the basis for educational reform. The research described in this volume provides compelling examples of how cognitive science can contribute to educational practice.

This introductory chapter summarizes several theories and methods from cognitive science that are directly relevant to educational practice, and provides examples of their educational application. This summary is intended primarily for the educational practitioner who might be unfamiliar with principles of cognitive science. Following the summary is an overview of the volume's chapters.

Principles of Cognitive Science

To understand cognitive research, one must be familiar with the concepts of information processing, knowledge types and knowledge representation, and human memory.

Information Processing.   Information-processing theory is the central theory of cognitive science. According to this theory, humans are symbol or information processors, much like a computer (cf. Newell and Simon 1972). Information, in the form of symbols or symbolic representations, enters the system and activates particular cognitive pro-cesses that result in physical or mental actions. Cognitive scientists study how information is encoded in symbols or, as they say, represented, the processes that act on and transform information, and the memory capacity limitations that constrain information processing.

Knowledge Types and Knowledge Representations.   Cognitive scientists distinguish between two major types of knowledge, "declarative" and "procedural" knowledge. Declarative knowledge is knowledge about the world and its properties. Procedural knowledge is knowledge of how to do things. Cognitive scientists also refer to "metacognitive" knowledge. Metacognitive knowledge is knowledge about one's own knowledge, skills, and abilities. Examples are knowing what one knows about poisonous snakes, about how to summarize a text, or about one's proficiency at long division. Authors in this volume also often refer to the metacognitive skills or strategies needed to monitor and regulate one's own learning. Examples include planning activities (e.g., planning which study strategy to use), monitoring activities during learning (e.g., monitoring one's understanding as one reads a passage of text), and checking outcomes (e.g., comparing an actual outcome to a predicted one) (Brown 1987).

Knowledge is organized and stored in memory in a number of possible representational forms. It can be stored as isolated and disconnected pieces of information. This is often the result of learning by rote. Imagine memorizing a list of the names of ten dinosaurs, a list of the types of food dinosaurs ate, and a list of dinosaur defense mechanisms. Knowledge in this form is useful in limited and isolated situations, specifically answering questions about the names, food types, or defense mechanisms of dinosaurs (e.g., name five foods dinosaurs ate). All too often, knowledge that students acquire in school seems to be in this form.

In contrast, knowledge can be organized in large, interconnected bodies, where pieces of knowledge are conceptually linked to other pieces. A network of dinosaur information might include names of dinosaurs, similarities and differences in their physical characteristics, habitats, food sources, and predators, and information about evolutionary forces and conditions that led to their extinction. The interconnections can extend further; for example, information about dinosaur habitats and defense mechanisms could be linked to information about other animals' habitats and defense mechanisms. The critical difference is not the amount of information, but how the information is organized. An interconnected knowledge network can be used for a broader range of cognitive activities, including answering a wide variety of domain-specific questions, drawing analogies, making inferences, and generalizing to new content areas.

Experts and novices in a knowledge domain (e.g., dinosaurs or physics) differ not only in the amount and organization of knowledge they have; they also differ in what they choose to represent. Novices often represent and connect pieces of domain knowledge in terms of surface-level features. Experts organize information in terms of deeper-level, conceptual features. For example, Chi, Feltovich, and Glaser (1981) asked physics novices and experts to categorize physics word problems according to similarities in solution procedures, and then to explain their categorization scheme. Results indicated that novices tend to group problems in terms of the objects in the problems (e.g., inclined planes, pulleys)—surface-level features. Experts grouped problems in terms of the physics principles embodied in the problem (conservation of energy, Newton's laws)—deep-level features. These differences in representational level are also linked to differences in experts' and novices' abilities to reason about and solve physics problems.

Memory.   Cognitive researchers posit that we have at least two types of memory stores; working memory (WM), and long-term memory (LTM) (Atkinson and Shiffrin 1968; Baddeley and Hitch 1974). WM is a limited-capacity store that contains information that is active for current processing. Information enters WM from the external world through the senses, and through activation and access of related information in LTM. Information moves in and out of WM relatively fast (within seconds) unless continual processing efforts keep it active. In contrast, information in LTM is in principle stored indefinitely and retrievable any time.

Learning occurs when information is transferred from WM to LTM. A mechanism called "elaboration" is important in this transfer process. *Elaboration* is the process of using facts stored in LTM to embellish on new, to-be-learned information; this connects new information to existing information, making it more memorable (Anderson 1982; Anderson and Reder 1979). Elaboration provides the learner with multiple "hooks" or routes for accessing information in LTM. Elaboration is a key process in building interconnected knowledge networks; information acquired without elaboration tends to be in the form of less memorable, isolated pieces of information.

Elaboration is at the root of laboratory-based studies that show it is easier to learn new information when it is linked to existing, related, knowledge already in LTM (Anderson 1982; Chase and Simon 1973a, 1973b). It partly explains why it is better to acquire procedural knowledge in the context in which it is to be used, as opposed to isolated contexts unrelated to those in which the skill will be used (e.g., learning to repair a car engine from studying a book rather than from practicing on an actual engine) (Anderson 1982). Without connections to the applied context, the procedural skill will not be associated with, and hence will not be used in, appropriate situations.

Methods of Cognitive Science

Three techniques widely used in cognitive research and featured in the following chapters are task analysis, analysis of verbal protocols, and simulations.

Task Analysis.   Task analysis involves detailed, fine-grained examination of performance on a task or problem. A task analysis provides testable hypotheses about the knowledge, skills, and psychological processes required to complete the task (Resnick 1976). Figure 1.1 shows a detailed analysis of the task of counting a fixed, ordered set of objects (Resnick, Wang, and Kaplan 1973). "The top box . . . shows

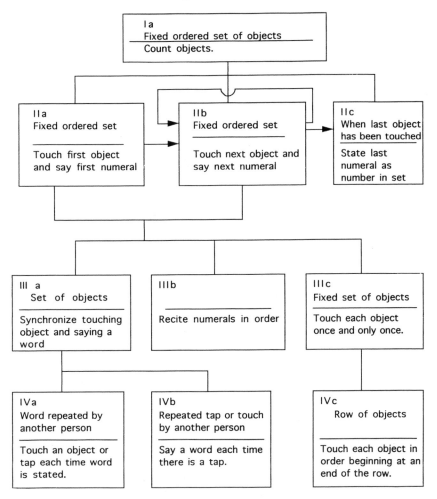

Figure 1.1
Analysis of the task of counting a fixed set of objects. Adapted from Resnick, Wang, and Kaplan 1973. Reprinted with permission.

the task being analyzed, the entry above the line describing the presented stimulus and the entry below the line the expected response. The second row . . . shows a hypothesized sequence of behaviors engaged in as the presented task is performed. Arrows indicate a temporally organized procedure. The [third and fourth rows] identify capabilities that are thought to be either necessary to performance . . . or helpful in learning the main task" (Resnick 1976, 65–66).

Verbal Protocol Analysis.   A verbal protocol consists of an "on-line" verbal description of what people are doing—what they are thinking about, what actions they are planning—while they solve a problem or complete a task. Here is an example of a problem and a student's verbal protocol for solving it:

> *Problem:* Twenty-nine students went on a field trip. Each van could hold 8 students. How many vans were needed?
>
> *Protocol:* I wrote all the 29 kids that there are, and then there are 8 vans, and how many vans are needed. No, there were 29 kids. Each van could hold 8 students. You could only have 8 students. You could count out 8 and circle them. So you would need 4, 5 vans, but you would have 4 of the vans that could hold the 8 kids, and then you would need an extra van that would hold the 4 extra kids that are left over.   (Swing, Stoiber, and Peterson 1988, 158)

A verbal protocol provides a "window" that looks in on what features of the problem people attend to, what factors influence their decisions about problem-solving steps to take, and what different strategies they have at their disposal. It reveals to the investigator what might be going on in a subject's WM during problem solving. Protocol analysis is particularly useful for examining differences in how experts versus novices reason about particular topics. For example, in the Chi, Feltovich, and Glaser (1981) study described above, protocols from physics novices and experts revealed differences in how they think about physics word problems and provided insights into expert and novice differences in problem-solving approaches.

Computer Simulation.   Computer simulations are computer programs designed to solve problems using the same information-processing techniques that a human would. They serve as both tests and validations of hypothesized models of people's thinking. A simulation is programmed according to a cognitive model which often is derived from prior task and protocol analyses. The programmer codes into the simulation the facts and concepts that constitute a particular task or problem, and the subject's declarative and procedural knowledge of the problem, as ascertained directly or inferred from the protocols. If the simulation behaves like the person did in the same problem situation, then the skills and knowledge built into the simulation, and the rules the simulation uses to solve the problem, provide an explanation or theory of how the human cognitive system solves the problem. Often, though, simulations go beyond informing us about how a particular task is performed to give us general insights into learning and skill development (e.g., Siegler and Shrager 1984).

Educational Applications of Cognitive Principles and Methods

Cognitive scientists study processes that produce complex human behaviors, including behaviors that occur in instructional situations—learning, reasoning, problem solving, studying, and teaching. In a general sense, all cognitive research has implications for education. Some general examples from research or precursors of research presented in this volume will illustrate the potential educational applications of the cognitive principles and methods described above. The subsequent chapters will present more explicit examples in a variety of educational settings.

Information Processing.   An information-processing approach to educational research shifts attention away from the products or outcomes of learning towards the processes involved in learning and teaching.

Annemarie Palincsar and Ann Brown (1984) recognized the need to teach children the fundamental skills needed for reading with comprehension. They used an information-processing approach to develop an instructional technique called reciprocal teaching (see also Brown and Campione, chapter 9; Bruer, chapter 10). Reciprocal teaching teaches comprehension-fostering and comprehension-monitoring processes that facilitate learning from text. The technique was based on an analysis of the cognitive and metacognitive skills or strategies a person applies to comprehend a written text. Palincsar and Brown identified six expert strategies: understanding the purpose of reading; activating relevant background knowledge; allocating attention to relevant rather than irrelevant content; evaluating content for internal consistency and compatibility with prior knowledge; monitoring comprehension as reading progresses; and drawing and testing inferences (Palincsar and Brown 1984). They developed activities that engage students in acquiring these strategies, and a process that teaches children to use these strategies while trying to comprehend text. The key activities are summarizing, questioning, clarifying, and predicting.

In reciprocal teaching, a teacher works with a small group of children as they discuss a text. Initially the teacher leads the discussions, models the key activities, encourages all the children to engage in the activities and to participate in the discussion, and provides feedback. Gradually, the students assume responsibility for leading the discussions, and the teacher's role becomes one of providing guidance and praise. Reciprocal teaching has proven immensely successful in improving students' reading comprehension (for details, see Palincsar and Brown 1984).

Reciprocal teaching is a classic example of an application of the information-processing approach to an educational problem. Such applications result in instructional programs that emphasize the cognitive processes that underlie desired learning outcomes. As the chapters of this volume demonstrate, this approach also fundamentally changes the roles of students, who become active participants in their own learning, and teachers, who become guides and mentors, or co-constructors of knowledge rather than distributors of information to passive recipients. This can profoundly alter the structure and course of classroom activities.

Knowledge Representation. Research on knowledge representation is also useful to educators. Studies of experts and novices in a particular domain, such as the physics experts and novices described above, elucidate the differences between expert and novice representations. Novice representations can inform educators about where their students start from. Expert representations present explicit instructional goals.

Kathryn Spoehr (chapter 4) reasoned that high school students would think more like history and literature experts if they organized their history and literature knowledge the way experts do. To help them do this, she had experts create a computer-based hypermedia[1] database of information about American history and literature that was organized and interconnected in a way analogous to their own mental representations of this knowledge. Interacting with the hypermedia system encouraged students to learn the information in the system, and more important, to develop an organizational structure for this knowledge like the experts.

Memory. Memory processes are, of course, fundamental to educational processes. Processes that transfer information from WM to LTM are particularly important. Teaching methods that stimulate memory processes, such as elaboration described above, can improve learning outcomes.

Teaching methods that stress connecting new information with prior knowledge are classroom applications of the principle of elaboration. Teachers can apply such an approach if they (1) identify their students' prior knowledge; (2) create learning situations that overlap with it; and (3) provide opportunities for students to see the connections. Hunt and Minstrell (chapter 3) apply such an approach in their instructional technique. They administer preinstruction quizzes to determine their students' prior conceptions about physical phenomena (derived mostly from their real-world experiences with physical objects). Subsequent instruction builds on the students' prior physics concepts. For example, the teacher uses a real-world example to introduce and reason about a concept from formal physics. Classroom discussions, where students reason about physical phenomena, help students connect what they are learning to what they already know.

Elaboration is also at the root of instructional techniques that teach procedural skills in contexts similar to those in which the skills should be used. This is one goal of the Cognitive Technology Group at Vanderbilt (CTGV) project (chapter 7). Students learn to apply mathematics to complex, real-world problems by solving complex, real-world mathematics problems, not by doing meaningless, artificial one-line word problems as found in most textbooks. In this way, students acquire the ability to define problems, plan solution strategies, consider alternative answers, and develop skills relevant to the way mathematics is actually used in daily life.

Finally, elaboration is involved in the metacognitive skills stressed in some educational programs described below. Monitoring one's comprehension, for example, involves searching LTM for related knowledge that can help make sense of new knowledge.

Irene Gaskins's instructional program (chapter 6), teaches students how, when, and why to use metacognitive strategies. Students learn how their WM and LTM function, and how using strategies such as drawing inferences, generating questions, and monitoring comprehension helps transfer information from WM into LTM through processes such as elaboration.

Task Analysis. Task analysis can contribute to instruction to the extent that it (1) analyzes tasks that are instructionally relevant; (2) yields task descriptions that are psychologically meaningful and task elements which can be taught effectively; and (3) recognizes distinctions between the performance of experts and novices (Resnick 1976). When it meets these criteria, a task analysis can be used in planning what to teach and how to teach it, and in diagnosing whether a student lacks some of the prerequisite skills and knowledge needed for a certain task. The task analysis can serve as an idealized model of how the student should perform and what instructional goals the teacher should strive for.

Task analysis was instrumental in each project in this volume. The CTGV (chapter 7), for example, analyzed the task of solving complex mathematics word problems; ones that cannot be solved by rote application of arithmetic algorithms. The analysis suggested a four-stage process: identify the problem, define it, generate subgoals and subproblems, and solve them. The CTGV studies revealed which stages students have difficulty with, and helped the research team devise instruction on how to plan, formulate, and solve complex, real-world mathematics problems.

Gardner, Krechevsky, Sternberg, and Okagaki (chapter 5) analyzed a considerably larger task: succeeding in middle school. Their theoretical analysis of success in school suggested the need for capacities that go well beyond traditional academic skills (how to read, write, and do arithmetic) to include skills for understanding the demands of the school context (e.g., teachers, peers, and assignments). They refer to these as "practical intelligences for school." The analysis formed the basis of a curriculum to foster these skills in middle school students.

Protocol Analysis.   Protocol analysis, a complex, labor-intensive technique, is impractical for direct use in classroom settings. However, encouraging students to verbalize as they plan to solve problems, as they solve them, or just after they have solved them, is a technique that can benefit both teachers and students. Students' verbalizations often reveal more about what they do and do not know than a teacher can determine from answers on tests. These verbalizations can therefore be a useful diagnostic tool. Also, verbalizing thoughts or beliefs, especially in the context of group discussions, allows students to reflect and expand on their own and other students' understanding.

Verbalization is a key component in several of the instructional programs in this volume (Hunt and Minstrell, chapter 3; CTGV, chapter 7; Scardamalia, Bereiter, and Lamon, chapter 8; Brown and Campione, chapter 9). In Hunt and Minstrell's physics instruction program, more that 50 percent of class time is spent in group discussions about physics problems and the results of classroom physics experiments. Discussions are an important vehicle for getting students to reflect on their own understanding and for helping teachers decide what concepts or ideas they need to focus on as instruction proceeds.

Verbalizations are a principal component in both reciprocal teaching (Palincsar and Brown 1984) and in the Communities of Learners project (Brown and Campione, chapter 9). Classroom discourse involving questioning, clarifying, summarizing, predicting, and criticizing is the primary way students construct knowledge. It is also the vehicle through which they acquire and develop the metacognitive skills needed for monitoring their own and each other's understanding.

Written protocols, in the form of written questions, explanations, comments, and justifications can serve a similar role. In Scardamalia, Bereiter, and Lamon's project (chapter 8), written protocols serve much the same function that verbal discussions do in Brown and Campione's classrooms in helping students and teachers generate and monitor knowledge and understanding.

Simulations.   A simulation based on a computer model provides explicit and detailed information about the factual and procedural knowledge needed to solve problems in particular domains and can therefore serve as an instructional guide. Simulations can aid teachers in setting realistic expectations about what students with specific skills can do, and serve as a potential diagnostic tool for identifying what knowledge and skills students already have and what they should acquire. Hunt and Minstrell's (chapter 3) program to teach high school physics includes a tool called the DIAGNOSER, which has some features of a simulation. The DIAGNOSER is a computer program that contains information about how people with different levels of physics knowledge and understanding (from naive to expert physicist) answer physics questions and justify their answers. The DIAGNOSER compares students' reasoning to its own expert database, and gives the students feedback on the consistency of their answers and reasoning. The DIAGNOSER also keeps a record of each student's problem solving. Thus, both the students and the teachers gain greater insights into the student's understanding than could be revealed through more traditional pencil-and-paper tests. This helps the teacher plan instructional activities that address particular areas in which students might be having difficulties.

Clearly, issues central to cognitive science—knowledge and skill acquisition, problem solving, memory—are relevant to educational issues, and the theories and methods of the psychology laboratory can be applied in educational settings. Yet there remains a wide gap between the basic science of cognition and the applied practice of classroom teachers. For the educational community to benefit from cognitive research, efforts must be made to bridge the gap.

Bridging the Gap: From Laboratory to Classroom

Each of the following chapters describes an extension and application of cognitive research to issues of educational significance in actual classroom settings, and each involves close collaborations among researchers and teachers. And, as is usually the case with compelling research, the practical applications and the teacher-researcher collaborations in turn prompt further questions about cognitive theory and its role in educational settings. The further challenges facing these researchers and other members of this research community are addressed in several of the chapters, particularly in the final one.

The volume is divided into three sections: (1) applications of cognitive research to teaching specific content areas, (2) applications for learning across the curriculum, and (3) applications that challenge traditional conceptions of classroom-based learning environments. The concluding chapter reviews the evidence in support of restructuring schools, starting from a cognitive research base, and discusses future challenges both to cognitive research and classroom practice.

Applications in Specific Content Areas
The three chapters in the first section describe instructional programs to improve knowledge and reasoning in three specific content areas: first grade arithmetic (Griffin, Case, and Siegler), high school physics (Hunt and Minstrell), and American history and literature (Spoehr). Two of these use technological innovations. Each instructional program and the associated technology evolved from cognitive research on how students learn, reason, and represent information. In these chapters, cognitive theory also informs the students' assessment and the evaluation of the instructional programs.

Griffin, Case, and Siegler's Rightstart project (chapter 2) is a classic example of how cognitive science can guide educational practice. Their previous research had revealed that large proportions of kindergartners from low-income, inner-city communities lacked basic number knowledge—what they refer to as the "central conceptual structure" for understanding early mathematics—that their peers from middle-income families possessed. This knowledge gap put them at a disadvantage from the very start of their formal education.

Griffin and her colleagues developed a curriculum that successfully teaches kindergartners the number knowledge they need to succeed at first grade arithmetic. The curriculum and evaluation were directly based on cognitive research about how number knowledge develops. One component of the prerequisite central conceptual structure for early mathematics understanding is a mental number line (see figure 2.2, below), which resembles a ruler numbered from 1 to 10. A child with such a mental representation can count from 1 to 10, make one-to-one mappings between objects and the numbers in the counting sequence, and tell that the size of a set of objects is indicated by the cardinal number assigned to it through counting. These skills are fundamental for solving first grade addition and subtraction problems. They are also among the skills that the low-income kindergartners lacked. The curriculum consisted of interactive games such as the Number Line Game that gave children practice with exactly those skills. Similarly, the Number Knowledge test, one of the tests used to assess children's number knowledge prior to and after the Rightstart instruction, assessed whether children acquired the knowledge implicit in the conceptual structure (e.g., knowledge of what number comes after 7, or of which number is bigger, 7 or 9).

Hunt and Minstrell (chapter 3) began with a theory of how students organize their "naive" knowledge of physical phenomena and how existing physical knowledge influences learning high school physics. This theoretical foundation, together with Minstrell's experience as an expert physics teacher, formed the basis of a multistep teaching program for high school physics that bridges the gap between naive and expert physics understanding, and connects school physics with the everyday world. The program has four parts: (1) the preinstruction quiz, (2) the benchmark lesson, (3) experimentation and discussion, and (4) assessment. The preinstruction quiz requires students to answer open-ended physics questions. The quiz gets the students to think about the issues they will cover in class, and informs the teacher about students' existing knowledge on the topic. In the benchmark lesson, a physics problem is presented, the students discuss it, predict answers, and give rationales for their answers. Then the solution to the problem is demonstrated, and the students discuss different interpretations of the results, and what the results tell them about the accuracy of their theories. After the benchmark lesson, additional discussions and laboratory experiments allow students to further explore their ideas and theories, extract general principles, and apply them in different contexts. Finally, there is an assessment stage. This involves the DIAGNOSER program described above. The DIAGNOSER enables individual students to assess their own understanding of the lesson's key concepts.

The majority of students in this instructional program show improved ability to reason like physicists after the instruction; they reason about physical situations using formal scientific principles, and they understand when a problem calls for a particular physics equation and why. These students also outperform students from more conventional physics classes on their final exams.

Spoehr (chapter 4), in collaboration with experienced classroom teachers, has developed a system to help students to understand the complex and multiple relationships that link American history and literature—bodies of social studies knowledge often taught in isolation. The system, called ACCESS (American Culture in Context: Enrichment for Secondary Schools), is a hypermedia system (see note 1 below) containing material in the form of text, video images, audio selections, computer graphics, and animation on American history and literature from 1607 to 1970. The information is organized into themes and subtopics, each of which is linked to other conceptually related themes and subtopics.

The theoretical framework guiding the development of this system is a cognitive analysis of the knowledge representations of experts engaged in historical and literary thinking. Spoehr's hypermedia system encourages students and teachers to develop a structural organization that links concepts and the relationships among concepts. This kind of organization is associated with creative, productive, and expertlike reasoning. After using the ACCESS system to prepare for class discussions or assignments, students did in fact demonstrate more expertlike and more complete representations of at least one topic they had studied.

In her chapter, Spoehr also examines some of the constraints cognitive researchers face when doing classroom-based research, particularly when teachers are either unfamiliar with a component of the instructional intervention (such as the technology) or when they are uneasy about deviating from their traditional instructional activities.

Applications for Learning across the Curriculum

The two research projects in the second section have a broader focus: imparting to students cognitive and metacognitive skills that apply across all school domains and that are important to overall school success, but that are not traditionally part of the curriculum—skills such as taking notes, apportioning study time, revising answers, making predictions, and assessing one's own cognitive strengths and applying them effectively. The two projects challenge traditional views on the roles of students and teachers: students in terms of what they should be learning and what constitutes "success" and "intelligence" in school, and teachers in terms of what and how they should teach to help their students be successful both in and out of school. The chapter by Gardner, Krechevsky, Sternberg, and Okagaki focuses more on the former; the chapter by Gaskins more on the latter.

The instructional program developed by Gardner, Sternberg, and their colleagues is the result of an amalgamation of two current theories of intelligence: Sternberg's triarchic theory of intelligence and Gardner's theory of multiple intelligences. These two theories emphasize that individuals have different intellectual strengths and weaknesses, and that the extent to which intelligence develops depends in part on the social and cultural contexts in which individuals find themselves. Their program, called Practical Intelligence for School (PIFS), stresses the development of intelligence in areas that go beyond traditional academic disciplines but that are also important for success across the entire school curriculum—areas such as knowing one's own strengths and weaknesses and how to capitalize on the former and improve the latter, knowing how to identify and solve problems, how to take notes, how to take tests, and how to cooperate with others and solve problems in social situations. In one version of the PIFS program, instruction was given as a stand-alone course taught over a semester or school year. A second version consists of infused units, where PIFS skills were taught in the context of social studies, mathematics, reading, and writing classes.

Assessments of students who completed the PIFS program included measures of their understanding of the issues addressed in the PIFS units, how well they learned the skills targeted in the units, and their ability to reflect on the processes or skills involved in particular tasks. Students in the PIFS program outperformed students with no PIFS instruction on all these measures.

As with Spoehr's ACCESS project, Gardner and his colleagues had to contend with variations in how successfully different teachers in different schools implemented the PIFS curriculum. They acknowledge the need for extensive staff development for schools participating in research-based instructional implementations. This issue is taken up as a central component of Irene Gaskins's strategy curriculum project.

Like Gardner et al., Irene Gaskins and the teachers at Benchmark School in Media, Pennsylvania, have developed a program for teaching middle school students about their own learning, thinking, and problem-solving skills and strategies as well as how to apply those skills across the curriculum. The description of Gaskins's project diverges somewhat from the others here in the amount of detail provided about the professional development program that prepared the Benchmark teachers to apply cognitive science in the classroom.

Gaskins describes a unique and extensive research-based professional development process she and the teaching staff at Benchmark School followed to prepare them to meet the challenges of applying the strategies-across-the-curriculum program. The challenges included acquiring knowledge and understanding of cognitive principles and developing new, nontraditional instructional practices. The teachers collaborated and consulted with each other and with educational and cognitive researchers around the United States throughout all stages of their project.

The broad application and long-term success of the types of classroom implementations described in this volume depend on how effectively they can be taken over and applied by regular classroom teachers, without needing the researchers' constant support and monitoring. Gaskins's professional development program is a compelling example of the kind of commitment required from both researchers and teachers to ensure that cognitive research is applied in the classrooms to the mutual satisfaction and benefit of researchers, teachers, *and* students.

Applications that Challenge Traditional Classroom-Based Learning Environments

A basic goal underlying each of the instructional programs described in these chapters is to encourage students to be active, self-directed, and intentional learners. An intentional learner is one for whom learning is a goal rather than an incidental outcome of cognitive activity (Bereiter and Scardamalia 1989). One strategy to achieve this goal is to create innovative new learning environments where students engage in a continual, largely self-directed process of inquiry and knowledge building, and share their knowledge with other members of the "learning community" to which they each belong. The learning community can include students and teachers in their own and other classrooms, as well as people outside the immediate school environment. Projects described in the third section of the book elaborate this strategy.

The "communities of learners" concept is central to the projects of the CTGV (chapter 7), Scardamalia, Bereiter, and Lamon (chapter 8) and Brown and Campione (chapter 9). It is central as a model of how cognitive research can dramatically and positively affect educational practice. It is also an educational model that raises a number of critical questions that the research and education communities will need to address as they continue to develop research-based educational applications: questions about educational goals and about the roles of teachers, students, the learning environment, and the community at large in the educational process.

For the CTGV, the community of learners model evolved over the course of a $5^1/_2$-year project that began with research-based attempts to improve performance on mathematics word problems among fifth and sixth graders. The instructional program, known as *The Adventures of Jasper Woodbury*, is a set of adventures on videodiscs that provides realistic and motivationally challenging contexts in which students identify, formulate, and solve mathematics problems. The project expanded from a program to change one aspect of the math curriculum, to a curriculum approach designed to change the nature of teaching and learning processes in the classroom, and finally to a 9-state, 17-classroom implementation network.

Students who complete the *Jasper* adventures develop complex problem-solving skills, such as the ability to plan solution procedures and generate the subproblems and subgoals required to solve complex, multistep problems. They also develop positive attitudes towards mathematics and their own mathematics abilities.

As the project expanded, so did the CTGV's conception of the learning community. The number and types of people involved in the *Jasper* community grew to include students and teachers in and outside a particular classroom or school, along with educational administrators, parents, and members of the business community.

The Computer Supported Intentional Learning Environment (CSILE) is a computer environment that stores the combined knowledge of a group (e.g., all the students in a single classroom) in a communal database (Scardamalia, Bereiter, and Lamon, chapter 8). All CSILE users can access the entire database, contribute text and graphical notes to the database, and add comments and queries about other people's notes. A learning community evolves as a natural by-product of the CSILE system. CSILE makes knowledge communal property, and makes the construction of knowledge a social event, shared and mediated by others. By design, therefore, CSILE changes a classroom of individual learners into a knowledge-building community.

Students who use CSILE develop cognitive and metacognitive skills as they reason about and contribute to the communal knowledge base. They also come to apply these cognitive and metacognitive skills as they reason about and reflect on their own knowledge and understanding. CSILE students report that their classroom activities are directed more towards learning than to completing tasks or assignments. There is evidence that CSILE students independently pursue collaborative knowledge-building activities. It is membership in a community of learners that seems to drive these effects.

The community of learners concept was built into Ann Brown and Joe Campione's instructional program from its inception. The goal of their program is to create a learning environment that takes advantage of and encourages distributed expertise within the environment. In their learning community, members each have expertise in different content areas related to a middle school biology curriculum. Each member is responsible for sharing their expertise with others and for seeking out others whose expertise can further their own understanding and knowledge. Brown and Campione employ several research-based pedagogical techniques to establish and sustain the learning community: reciprocal teaching, the jigsaw classroom, cross-age tutoring, and electronic mail connections with outside experts.

Reciprocal teaching, described above, is a technique for promoting reading comprehension, where small groups of students question, summarize, clarify, and predict as they discuss texts or topics together. The jigsaw method of cooperative learning consists of placing together in small groups students who are each experts on one subtopic, and making all students responsible for sharing their knowledge with the other members of their group (Aronson 1978). Cross-age tutoring involves older, here fifth and sixth grade, students working with younger, here second and third grade, students. Tutoring gives students further opportunities to talk about learning and to be responsible for sharing their knowledge with others, and reinforces the collaborative structures in place in the school. Finally, electronic mail connections to members of the research and scientific communities extends the learning community beyond the school walls.

A big challenge for researchers who develop these new learning environments is to delineate the learning principles that are central to the success of these environments. This is necessary for projects like CSILE or the Community of Learners to be disseminated on the basis of more than surface features (Brown and Campione, chapter 9). Brown and Campione, the CTGV, and Scardamalia and Bereiter are currently attempting to define the learning principles embodied in their learning communities approach. These principles are the building blocks to a new theory of learning, one with direct and important implications for improving schools and broadening learning environments for students and teachers.

As this new learning theory develops, new research questions arise to challenge the research community, including questions about how and why social contexts such as learning communities improve the quality of the learning experience; why group discourse processes are so effective for transmitting knowledge; and what the implications of communities of learners studies are for cognitive science's understanding of individuals' learning processes and of higher-order brain function. In his concluding chapter, John Bruer (chapter 10) elaborates on these and other research questions now facing the research and education communities.

Conclusion

"Classroom Lessons" in this volume's title refers to lessons of two types: there are the lessons that the researchers and their teacher-collaborators developed and applied in classrooms—the interventions, curricula, educational technologies—and perhaps more important, there are the lessons that the research teams themselves learned from their experiences applying cognitive principles in classrooms.

Because of their demonstrated successes, most of the programs described in this volume have already been or may soon be implemented in multiple sites (Griffin, Case, and Siegler, chapter 2; Hunt and Minstrell, chapter 3; Spoehr, chapter 4; Gardner et al., chapter 5; CTGV, chapter 7; Scardamalia, Bereiter, and Lamon, chapter 8; Brown and Campione, chapter 9). Many students, teachers, and educators will therefore benefit from these classroom lessons.

Conversely, the research community has benefitted from the lessons that have arisen from extending their work into the educational arena. These lessons have influenced what the researchers know and what they want to know about learning and, more generally, about our mental functioning. Thus, this volume reports on progress towards a symbiotic union that may bridge the gap between cognitive research and educational practice.

Note

1. A hypermedia system is a computer learning environment in which informational units are in the form of text, video images, computer graphics, animation, and sound. The information is interconnected within the system, and organized along multiple dimensions, so that it can be explored in a variety of ways following those multiple connections (Spiro and Jehng 1990).

PART I

Domain-Specific Applications

Chapter 2

Rightstart: Providing the Central Conceptual Prerequisites for First Formal Learning of Arithmetic to Students at Risk for School Failure

Sharon A. Griffin, Robbie Case, and Robert S. Siegler

A desire to improve mathematics education is not a new phenomenon in the history of U.S. schooling. Although it has been expressed for decades, in various quarters and with varying levels of intensity (Case and Garrett 1992), it assumed significant and widespread proportions in the mid-1980s when the results of international comparisons were widely circulated.

These findings suggested that American children were not acquiring the mathematical knowledge possessed by their Asian peers or the skills needed to succeed in a technologically advanced society (NAEP 1983, 1988). This knowledge gap was found to be minimal in grade one, to become increasingly pronounced as schooling progressed, and was apparent on a wide array of measures that tapped conceptual understanding, as well as knowledge of facts and procedures (Stevenson, Lee, and Stigler 1986; Stigler and Perry 1988). Of significance to the work described in this chapter, this knowledge gap was most pronounced in the performance of American children living in economically deprived inner-city communities (Case 1975; Saxe, Guberman, and Gearhart 1989).

A dominant explanation that was offered for these findings was that the formal learning opportunities provided in American schools are divorced from children's intuitive, informal understandings (see, for example, Ginsburg and Russel 1981; Hiebert 1986). Armed with research findings that accumulated in the 1980s, and that documented the manner in which children's intuitive knowledge of number develops across the school-age years (e.g., Resnick 1989; Siegler and Robinson 1982; Case 1985), the response from the educational community was swift and sure. The National Council of Teachers of Mathematics published a mandate (NCTM 1989b) requiring that mathematics instruction be grounded in children's intuitive knowledge. Several programs that implement this mandate are currently being developed (see, for example, University of Chicago School of Mathematics Project

1990; Resnick, et al. in press; Cobb et al. 1991; Fennema and Carpenter 1989; Kamii 1985). These solutions promise to do much to reduce the knowledge gap described above.

However, in recent cognitive developmental work we have conducted, another, potentially more fundamental, source of the knowledge gap became apparent. Although many children start school with a well-developed intuitive understanding of number (e.g., Hiebert 1986; Case 1985; Siegler and Robinson 1982), not all children do so.

In particular, when tests of conceptual knowledge were administered to groups of kindergarten children attending schools in low-income inner-city communities, a significant number were unable to demonstrate the knowledge possessed by their middle-income peers (Case and Griffin 1990; Griffin, Case, and Capodilupo in press). When tests of procedural knowledge were administered to groups of kindergarten and first grade children in similar communities, a significant number used strategies that were "non-adaptive," that appeared to prevent the development of more adaptive strategies, and that were never found in the strategy choices of their middle-income peers (Siegler in press). If children start school without the intuitive knowledge that is explicitly assumed by the mathematics programs being developed for the 1990s, the risk for school failure may continue, in spite of the excellence of the new programs.

The Rightstart program was designed to remedy this knowledge gap at its source, at the very start of formal schooling. By developing a program to teach the central conceptual prerequisites for first formal learning of arithmetic (i.e., the intuitive knowledge on which success in addition and subtraction depends), we hoped to ensure that all children who had not already acquired the critical knowledge had an opportunity to do so before they started first grade. In the following sections, we describe the research evidence that suggested a need for the Rightstart program, the theoretical framework that was used to develop it, the program itself, and the results that were obtained when this program was implemented over a three-year period.

Research on Young Children's Strategy Use

Information processing research has revealed a great deal about how young children solve arithmetic problems. They appear to use a variety of strategies to do so, including counting from one, counting from the larger addend, decomposing a single problem into two or more simpler ones, and retrieving answers from memory (Fuson 1982; Groen and Parkman 1972; Siegler in press). Choosing wisely among these strategies offers children the opportunity to fit the characteristics of the strategy to the demands of the task. However, not all children make wise choices. Some use fast and easy approaches, even when these approaches have little likelihood of success; others use unnecessarily slow and time-consuming approaches, even when they could succeed with faster and easier ones.

These individual differences in children's strategy choices are apparent as early as first grade. In a series of studies conducted with children from middle income communities, Siegler (1988) examined individual differences in 6-year-olds' strategy choices in addition and subtraction, using the model he had developed and validated earlier with Shrager (Siegler and Shrager 1984). What he found was that children could be clustered into three distinct groups. "Good students" had a core set of problems they knew "by heart," and for which they would retrieve the answers from memory. For problems they did not know as well they also had a set of efficient "backup strategies," which would allow them to compute the answers from first principles (e.g., via counting). By contrast, "not-so-good" students were poor both at retrieving answers and at using counting strategies. They also used retrieval on many problems where they had little chance of doing so correctly. Finally, there was a group of "perfectionists," whose knowledge of the basic problems was about the same as that of the good students, and whose backup strategies were just as efficient, but who employed a far stricter criterion for retrieving answers from memory, thus laboriously computing a great many answers for which they knew the answers quite well already.

This analysis of individual differences received a number of types of external validation. For example, good students' and perfectionists' achievement test scores averaged at the 81st and 80th percentiles respectively, whereas the not-so-good students' scores averaged at the 43rd percentile. Further, all of the children who were assigned to learning disabilities classes or held back at the end of the year were in the not-so-good group. Thus, the differences between not-so-good students and the other two groups were evident on standardized tests as well as in the children's strategy choices. Only the strategy-choice test, however, revealed the stylistic differences between the perfectionists and good students. In addition, only the strategy-choice test could specify the precise locus of the poor students' difficulties.

Recently, Siegler and Kerkman (Siegler in press; Kerkman and Siegler in press) examined whether first graders from low-income communities would show similar patterns of strategy use and strategy choice, and similar individual differences in these properties, to those observed with middle-income children. The study exactly paralleled the Siegler (1988) study of individual differences, except that the children were examined somewhat later in first grade (April rather than November and December). The reason for the later testing was to achieve greater similarity in absolute levels of performance (it was the individual differences in *patterns* of performance that were of interest).

As hoped, absolute levels of accuracy, speed, and strategy use of the lower-income first graders were comparable to those of the middle-income children tested five months earlier in the school year. The lower-income children also showed highly adaptive choices among alternative strategies, and the general pattern of strategy use closely resembled that found in the middle-income samples. On more than 90 percent of trials, children used strategies that had been observed relatively often in previous studies. In order of frequency of use, these strategies were retrieval (51 percent of trials), counting from the larger addend (16 percent), counting from one (14 percent), finger recognition (7 percent), guessing (3 percent), and saying, "I don't know" (3 percent).

On the remaining 5 percent of trials, however, the children used two other strategies. One was an approach that had rarely been seen in previous detailed strategy assessment studies (all of which had been conducted with middle-class children); the other strategy of interest was one that had literally never been seen. The more common of the two approaches was counting-on from the smaller addend. On a problem such as 5 + 9 or 9 + 5, the child would count-on from the 5. The less common of the approaches was counting on from neither addend. On 5 + 9 or 9 + 5, the child might count on from 7 or 8.

Analyses of individual children's counting from the smaller addend were especially revealing. One group, including 36 percent of children, counted from the smaller addend on fewer than 10 percent of the trials on which they counted from one of the two addends. Another group, including 11 percent of children, counted from the smaller addend on at least 50 percent of trials on which they counted from one or the other addend. However the largest group—53 percent—counted from the smaller addend on between 10 percent and 50 percent of such trials. These data demonstrate that counting from the smaller addend could not be attributed to a small number of children engaging consistently in the activity. Rather, it seemed to be something that many of the lower-income children did sometimes. The pattern contrasted with the findings of Siegler (1987) and Siegler and Jenkins (1989), studies that applied the same strategy assessment methodology to middle income samples. In both of the studies with middle income samples, counting from the smaller addend was an extremely rare activity. Only one of the 4- and 5-year-olds in the Siegler and Jenkins study and none of the middle-income 6- and 7-year-olds in Siegler

(1987) were observed to use it (versus three of four children from the low-income families in Siegler and Kerkman, in preparation).

The other strategy of interest was counting from neither addend, an approach that had never been observed in any previous studies of children from middle-income backgrounds. Even in Siegler and Jenkins (1989), where 4- and 5-year-olds' very first uses of counting from a number larger than one were focused on, the children never counted from a number different than either addend.

Although counting from the smaller addend fairly often generates correct answers, and counting from neither addend hardly ever does, it seems quite likely that the two strategies reflect different degrees of a similar problem: an early gap between these children's use of a strategy and their understanding of why the strategy works and what goals it achieves. In short, the pattern apparent in these findings suggests that many children in the lower-income groups may not have acquired the intuitive understanding of number that was demonstrated in the strategy use of the middle-income group.

Research on Young Children's Intuitive Knowledge of Number

After reviewing the literature on young children's arithmetic, Resnick (1983) concluded that children represented the addition process in terms of something like a mental number line, and that this number line provided the conceptual underpinning for children's use of arithmetic strategies. According to her analysis, children see the use of a strategy such as counting on their fingers as being justified, because it is like traversing a mental number line and arriving at the answer. The lack of such a representation may be part of the reason that some students have difficulty in learning to add or subtract or are poor at executing these strategies; lack of understanding of why the strategies work may interfere with skillful execution of the strategies. This, in turn, may lead to such strategies not being used very often, and may prevent a core set of problems from being learned "by heart."

In subsequent work, Case, Griffin, and their colleagues (Case and Sandieson 1987; Case and Griffin 1990; Griffin, Case, and Sandieson 1992; Okamoto 1992) developed, tested, and refined a measure to assess children's conceptual knowledge of number. The test was used initially with middle-income American children, and normed for the age levels of 4, 6, 8, and 10 years. The developmental theory that guided construction of these measures is described in the following section but one set of findings is relevant to the present discussion.

When the number knowledge test (see table 2.1) was first administered to a group of low-income 5- to 6-year-olds, they were found to

Table 2.1
Number knowledge test

Preliminary: Let's see if you can count from 1 to 10. Go ahead.

Level 0: (4 years)

1. (Present mixed array of 3 red and 4 blue poker ships.) Count the blue chips and tell me how many there are.

2. I'm going to give you 1 candy and then I'm going to give you 2 more. (Do so.) How many do you have altogether?

3. (Show stacks of 5 and 2 poker ships, same color.) Which pile has more?

4. (Present mixed array of 7 circles and 8 triangles, same color.) Count the triangles and tell me how many there are.

Level 1: (6 years)

1. If you had 4 chocolates and someone gave you 3 more, how many chocolates would you have altogether?

2. What number comes right after 7?

3. What number comes two numbers after 7?

4a. Which is bigger: 5 or 4?
4b. Which is bigger: 7 or 9?

5a. Which is *smaller:* 8 or 6?
5b. Which is smaller: 5 or 7?

6a. (Present visual array.) Which number is closer to 5: 6 or 2?
6b. (Present visual array.) Which number is closer to 7: 4 or 9?

Level 2: (8 years)

1a. Which is bigger: 69 or 71?
1b. Which is bigger: 32 or 28?

2a. Which is smaller: 27 or 32?
2b. Which is smaller: 51 or 39?

3a. (Show visual array.) Which number is closer to 21: 25 or 18?
3b. (Show visual array.) Which number is closer to 28: 31 or 24?

---

perform much like middle-income 3- to 4-year-olds. Unlike middle-income 5- and 6-year-olds, a significant number of these children were unable to tell which of two numbers is bigger (e.g., 6 or 8), or which number is closer to 5: 6 or 2. They were also unable to answer the verbally presented problem involving the receipt of four objects followed by three more objects.

While the difficulties on the first two items suggest an absence of the general conceptual knowledge inherent in a mental number line representation, the latter difficulty indicates the absence of that aspect of this knowledge on which the solving of first grade addition and subtraction problems is most directly dependent. Most middle-income kindergarten children already knew how to solve simple addition problems when these were presented orally. Thus, the only training

Table 2.2
Kindergartner's performance on number knowledge task: Percent correct on selected items

Level	Items	High SES (n=60)*	Mid SES (n=13)**	Low SES (n=261)***
0	How many candies altogether	100	100	92
(4 yrs.)	Which pile has more chips	100	100	93
	Count triangles	85	92	79
1	How many chocolates altogether	72	69	14
(6 yrs.)	What number comes two numbers 7	64	69	28
	Which is bigger/smaller (4 items)	96	77	18
2	Which is bigger/smaller (2 items)	48	15	1
(8 yrs.)	Which is closer to 21: 25 or 18	53	31	2
	How much is 54 + 12	15	0	0

* 2 schools (public and private) in CA
** 1 school (private, Catholic) in CA
*** 6 schools (public) in CA and MA

they really needed was in conventional numerical notation, such as $4 + 3 = ?$. By contrast, the low-income group often gave answers that seemed like wild guesses (e.g., $4 + 3 = 13$) or simple associations based on their knowledge of counting (e.g., $4 + 3 = 5$). In short, they appeared to be missing precisely those conceptual prerequisites on which success in arithmetic depends.

On the basis of the findings described thus far and the theoretical formulations described in the following section, the Rightstart project was launched. Subsequent findings as the project progressed, and as the number knowledge test was administered to an increasing number of children from low-income communities, provided evidence that the knowledge gap identified in the first study was not an isolated phenomenon. It was apparent in each of the studies reported in this chapter, in the performance of kindergarten children attending schools in Canada, California, and Massachusetts. An overview of these findings for selected items on the Number Knowledge test is provided in table 2.2.

Theoretical Framework

In the past decade or so, a number of neo-Piagetian theorists have proposed that a major reorganization occurs in children's thought at 5–6 years, about the age when arithmetic is normally introduced in schools (Case 1985; Fischer 1980; Halford 1982).

Our own efforts to investigate this reorganization began with Siegler's (1976) observation that 6-year-olds use a quantitative rule for solving balance beam problems ("Pick the side that has the greater number of weights as the one that will go down"). Four-year-olds cannot usually solve balance beam problems that demand a rule of this sort. However, they can solve problems that are solvable with a qualitative version of this rule, that is, problems where one side has a very large weight and the other side a very small one (Liu 1981). Four-year olds also can solve problems where their only task is to count small arrays of objects. Given this pattern of strengths and weaknesses, Case and Sandieson (1987) proposed that what 4-year-olds lack is the ability to coordinate these two schemes into what they termed a "dimensional structure", that is, a structure in which properties such as weight are represented as quantitative dimensions with two poles and a continuum of values in between.

In a series of studies conducted in the 1980s, this difference between 4- and 6-year-olds was found to be quite general. It was apparent on tasks of moral reasoning (Damon's Distributive Justice task), tasks of social reasoning (Marini's Birthday Party task), and tasks of scientific reasoning (Piaget's Projection of Shadows task). Children's performance across all of these tasks was also found to be highly consistent at the age-levels of 4, 6, 8, and 10 years (Marini 1992). To account for these findings, we proposed that each task had some (often implicit) quantitative component and that children's performance on all these tasks, drawn from distinct content domains, could be explained by their growing understanding of number (Case and Griffin 1990; Griffin, Case, and Sandieson 1992). Using postulates of neo-Piagetian theory (Case 1985, 1992), we modeled the quantitative understandings that appeared to be central for successful performance at four age-levels as depicted in figure 2.1.

What this figure is meant to suggest is that, at the age of 4 years, children tend to represent all possible variables in a global or polar fashion, so that they can make mappings of the sort: "Big things are worth a lot; little things are worth a little." At the age of 6 years, children tend to represent variables in a continuous fashion (i.e, as having two poles and a number of points in between). Moreover, they realize that these points can be treated as lying along a mental number line, such that values which have a higher numeric value also have a higher real value associated with them. At the age of 8 years, children can think in terms of two independent quantitative variables (e.g., hours and minutes on a clock; dollars and cents), but cannot yet make successful comparisons between variations along each. Finally, at the age of 10 years, children can make these sorts of

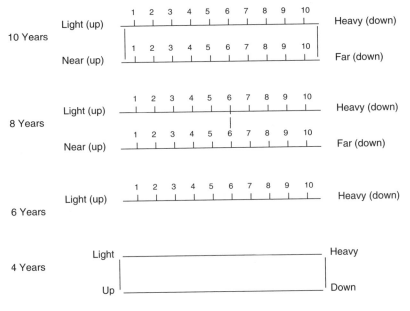

Figure 2.1
Conceptual representation hypothesized to underlie children's progress on quantitative problems

comparisons, by thinking in terms of the "trade-offs" between two quantitative variables.

To test this model, two additional instruments were constructed, a time-telling test and a money-handling test. Items included in these tests were drawn from the domain of everyday experience and were assigned to four age-levels in accordance with the model's predictions. When these tests were administered to populations of children from middle-income communities, the predictions were found to be highly accurate. At four age-levels (4, 6, 8, and 10 years), children's performance was consistent with the model and consistent with the pattern found in previous studies (Griffin, Case, and Sandieson 1992). Given the generality of the findings, we proposed that the numerical understandings implied in the model were powerful organizing schemata, "central conceptual structures," that mediate performance on a wide variety of tasks with some quantitative component (Case and Griffin 1990; Case 1992).

The number knowledge test that was described in the previous section was developed to assess the knowledge implied in these structures. When the findings suggested that kindergarten children in one at-risk community could not pass the 6-year-old level of the test, we

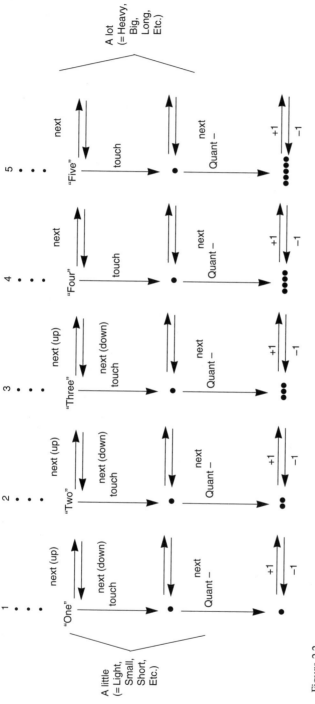

Figure 2.2
Central conceptual structure hypothesized to underlie six-year-old's early understanding of mathematics (dotted lines indicate "optional"—i.e., non-universal—notational knowledge)

began to speculate that the reason some American children do poorly in school is that they haven't acquired the central conceptual structure on which success in arithmetic depends. If we could develop a program to teach this structure, we might give children who did not already possess it, a solid conceptual foundation for first formal learning of arithmetic as well as a foundation for higher-order mathematical understandings. The Rightstart program was designed to serve this purpose.

To teach this structure, we required a more detailed model of the knowledge implied in a single mental number line. Relying on a rational analysis to identify central components of this structure, results of the number knowledge test, findings in the mathematics research literature (e.g., Resnick 1983; Gelman and Gallistel 1978) which helped us identify knowledge components that serve as precursors to a full understanding, and in-depth interviews with children, we proposed the elaborated structure depicted in figure 2.2.

The understandings implied in this figure, and presumed to be conceptual prerequisites for all arithmetic operations with single-digit numbers, can be described as follows: (a) a knowledge of the number sequence from 1 to 10, and an awareness of each number's position in the sequence; (b) a knowledge of the one-to-one manner in which this sequence is mapped on to objects when counting; (c) an understanding of the cardinal value of each number (i.e., that when touching the third object and saying "3," one has formed a set whose size is indicated by this number); (d) an understanding of the generative rule which relates adjacent cardinal values (e.g., that 3 represents a set that's just like 2 except that 1 object has been added, or that 3 represents a set that's just like 4 except that 1 has been subtracted); and (e) an understanding of the consequence of this fact: namely, that each successive number represents a set which contains more objects, and thus has a greater value along any particular dimension. The first three elements specified above are known to develop in the preschool years (Gelman and Gallistel 1978).

To summarize, the theoretical assumptions on which the Rightstart program was based are as follows: (1) In the course of their preschool experience, many (but not all) children develop powerful organizing schemata that are central to their understanding of the school tasks that they encounter in subsequent years. These schemata may be called "central conceptual structures" (Case and Griffin 1990). (2) The central conceptual structure on which early addition and subtraction are dependent is one for conceptualizing the world in terms of quantitative dimensions. Once this structure is in place, children see the world as comprised of dimensions having two poles, and a large number of points between these poles, whose relative magnitude can be indexed by the number system (see figure 2.2). (3) In comparison to their peers, children who are at risk for early school failure in math are less likely to have developed this structure by the time they enter first grade. (4) If these children are provided with experience that enables them to develop this structure—before they enter grade one—their first learning of addition and subtraction should improve considerably.

The Rightstart Program

The curriculum we developed was more limited in scope than many kindergarten programs. It was designed to teach the specific set of nodes and relations specified in the structure depicted in figure 2.2 (i.e., the cognitive structure underlying a 6-year-old's numerical understanding) and to give children multiple opportunities to assemble these components into a well-consolidated whole.

To teach this structure, we developed a series of thirty interactive games (some with several variations) that provided hands-on opportunities for children to construct, and to consolidate, the understandings depicted in each set of nodes and relations within the structure. Sufficient games were developed so that each knowledge component included in the structure could be explicitly targeted in one set of lessons. In addition, each game implicitly targeted several other components of the structure as well, to provide opportunities for multiple levels of learning and to ensure that the integrated structure we were attempting to teach was adequately represented in each learning activity.

The games themselves were designed to be played by a group of 4–5 children, with teacher supervision. Activities that could be used with a whole class of children to reinforce the knowledge acquired in particular games were also included in the program, as were Learning Center activities that children could engage in without teacher supervision. To support these games and activities, we selected props that were congruent with the structure we were attempting to teach, and that represented this structure in a variety of ways.

The Number Line Game

The number line game exemplifies our approach. This game is played by a small group of children on a game board that portrays a series of number lines (one for each player) coded in different colors. To play, children roll a die and compute the quantity shown to determine who goes first. The first player then rolls the die, computes the quantity, asks the banker for that many counting chips, places the chips in sequence along his or her number line while counting, and then moves his or her playing piece along the counting chips (while counting once again) until the playing piece rests on the last chip (which itself rests just below the numeral that corresponds to the quantity rolled and moved). Play then moves to the next player; the first child to reach the winner's circle (beyond the 10 square) wins the game. Children are asked to watch and listen carefully while others are counting and moving to ensure that no one makes a mistake. When a mistake is made or a computation is challenged, it is typically resolved by re-counting and/or group discussion.

These aspects of game play give children repeated exposure to the vertical nodes and relations illustrated in figure 2.2. They were de-signed to help children consolidate knowledge of: the number se-quence up and down, the corresponding numerals, the one-to-one manner in which numbers map onto objects when counting in either direction, and the cardinal value of each number.

When children are comfortable with this level of play (i.e., when they can reliably count, quantify sets, and match sets to numbers), several variations are introduced. Children are asked to make relative quantity assessments with questions such as "Who is closest to the goal?" and to map these assessments onto the number sequence with questions such as "How do you know?" They are asked to draw chance cards during game play which require that their quantities, and their position on the number line, be incremented or decremented by one. They are asked to use numerosity to make predictions about who is likely to win, or lose, the game. These variations provide plenty of exposure to the horizontal nodes and relations illustrated in the figure. They were designed to help children acquire the increment and dec-rement rules, and understand that numbers can be used to make relative quantity assessments (e.g., if Maria has 5 and Stephen has 4, then Maria has more/is further ahead/is closer to the goal).

The twenty-nine other games included in the program are distinct from this one, but they also provide opportunities for children to construct and to consolidate the same knowledge structure, at their own pace and in contexts that are highly motivating for a wide variety of children. In contrast to the competitive format of the game just described, over 50 percent of the games included in the module use a cooperative format in which children must work together in pairs, or in a small group, to achieve the goal. Opportunities or requirements to justify and explain a particular quantitative assessment are built into many of the games. Prompts for verbal communication are scripted in the teacher's manual, in the form of "How do you know?" questions, for several other games.

Finally, the entire set of games is sequenced within the module to provide a natural bridge between children's entering understanding of number and quantity, and the complete set of understandings implied in the central conceptual structure. In other words, the knowledge components that are targeted early in the instructional sequence are those that children are known to acquire earliest in development. With room for adaptation to accommodate the particular group of learners, the entire sequence was designed to recapitulate the natural developmental progression.

The instructional principles that were used to develop the program are apparent in the above discussion. They can be summarized as follows:

1. *Conceptual bridging:* The activities included in the module should serve as a "conceptual bridge" between children's current understanding of number and quantity and the sorts of understanding implied in the "mental number line" structure.

2. *Representational congruence and diversity:* The props used to accompany these activities should be congruent with the "mental number line" structure and should represent this structure in diverse ways.

3. *Multiple levels of understanding:* The activities should allow for multiple levels of understanding so children with different entering knowledge, and different learning rates, can all learn something from each activity.

4. *Affective engagement:* The activities should be affectively, as well as cognitively, engaging.

5. *Physical, social, and verbal interaction:* The activities should provide opportunities for children to interact with the materials and to use the knowledge they are constructing in a variety of ways (e.g., to solve game problems; to communicate with peers).

6. *Developmental sequencing:* The activities should be sequenced in their normal order of acquisition.

Program Evaluation

The Rightstart program was used over a period of three years with small groups, or whole classes, of kindergarten children attending schools in Canada, California, and Massachusetts. In four of the studies reported in this chapter, the children were taught in small groups of 4–5 children, for about 20 minutes a day. Most of the teachers were research assistants who were trained to teach the curriculum. In a fifth study (i.e., study 4), the program was taught by a teacher-researcher to two whole classes of children, with 20 to 25 children in each class. The entire program extended over a 3- to 4-month period in each study.

The children who received the program were all attending kindergarten in inner city schools with large minority populations. Most of the children came from low-income communities and were drawn from school populations considered to be at risk for school failure. Prior to training, in the middle of their kindergarten year, the vast majority of the children who received the program (in most studies, the majority of children in each kindergarten class) failed the 6-year-old level of the number knowledge test described earlier in this paper. Many of these children also failed items at the 4-year-old level of this test.

In three studies (i.e., studies 1, 2, and 4), we created matched control groups of children, on the basis of number knowledge test scores, age, school placement, and ethnic background. Two control groups were established for study 1, which was conducted in a public school in metropolitan Toronto that drew children, almost exclusively, from a Portuguese immigrant community. Most children included in the sample had received a year of preschool training (i.e., junior kindergarten) and all were proficient in English when the study began. Pretesting was conducted in the language the child was most comfortable with and number knowledge pretest scores, as well as classroom placement, were used to establish three matched groups. One group received the Rightstart program. Control group 1 received an equal amount of small-group attention with a more traditional math program that was specifically designed to provide a level of affective engagement that was commensurate with the Rightstart program. Control group 2 received a language program designed with similar criteria in mind and administered in a similar format.

Studies 2 and 4 were conducted in three public inner-city schools in central Massachusetts that drew children from a variety of cultural backgrounds (e.g., Hispanic, Southeast Asian, Afro- and Anglo-American). All children included in these samples were comfortable with the English language and the number knowledge pretest (administered in all studies in the child's preferred language) was used, along with the other criteria mentioned above, to establish matched treatment and control groups. In these studies, the control groups were given no additional training beyond their regular classroom instruction. In all studies, matching was nearly perfect for number knowledge performance and cultural background, and less perfect with respect to age. With the exception of study 4, where the Rightstart program was administered in a whole-class format and the control group was drawn from a separate classroom, matching was nearly perfect for classroom placement as well.

Assessment Objectives and Procedures

Our program evaluation was designed with three objectives in mind. First, we wanted to see whether the Rightstart program was sufficient to teach the knowledge specified in the central conceptual structure and whether it did so more efficiently than other, more traditional, kindergarten mathematics programs. Second, we wanted to see whether the knowledge acquired was central to children's performance on a broad range of tasks with some quantitative component, as suggested by the theory. Third, we wanted to see whether the knowledge acquired would enhance children's ability to profit from early formal instruction in arithmetic, as the theory also predicted.

To realize these objectives, we administered a battery of tasks to all children in each sample. The number knowledge test was administered before and after training and the pre- posttest gains were used as a measure of the extent to which children had acquired the knowledge implied in the central conceptual structure. In two studies, children's responses to one item on this test were further analyzed to obtain a measure of strategy use and a probe (i.e., "How did you figure that out?") was included in the test administration to obtain additional information for this analysis.

To see whether the knowledge acquired was central to children's performance in content domains that had *not* been addressed in the Rightstart program, we administered a battery of developmental tasks (i.e., those mentioned in a previous section) after training in all studies and before training in the majority of studies. These included the balance beam task, which requires predictions of relative weight; the birthday party task, which requires predictions of relative happiness; the time knowledge task, which poses a variety of time problems; the money knowledge task, which poses a variety of money problems; and the distributive justice task, which requires attention to issues of fairness.

Each of these tasks has some quantitative requirement in that a successful solution to the problem posed (e.g., "Which side of the beam will go down?" "Who will be happier?" "What time is shown on this clock?") is possible only when the problem array is quantified in some fashion. Each of these tasks also has specific content that was purposely excluded from the Rightstart program. In the entire curriculum, any mention of balance systems, birthday parties, time, and money was scrupulously avoided. Our purpose in administering these tests was to see whether the central conceptual structure—if it could be taught—had the broad range of application the theory suggested. These tasks are described in greater detail in Griffin, Case, and Capodilupo (in press).

The third question we sought to answer was, Does this knowledge enable children to profit from early formal instruction in arithmetic? To answer this question, we retested one sample of treatment and control children (i.e., those included in study 2) one year later, at the end of grade one. Because many children had moved out of the geographic area, the sample was appreciably reduced when the first grade follow-up study was conducted. The children who were located (11 from the treatment group and 12 from the control group) were attending six different schools within a 30-mile radius, and were in 12 different classrooms. The children's first grade teachers had no knowledge of the Rightstart project, or of the treatment status of the children.

To assess arithmetic knowledge at the end of grade one, four instruments were developed or adapted. These included: an oral arithmetic test (e.g., "How much is 2 + 4?"); a written arithmetic test, which presented simple arithmetic problems in a typical worksheet fashion; a word problems test, which was a modified version of one developed by Riley and Greeno (1988) and which required children to provide verbal answers to orally presented word problems; and a teacher rating scale, which required the classroom teacher to rate each child's mathematics performance, in relation to other children in the class, on eight items taken from the school report card. The number knowledge test was also included in this battery to assess the stability of the knowledge acquired in kindergarten, over a one-year period.

Results and Discussion

Number Knowledge
Table 2.3 shows the percentage of children passing the number knowledge test, before and after training, in five separate studies conducted over a three-year period. As the table indicates, almost all children included in each sample failed the number test prior to training. Four or five months later, the vast majority of the children who had received the training passed the test. By contrast, only a minority of the children in the control groups passed. Note that two of the control groups (i.e., the groups established in study 1) had received training programs that provided an equal amount of individual attention and that contained the same number of games as those developed for the Rightstart program. Multivariance analyses indicated that the gains made by the

Table 2.3
Percentage of children passing number knowledge test before and after training

	Treatment groups*	
	Pretest	Posttest
Study 1 (*n* = 20)	15	80
Study 2 (*n* = 23)	0	87
Study 3 (*n* = 7)	0	71
Study 4 (*n* = 38)	7	53
Study 5 (*n* = 10)	10	70
	Control groups*	
	Pretest	Posttest
Study 1:		
Math control (*n* = 20)	15	37
Language control (*n* = 20)	15	35
Study 2 (*n* = 24)	0	25
Study 4 (*n* = 38)	7	14

* Groups drawn from twelve classrooms in six schools located in Canada, California, and Massachusetts.

treatment groups were superior to the gains made by the control groups at the .05 level or better, in each study.

The consistency of these findings, across five separate studies, indicates that the curriculum did what it was supposed to do with considerable effectiveness. Even in the fourth study—where training was conducted with a ratio of one teacher to twenty-five children—the gains were substantial, although lower than the gains shown in the other studies where training was conducted in small groups. Since the curriculum was taught by several different teacher-trainers, to groups of children from widely divergent cultural backgrounds (e.g., Portuguese immigrants in Toronto, Caribbean immigrants in Massachusetts, Afro-Americans in California, and Anglo-Canadians or -Americans in all sites), these findings indicate that the curriculum enabled a wide variety of children to construct, and to consolidate, the knowledge implied in the central conceptual structure. It also appeared to be effective in a variety of educational contexts.

Strategy Use
Strategy use was examined on the number knowledge test item (i.e., "If you had 4 chocolates and I gave you 3 more, how many would you have altogether?") that assessed arithmetic knowledge most directly and that assessed children's ability to apply the +1 increment rule they

had been taught in the Rightstart program to problems with larger addends. It is worth noting here that none of the activities in the Rightstart program provided training in incrementing quantities larger than one, and the activities that addressed this knowledge objective most directly were the games, which required a small-group instructional format.

Two indices were adopted to obtain a global measure of "reasonable" versus "wild guess" strategy use. The major index was children's responses to the 4 + 3 test item itself. For this measure, a response of 5, 6, 7, or 8 was coded as reasonable on the assumption that each was in the neighborhood of the correct answer and each indicated some awareness that the largest addend should be incremented. A response of "I don't know" was also coded as reasonable on the assumption that it indicated some awareness that the problem required a particular strategy that was not yet available to the child. All other responses, which ranged from 0 to 400, were coded as wild guesses.

The second index available in two studies was children's response to the probe "How did you figure that out?," which was included in the posttest administration of this item. As might have been expected, this question was difficult for many children to answer and these data were used only to provide supporting evidence for the coding categories described above. Children's responses to the probe included "I just knew," "I guessed," "I counted," "I don't know," and blank stares. An analysis of these results indicated that the majority of children who produced responses that were coded as wild guesses also responded to the probe with an "I just guessed" response or a blank stare, lending convergent support to the coding categories that were established for this analysis.

Table 2.4 shows the percentage of children producing wild guess responses to this item in study 2 (small-group instructional format) and study 4 (whole-class instructional format). These data indicate a substantial difference between the treatment and control groups in both studies and a difference of greater magnitude in study 2, where the program was taught in its entirety and in a more ideal instructional

Table 2.4
Percentage of children using "wild guess" strategies on number knowledge test item (numbers in brackets indicate percent children achieving correct answer of 7)

	Treatment group	Control group
Study 2 ($n = 47$)	4 (87)	33 (21)
Study 4 ($n = 72$)	11 (53)	39 (25)

format. Although pretest measures on strategy use were not available, the groups were well matched on several other indices of mathematical knowledge, and it seems reasonable to assume that pretest strategy use was comparable as well.

These data suggest that the children who received the Rightstart program were better able than children who had not, to employ a reasonable strategy in their attempts to solve a novel addition problem and to achieve a higher success rate on this problem. Since children who received the program also gave evidence they had acquired the central conceptual structure the program was designed to teach, it seems reasonable to attribute the superior strategy use of these children to a conceptual knowledge base that enabled them to make sense of the problem and to adopt, thereby, a reasonable strategy to solve it.

Transfer Effects

Table 2.5 shows the percentage of children passing five transfer tests before and after training. The data used for this table were an aggregate of three sets of findings, collected over a three-year period, and they provide a reasonable estimate of transfer effects in each study. As the table indicates, very few children were able to pass any of these tests prior to training. By contrast, on the posttest, the majority of the treatment group passed four of the five transfer tests and the majority of the control group failed. Even on the money knowledge test—where the absolute magnitude of children passing was lower—the difference between the treatment and control groups was still significant at the .01 level. Multivariance analyses provided similar or higher confidence levels on each of the remaining tests. These findings provide strong evidence that the knowledge implied in the central conceptual structure, and acquired through our readiness training, has the broad range of application the theory suggests.

Table 2.5
Percentage of treatment and control children passing five transfer tests (aggregate data from five studies)

	Pretest	Posttest treatment group	Posttest control group
Balance beam ($n = 183$)	10	77	37
Birthday party ($n = 107$)	16	81	37
Time-telling ($n = 183$)	11	65	28
Money-handling ($n = 183$)	8	38	18
Distrib. justice ($n = 47$)	—	87	37

First Grade Follow-Up

When the number knowledge test was readministered, one year later, to the first grade follow-up sample, the results indicated that all of the children who had received the Rightstart program in kindergarten passed level 1 of this test at the end of grade one (versus 87% passing one year earlier). At this point in time, 83 percent of the control group also demonstrated this knowledge (compared to 25% one year earlier). These findings suggest that: first, the knowledge the treatment children acquired in kindergarten was stable over a one-year period and was very likely available to them when they started first grade; and second, at some point during their first grade experience, many children in the control group also acquired this knowledge. These findings raise an interesting question, namely: If many children can acquire the knowledge taught in the Rightstart program in the course of their first grade experience, why bother to teach it in kindergarten? The results described below provide an answer to this question.

Table 2.6 presents the results of the number knowledge test and the arithmetic tests that were included in the first grade battery. These findings indicate that some children in the treatment group were now able to solve double-digit problems that were included in level 2 of the number knowledge test. No child in either group passed these items at the end of kindergarten and none of the control children passed them at the end of grade one.

When children's performance on the first grade arithmetic tests is examined, the findings indicate that the majority of the treatment group passed two of these tests, the oral arithmetic test and the word problems test, whereas a large proportion of the control group failed.

Table 2.6
Percentage of treatment and control children passing battery of tests at the end of grade one

	Treatment group (*n* = 23)	Control group (*n* = 24)
Number knowledge:		
Level 1	100	83
Level 2	18	0
Oral arithmetic	82	33
Written arithmetic	91	75
Word problems:		
Level 1	96	54
Level 2	46	13

Table 2.7
Percentage of treatment and control children achieving teacher ratings of average or above at the end of grade one

	Treatment group ($n = 11$)	Control group ($n = 12$)
Number sense	100	24
Meaning of numbers	88	42
Use of numbers	88	42
Addition	100	66
Subtraction	100	66
Accuracy	63	59
Speed	75	42

On each test, the groups differed significantly. On the third test, the written arithmetic test, a large proportion of both groups passed and the difference between the groups was not significant. Since the written test required children to solve the sort of worksheet problem they encountered on a daily basis in their classrooms, this finding is not surprising. It suggests that most children were able to profit from extensive exposure to a particular problem format.

On the teacher rating scale, almost all children in the treatment group received a rating of average or above average on five of the the seven items included on this scale (see table 2.7). The proportion of children in the control group receiving this rating was significantly lower. The differences between the groups are especially striking on the three items that indexed the conceptual knowledge the Rightstart program was designed to teach, namely: "demonstrates number sense," "understands the meaning of numbers," "understands the use of numbers." Conversely, on the two items that were not addressed or considered important in the Rightstart program—"works with reasonable speed," "works accurately"—there was no difference between the groups. The high ratings the treatment children received from their first grade classroom teachers are also striking when it is recalled that these children had been performing in the below-average category in kindergarten and had been included in the Rightstart training sample for this reason.

When the data from the first graders are considered as a whole, they suggest that both groups (i.e., treatment and control) acquired some new knowledge in their first grade experience. Both groups learned to solve the sort of arithmetic problem they encountered on a daily basis in their classroom. However, when children were required to use this knowledge more flexibly, to solve formal problems presented orally, to solve word problems, or to demonstrate to their classroom teachers that they possessed number sense, a large proportion of the control group was unable to do so. By contrast, the treatment children appeared to have acquired new knowledge that was general, and that could be applied in a more flexible fashion.

One possible interpretation of these findings would be to suggest that the treatment children had a central conceptual structure in place, at the beginning of grade one, which lent meaning to the facts, algorithms, and strategies that were taught in their first grade classrooms. By assimilating this procedural knowledge into their conceptual structure, they were able to construct new knowledge that was general, and that could be deployed in a variety of situations. Lacking such a structure, the control children were able to master some of the procedural knowledge that was taught in their first grade classrooms, but were unable to make sufficient sense of it to permit generalization to new problem contexts.

We ourselves were surprised at the magnitude of these findings. We had hoped that the Rightstart program would have some long-term effects, but we had also feared that these effects might be lost when children were exposed to a whole year of traditional instruction that provided little support for the conceptual understandings taught in the kindergarten year. The findings provide evidence that training effects are robust and that the Rightstart program does, indeed, facilitate first formal learning of arithmetic.

Conclusions

Taking the data we have gathered across the past three years as a whole, we draw the following general conclusions:

1. Children from different social strata in America enter school with substantial differences in their understanding of numbers. Those in middle and high SES groups view the number system in the dimensional fashion indicated in the central conceptual structure (figure 2.2). Many children from low-income families appear to lack this conceptual knowledge; they see numbers in a predimensional fashion or they cannot apply their dimensional understanding in the sort of context that our schools provide. Given the problems that American schools have in fostering conceptual understanding in children from all backgrounds (Stigler, Lee, and Stevenson 1990), this sort of early difficulty seems particularly unfortunate, since it increases the likelihood that children will treat school math from the start as a rote activity.

2. The Rightstart program appears to be effective in eliminating these differences and in enabling a wide variety of children, who come to school from different starting points and/or with different linguistic conventions, to acquire the conceptual knowledge it was designed to teach. Its effectiveness has now been demonstrated in two countries (Canada and the United States), in six separate schools, and with five lower- and lower-middle-income groups. It has also been shown to be effective when implemented by eight different teacher-trainers.

3. It seems clear that the program does not have its effect simply by familiarizing children with the procedure for counting, or for representing numbers with numerals. Nor does it have its effect simply by engaging children in a social process with which they have had little experience up to that point in time, namely, answering test questions by an adult, and justifying these answers in a "decontextualized" setting. If these were the only important aspects of the program, then one would have expected more progress to be shown by the control groups that were used in study 1.

4. Three of the main foci of the program were (1) teaching children to respond to questions about relative magnitude in the absence of any concrete sets of objects, (2) teaching children the "increment rule," i.e., the rule that dictates that the addition or subtraction of one element to a set alters the cardinal value of that set by one unit, and therefore moves the value one unit up or down on the number line, and (3) teaching children that knowledge of relative position on the number line is useful for determining relative quantity in various "real world" tasks, when it cannot be determined more directly. Since the sorts of questions on which children showed improvement on the post-test battery all dealt with one or another of these components, it can be assumed that the program had its effect for the reason hypothesized; namely, it enabled children to acquire the numerical understandings specified in the central conceptual structure.

5. On the basis of the transfer effects, it seems clear that the knowledge taught is central to children's performance on a range of quantitative tasks for which no specific training had been provided.

6. On the basis of the first graders' performance, it also seems clear that positive effects of the Rightstart program are apparent one full year after the program has ended. After being exposed to a standard first grade arithmetic curriculum in a variety of classrooms in a variety of schools, children who had received the

program in kindergarten did significantly better than their peers in the control group on several achievement measures administered at the close of first grade. The mathematics knowledge and learning they demonstrated at this point was commensurate with that of their middle-income peers and in sharp contrast to the learning potential these children had demonstrated in the middle of their kindergarten year.

In summary, the major conclusion we draw from these findings is a straightforward one. Although children from different backgrounds may still need different sorts of programs to accommodate their needs as they progress through formal schooling, the Rightstart program ensures that children from a diverse array of backgrounds will all start first grade with an understanding of quantities, numbers, and numerical terminology that builds on their existing insights and vocabulary, and that is well matched to the requirements of first grade.

Note

The Rightstart program and the research that supported its development and evaluation were made possible by a grant from the James S. McDonnell Foundation.

Chapter 3

A Cognitive Approach to the Teaching of Physics

Earl Hunt and Jim Minstrell

We see instruction as fostering reconstruction of understanding and reasoning, rather than as the memorization of correct procedures and answers.

Physics, in its broadest sense, represents a collective attempt by scientists to make sense of the physical world. Learners individually, in their daily interaction with natural phenomena, unconsciously or consciously make personal sense of that natural world. Physics is central to science itself, and is an important gateway to other courses in science and engineering. Failure to understand elementary physics may serve as a barrier to students' developing careers in a number of important and interesting fields. Nevertheless, in spite of the importance of the topic, fewer than 20 percent of high school students nationally take courses in physics, thus effectively shutting the majority of our students out of the career lines in science and engineering that the country so badly needs. Therefore, it is important to the progress of science, to society, and to learners that we learn effectively to bridge the gap between the specific, case-dependent understanding of the individual and the principled, collective understanding of the scientist.

How people learn physics is also an interesting question for cognitive psychology, because it offers us a chance to look at how people develop an abstract knowledge system that relates to phenomena they can observe in their daily life.

In this chapter we describe a teaching technique for introductory physics that is coordinated with a theory of how students organize their knowledge of physical phenomena prior to instruction. The teaching technique and the theory attempt to bridge the gap between students' physics and scientists' physics. It would be incorrect to say that the teaching program was dictated by cognitive science; much of it was dictated by the experience of physics teachers over the years. It is correct to say that the concepts of cognitive science can be used to examine the program in a systematic way, and to explain why the program works reasonably well.

We first describe the theoretical rationale for the program and then explain its implementation in the classroom. We then present some data demonstrating the effectiveness of the program, and close with a discussion of topics for the future.

A Psychological Framework for Thinking and Physics

The program is based on the idea that when students enter a physics classroom they have a number of ideas with which to predict or explain physical phenomena. Some early research labeled these concepts "misconceptions" or "naive views," and either implied or directly stated that the purpose of instruction was to stamp out these ideas. The ideas, however, do work in appropriate contexts. After all, high school students play basketball, ride skateboards, turn on lights, see water waves, and otherwise engage in physical activities and observation all the time. Therefore diSessa's (1988) term *knowledge in pieces* may more accurately describe the contextual relevance of students' understanding. The instructor's job, as we see it, is to help the students weave their bits of local knowledge into a coherent whole, based on more abstract principles than the students normally would consider.

In order to establish such a program in the classroom we need to operationalize our representations of the ideas that students have. Here our central concept is the *facet*.

A facet is a convenient unit of thought, an understanding or reasoning, a piece of content knowledge or a strategy seemingly used by the student in making sense of a particular situation. For the most part, our facet descriptions paraphrase the language used by students as they justify their answers, predictions, or explanations. We attempt to capture, in one facet statement, the intention of the expressed idea. Although each facet is a slight abstraction, we attempt to make it an accurate description of what students actually say or do. An example from free-fall and projectile motion is "Horizontal motion keeps things from falling as rapidly as they would if they were moving straight downwards."

Facets are organized into clusters of domain-specific knowledge. Facets may be associated with particular situations, like the forces on an object submerged in a surrounding fluid. They also may represent more strategic reasoning, such as the kinematics facet "average velocity can be determined by adding the initial and final velocities and dividing by two." The key point is that facets are defined with sufficient specificity to make their application recognizable in the writing, speaking, and other actions of learners. In other words, a teacher should be able to recognize a facet when a student uses one. By recognizing facets, teachers and developers can specifically address students' understanding and reasoning.

Our facets can be thought of as abstractions derived from combining even more basic psychological units or principles, which diSessa (1983) calls "phenomenological primitives" (*p-prims*). An example would be the idea of "springiness." In diSessa's scheme, our facets would be seen as specific instantiations of one or more p-prims. Using somewhat different terminology, other authors have argued that constructs (like our facet concept) represent a specific application of a student's overall approach, or *schema*, for a whole domain of problems. An example would be an impetus schema for explaining the motion of objects. For the purposes of working in the classroom (with teachers and students), we can remain theoretically neutral about such higher-order levels of mental organization and use facets that have concrete referents in the classroom. We shall, however, make some comments later about what our work with facets might reveal about constructs such as p-prims and schema.

The "truth" or utility of facets often depends on the context of the situation. For example, the horizontal motion of a paper airplane may keep it from falling as rapidly as a dropped paper airplane. The students' facet may not work for marbles rolled off tables or dropped, but it does work for beach balls thrown horizontally (with an underspin) versus dropped beach balls. Thus the facet "Horizontal motion slows vertical motion" is valid in some contexts in the real world, even though it may not be the more generalizable scientific principle that science teachers want to convey. In these examples, what is frequently lacking in the students' account are explicit considerations of the effects of the surrounding, fluid medium of air. However, in the typical science curriculum account, the effects of air are usually dealt with implicitly in a side note: "Assume no air resistance." Thus the curriculum sidesteps an effect that, in fact, is an important part of the students' initial understanding of the situation.

The key idea behind the instructional method is that students' facets can be used as a basis for focusing instruction. Consider one commonly encountered situation, in which students believe, "Active objects [like hands] can exert forces," but many also believe, "Passive objects [like tables] cannot exert forces." Students who appear to hold these two facets can be guided, through activities and discussion, to believe that consistent explanations for the "at rest" condition of an object would also involve believing that both active and passive objects can exert forces (Minstrell 1982). Rarely is the distinction between active and passive forces made in physics texts. The distinction is not necessary to a physicist, yet, for students, it proves to be very useful. It is a distinction students want to make, and it can be put to use later in energy-related discussions addressing questions such as which object is doing the work, and which object is "losing" energy in an interaction.

Sometimes students have a useful understanding of a relationship between factors even though they do not sufficiently understand the individual factors involved in the relationship. Consider the situation of a wagon being pushed horizontally on a smooth, level surface. We have found that most high school students (and most fourth graders) know that "a larger [horizontal] force on the wagon will make it go faster," and that when the same force is applied on a heavy and a light wagon, "the heavier wagon will go more slowly." Thus, they have the primitive idea that the greater push "influence" will produce the greater effect, and the greater resistive "influence" will produce the lesser effect. They can even put these two ideas together in a third situation, "How do you get the heavy and light wagons to move equally fast?" About 95 percent of the high school physics students and about 75 percent of the fourth graders said, "To get the wagons to move equally fast, you have to push harder on the heavier wagon." Thus, although they do not have completely productive understandings of force, inertial mass, and acceleration, they have a productive understanding of the relationship among these ideas (Minstrell & diSessa in press). We are designing curriculum and instruction to take into account the productive pieces of reasoning and understanding students bring to the learning situation.

Another important finding is that facets may be cued by contexts and, more importantly, not cued by some contexts even though they apply there. Consider the problem of understanding that inertia applies to all motion. We know, from their performance on the wagons problem, that although students do not have a complete understanding of inertial mass, they do have a primitive idea of the "heft" of an object as resisting motion in horizontal contexts. Yet in a context of downward vertical motion, inertial resistance to motion is not considered. Students remark, "It's not hard to get something going in the downward direction. All you have to do is let it go."

In order to show that the primitive concept of inertia generalizes to falling bodies, we provide a "benchmark experience" intended to illustrate the issue. In this particular case, students are taken outside and asked to push a softball and a shot put downwards so that the ball and shot put will be traveling as rapidly as possible when they

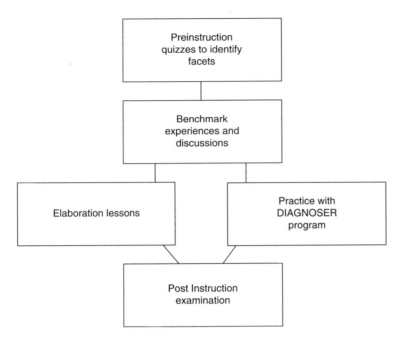

Figure 3.1
Sequence of instruction during a unit

hit the ground. After a bit of coaching so that the students can actually do this, each of them feels, perceptually, that it is more difficult to get the shot put going fast downward than to get the softball going fast downward. At the end of the year, nearly 80 percent of our students incorporate inertia into their explanations for the actions of falling bodies.

The Educational Program

The educational program is based on two simple principles. The first is that students should be encouraged to bring their current ideas, that is, their inconsistent but not incorrect facets, into the open for examination. We want them not just to "know what to do," but rather to ask, "Why does this work?" The second is that students should be exposed to situations and questions intended to help them develop their ideas toward an understanding of the concept of physics.[1] The methods are not *discovery learning*, in the sense that the term was used in the 1960s and 1970s, since the instructor does a great deal of guiding the discussion. However, throughout, and even in dealing with a computer program, instruction is carried on as a discussion, rather than as a didactic lecture. We see instruction as fostering reconstruction of understanding and reasoning, rather than as the memorization of correct procedures and answers.

We demonstrate how instruction is developed by considering a specific unit in the course dealing with the nature of gravity.

The goal of this unit is to develop an understanding of the nature of gravity and its effects. A related topic is understanding effects of ambient, fluid mediums on objects in them, whether the objects are at rest or moving through the fluid (e.g., air or water). This is a fairly important unit, because many students do not clearly understand the distinction between the effects of gravity and the effects of a surrounding fluid medium. When one attempts to weigh something, does it weigh what it does because the air pushes down on it? Or is the scale reading that would give the true weight of the object only distorted somehow, because of the air? Or is there absolutely no effect by the air?

The educational program is based on four steps. The steps themselves are shown in figure 3.1, which we now explain, using the nature of gravity as a running illustration.

The Preinstruction Quiz
In order to address students' understanding and reasoning, the first thing we do is to elicit student thinking about particular situations. To identify initial facets, we invite the students to record their initial understandings on a preinstruction quiz. One purpose of the quiz is to help students become more aware of the content and issues (including issues relating to their own initial ideas) involved in the upcoming unit. A second reason is to provide the teacher with knowledge of the related issues in the class in general and provide specific knowledge of which students exhibit what sorts of ideas. The quiz is intended both to extract information about facets that have been observed in previous classes and to let students express opinions in a way that might reveal new facets to us.

Figure 3.2 illustrates a question that is used in the nature of gravity preinstruction quiz. The students are asked to deal with the following situation:

> First we weigh some object on a large spring scale, not unlike the ones we have at the local market. The object apparently weighs ten pounds, according to the scale. Now we put the same apparatus, scale, object and all, under a very large glass dome, seal the system around the edges, and pump out all the air. That is, we use a vacuum pump to allow all the air to escape out from

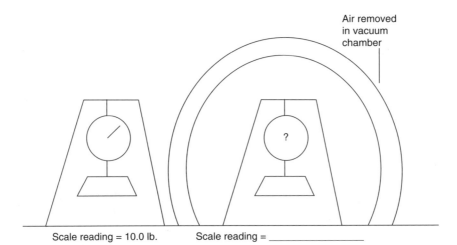

Scale reading = 10.0 lb.   Scale reading = _____

Figure 3.2
A problem used in the nature of gravity preinstruction quiz. A block attached to a scale weighs ten pounds when weighed on the bench (left). What does the block weigh when the scale is placed in a vacuum jar and all air is removed (right)?

under the glass dome. What will the scale reading be now? [pause] And, in the space provided, briefly explain how you decided.

Students write their answers and their rationale. The instructor can read these answers to identify the facets represented in them. To gain the flavor of this analysis, consider the following comments about students' thinking, offered to teachers using our materials:

Students who give an answer of zero pounds for the scale reading in a vacuum usually are thinking that air only presses down, and "without air there would be no weight, like in space."

Other students suggest "a little less than 10 pounds", because "air is very light, so it doesn't press down very hard, but it does press down some," thus, taking the air away will only decrease the scale reading slightly.

Other students suggest there will be no change at all. "Air has absolutely no effect on scale reading." This answer could result either from a belief that fluid media do not exert any forces or pressures on objects in them, or that pushes by the fluid on the top and bottom of an object are equal. (Note that the approach by the typical physics curriculum or instruction would reinforce these ideas. Since the actual effect by the air is so small, the effects of the air typically are dismissed, frequently without any reference to the appropriateness of that assumption.)

A few students suggest that while there are pressures from above and below, there is a net upward pressure by the fluid. "There is a slight buoyant force." (An acceptable, workable idea at this point.)

Finally, a very few students answer that there will be a large increase in the scale reading, "because of the [buoyant] support by the air."

Note that the open-ended question allows the possibility for students to express a facet that we have not previously observed. Therefore the instructional sequence, incorporating facets, can be refined continuously.

Benchmark Instruction

The next stage is to present students with a "benchmark" problem situation that will provoke group discussion in which different students put forth their ideas and discuss them. The lesson is a benchmark in the sense that it becomes a memorable lesson referred to in subsequent discussions. In the case of the nature of gravity unit, the appropriate benchmark is obvious, the teacher "just happens to be prepared" with a vacuum pump, bell jar, spring scale, and an object to hang on the scale. The students are then asked to discuss, publicly, what they think is going to happen.

The goal of this phase is to provoke a group discussion of the facets held by different students. This works well because the ideas behind the facets usually can be defined as reasonable conjectures. Let us consider a few:

The students who suggest that air pressure is involved in weight may be responding to the actual correlation between the presence of air and apparent weight on earth and the lack of air and apparent weightlessness in space. While all scientists learn that "correlation is not causation," looking for causal relations between correlated variables is a technique widely practiced in informal and formal reasoning, and in fact often leads to a correct answer.

A person who feels that air pressure might have something to do with weight also has a point. Air does push down upon an object. What has not been considered is that pressure due to displacement of a fluid medium also pushes upward, and for that matter in all other directions. However, the idea that something below, especially a fluid substance, exerts a force on something above is itself a subtle one (which, in fact, is addressed in another benchmark lesson).

Some people think that air pressure *reduces* apparent weight, by analogy to buoyancy in water. In fact, they are right, but buoyancy in air is small relative to gravitational effects unless the object in question has a large volume and low density, for example, a helium balloon.

As can be seen, an advocacy argument could be made for each of the different facets. The instructor's role at this point is to honor the attempted answer and encourage students to express their rationale, showing that these are real questions and that the resolution of the argument is not at all simple. In particular, students are urged to concentrate on such questions as "Is this idea ever true? When, in what contexts?" and "Is this idea valid in this particular context? Why or why not?"

The teacher attempts to maintain neutrality during the discussion (and, most importantly, does not present a voice of authority). However the teacher must have a clear idea of the various issues through which students will be guided. If all goes well, at some point in the discussion the students will be ready to take what is probably the most important step in scientific reasoning, resolving their disputes by appealing to data. Having gone as far as they can by reason, the students want to run the experiment.

After a preliminary demonstration that the vacuum pump really does evacuate the air from the bell jar, the experiment is run. Students see that there is no detectable difference in the scale reading in the vacuum versus in air.

Rather than presenting this as a triumph for the right reasoning, the instructor then initiates a discussion of the interpretation of the data. This part of the discussion is intended to illustrate the point that scientific experiments are seldom conducted to find out "what happens" in the sense of obtaining a definite fact. Rather, they are conducted in order to develop evidence in support of, or to refute, a conclusion. In this particular benchmark lesson, the teacher "revisits" some earlier concepts of measurement, by urging the class to consider the following questions: "What can we conclude from the experiment?" "Given the uncertainty of the scale reading, can we say for sure that the value is still exactly the same?" "What original suggested answers can we definitely eliminate? What answers can we not eliminate, knowing the results of this experiment?" and "What ideas can we conclude do not apply?"

The intended result of this discussion is that certain outcomes and arguments can certainly be eliminated. The students can confidently assert that the weight did not go to zero, nor did it increase greatly. Therefore, buoyancy effects due to air clearly do not have a major influence on apparent weight. On the other hand, it is clear we cannot discriminate between the possibilities that air has no effect or that it has some (positive or negative) effect that cannot be detected by our measuring scale. The students are led to the conclusion that the effects of gravity and of the surrounding medium are clearly different, and that gravity is the major cause of apparent weight for "most objects in air." However, there are many questions about apparent weight remaining to be resolved.

Not attaining complete closure, not obtaining "the" answer, at this point in the instruction is a source of frustration to some students and teachers. However, it does reflect the nature of scientific experimentation. We believe that an instructional method that emphasizes discovery of the "right" answer actually distorts students' views of what the scientific process really is.

Elaboration: In-Class Experiments, Problems, and Discussion

Subsequent discussions and laboratory investigations allow students to explore their ideas concerning the relationships between gravity, apparent weight, and the effects of a surrounding medium. Ordinary daily experiences are brought out for investigation: an inverted glass of water with a plastic card over the opening (the water does not come out), a vertical straw dipped in water with a finger placed over the upper end (the water does not come out of the lower end until the finger is removed from the top), an inverted cylinder lowered into a larger, tall cylinder of water (it "floats," and as you push the inverted cylinder down, you can see the water rise relative to the inside of the inverted cylinder), and a two-liter, water-filled soda bottle with three holes at different levels down the side (uncapped, water from the lowest hole comes out fastest; capped, air goes in the top hole and water comes out the bottom hole).

The important thing is that the students are encouraged to extract general principles from a variety of specific contexts. They are continually asked, "What can each experiment tell us that might relate to all of the other situations, including the original benchmark problem?" New issues are opened up as well, touching on such concepts as the "stickiness" of water, and the apparent "sucking" by vacuums. In addition to encouraging additional investigation of issues, the teacher can help students note the analogical similarity between what happens to an object submerged in a container of water and what happens to an object submerged in the "ocean of air" around the earth.

A final experiment for this unit affords students the opportunity to try their new understanding and reasoning in yet another specific context. A solid metal slug is "weighed" first in air, then partially submerged in water (scale reading is slightly less), totally submerged just below the surface of the water (scale reading is even less), and totally submerged deep in the container of water (scale reading is the same as any other position, as long as it is totally submerged). From the scale reading in air, students are asked to predict (qualitatively compare) each of the other results, then do the experiment, record their results, and finally, interpret those results in the form of general principles about the pushes by a fluid on a submerged object. For a last task, students are asked to relate these results and the results of the previous experiments to the original benchmark experience of weighing an object in air and in a vacuum. "What if we had a scale with infinite precision?"

The purpose of doing experiments in these different contexts is to give students experience in recognizing common, physics-relevant features that appear in different contexts. Note that this approach is completely consistent with current theories in cognitive psychology, which stress the importance of pattern recognition as a cue to the use of different methods of reasoning. Numerous authors have said that "novices react to surface features, experts look at the 'deep structure' of a situation." Without elaboration, this statement says little more than that experts look at the right things and novices do not. The teaching methods developed here are intended to give students experience in coding real-world problems into physics-relevant terms. This contrasts with much of traditional physics teaching, which emphasizes how to solve a problem after it has been appropriately coded.

Assessment Embedded within Instruction

The instructional techniques just described are conducted as group problem-solving sessions. In addition, students are given a chance to check their own understanding by completing a variety of quizzes on which they are given immediate feedback about the adequacy of their answers and reasoning. While some use has been made of paper-and-pencil quizzes, our preferred method of self-assessment is to have the students work through computer-presented problems, using a program called DIAGNOSER. We discuss the program in some detail here because it represents instructional innovation consistent with our theoretical perspective.

Technically, the DIAGNOSER is a Hypercard program, designed to run on a Macintosh LC or similar configuration. This restriction was placed on the programmers to ensure that the program would run on machines likely to be available to schools. A technical description has been presented elsewhere (Levidow, Hunt, and McKee 1991). Here we concentrate on the students' view of DIAGNOSER and its relation to our theoretical framework.

The DIAGNOSER is organized into units that parallel the units of instruction in our physics course. Within our example unit, a cluster of questions focuses on the effects of a surrounding medium on scale readings when one attempts to weigh an object. Within each cluster, the DIAGNOSER contains several question sets. Each set may address specific situations dealt with in the recent instruction, to emphasize to students that we want them to understand, and be able to explain, these situations. Other sets depict problems, consistent with our goal of encouraging students to generalize the context where they apply physics principles.

Each question set consists of five Hypercard screens. The first screen contains a phenomenological question, typically asking the student, "What would happen if . . . ?" The appropriate observations or predictions are presented in a multiple-choice format. Each of the choices represents the choice a student would make if he or she saw a particular facet as being applicable in this context. Naturally, one of the choices is always a "physicist-like" facet, representing one way a physicist would analyze the question that has been posed.

The second screen is a simple rating form, on which students indicate their confidence in their answer. Students are asked to tell us whether they are "just guessing" or have confidence in their reasoning. The data gathered from these responses have, to date, been used only for research purposes, and are not part of the teaching method itself.

The third screen asks the student, "What reasoning best justifies the answer you chose?" Again the format is multiple-choice, with each choice briefly paraphrasing a facet as applied to this problem context. We regard this as an extremely important step. It reinforces the idea that "gut feeling" answers are not sufficient; every time a student answers a question the student should attempt to justify it. "How do you know . . . ?" and "Why do you believe ?" are prominent questions in the class instruction.

At this point, the program has two pieces of information about a student; the answer that the student chose, which implies a facet, and the justification that the student gave, which also implies a facet. This means that the program can distinguish between three types of students: students who gave the physics-like answer and justified it correctly, students who gave some other answer associated with a non-physicist facet and justified their answer by appeal to the same facet, and students who gave an answer associated with one facet and justified it by reasoning associated with another facet. In more conceptual terms, the program can distinguish between students whose answers and reasons are consistent with each other and consistent with physics, students whose answers and reasons are consistent with each other but not consistent with physics, and students whose answers and reasons are not consistent with each other.

In the traditional sense, only the first type of student is correct. (Indeed, a traditional question that asked only for an answer could not distinguish between a person who understands and a person who gave the "correct" answer for problematic reasons.) However, we believe that there is an important distinction between the second and third types: students who reason consistently but not in accord with physics and students whose answers and reasons are inconsistent with each other. The second type of student needs to consider the context-specific nature of his or her argument, but there is nothing wrong with the student's reasoning style per se. It is consistent. The third type of student needs to note the apparent inconsistency in his or her reasoning and needs to be encouraged to address the apparent knowledge or reasoning difficulty associated with the inconsistency.

These possibilities are reflected in the fourth screen, which we call the "diagnosis" screen. What the diagnosis screen says depends upon precisely what the student did. Students who give the correct alternative and the physicist's explanation of it receive an encouraging message. When students provide an answer that is consistent with their reasoning, but not in accord with the principles of physics, the diagnosis message specifically acknowledges their consistent reasoning, and then suggests some further situations that ought to be explored. These situations are intended to illustrate the need to develop reasons that rely on generalizable physical principles rather than upon the specific context of a particular problem.

Students who display inconsistencies in reasoning are treated in a different way. If a student gives the "right" answer but cannot justify it, the situation is pointed out, and the inconsistency is called to the student's attention in a somewhat disapproving way. Finally, the student may choose a "wrong" answer, and give an inconsistent reason for it. The diagnosis message is slightly more curt, but only slightly. In general, DIAGNOSER messages clearly favor understanding and consistent reasoning.

The question, reasoning, and diagnosis screens have an additional option for the student. Instead of just answering the question, the student can "write a note to the instructor." Students who exercise this option are routed to a primitive electronic mail system, where they can leave a note about their interpretation of the question or about their difficulties with the content. These notes can be scrutinized by the teacher/researcher, and used to assist the individual student, to improve DIAGNOSER questions, and to modify activities to improve instruction.

Students are also allowed to move back and forth between the question and the reasoning screens. This is done to encourage them to think about why they have answered the question the way they have, and to seek more general reasons for answering questions in specific contexts.

The DIAGNOSER is run in parallel with other instructional activities going on in the classroom. Some students will be working on

DIAGNOSER while others are working in groups on problem-solving or additional laboratory investigations. In the case of our example subunit, the class may even be moving ahead into the next subunit. Although students work on the DIAGNOSER individually, they are not graded on their performance on it. It is a tool to help them assess their own thinking, and it is a tool to help the teacher determine additional instructional needs for the class as a whole or for students individually. It is also a device to assist the students and teacher in maintaining a focus on understanding and reasoning.

In terms of distribution of class time, we estimate that about 25 percent of the total class time is used for large group discussions, 40 percent for laboratory studies, 30 percent for small group discussions, and 5 percent for instruction with the DIAGNOSER. We stress that these are estimates of what happens, rather than goals we attempt to achieve. There also appears to be a fair amount of variation in the distribution of time across instructors, so that these numbers might vary by as much as 10 percent from one teacher to another.

Assessment of Knowledge States after Instruction
A unit of instruction may consist of several benchmark experiences and many more elaboration experiences together with the associated DIAGNOSER sessions. Sometime after a unit is completed, students are tested. Consistent with our general philosophy, the end of unit examination includes questions that require application of physics concepts beyond the specific contexts dealt with in class.

The postinstruction questions are clustered about related facets, in much the same way the DIAGNOSER frames are. In our example cluster, test questions would probe students' thinking about situations in which the local air pressure is substantially changed. Have students moved from believing that air pressure is the cause of gravitational force? Do they still believe that air pressure only pushes in the downward direction? Other questions focus on interpreting the effects of a surrounding fluid medium. In the situation with a smaller cylinder inverted and floating in the water of a tall cylinder, what is the meaning of the fact that the water level in the inverted cylinder rises as that cylinder is pushed deeper and deeper into the water of the tall cylinder?

In designing questions we also develop lists of expected answers and their rationales, in terms of facets. The resulting records, from preinstruction quizzes through the diagnoser and finally the postinstructional quiz, allow us to examine the trail of facets that students take as they develop an understanding of a topic in elementary physics.

Status of the Project: Educational Evaluation

This project can be evaluated from two different views: as an investigation to improve the teaching of physics, and, more generally, as an effort to apply the concepts of cognitive science in an instructional setting. We will first consider the former goal, and then the latter, more general one.

To give some flavor of the educational results, let us continue with the example unit. The statistics reported are from a physics course taught at Mercer Island High School in Washington State. The course enrolled 180 students, divided into sections of about 25 students each.

The greatest increases in the use of physics-like reasoning occurred during the instruction period, from the preinstruction quiz on through the time the DIAGNOSER was used. On a preinstruction quiz only 3 percent of the students wrote answers that indicated a clear understanding of the concepts of physics involved in buoyancy and gravity questions. When students from this class worked through the relevant DIAGNOSER problem, they correctly answered the question (i.e., stated what would happen in the problem as posed) 81 percent of the time, and gave answers consistent with general principles of physics 59 percent of the time. On the end of semester final exam 61 percent of the students chose appropriate answers to gravity and buoyancy questions, and defended them well in writing. Three relevant questions were included on the end of year final, and from 55 to 63 percent of the students answered them correctly.

These figures refer to students who gave answers that clearly agree with the correct answer, as reflected in physics textbooks. What about the 40 percent of the students who still did not provide a physics-like answer? It turns out that they did show evidence of moving toward physics understanding, although they were not quite all the way there.

In the preinstruction quiz two facets accounted for 49 percent of the choices: the ideas that "downward pressure causes gravity" and that "fluid mediums push mainly downward." These facets accounted for less than 20 percent of the responses in DIAGNOSER sessions and about the same percentage of the responses in the semester and end of year examinations. Apparently about half of our students came to physics instruction believing that air and perhaps even water pressure effects are mainly in the downward direction. By the end of the year, through early specific instruction and later revisiting, this belief was greatly reduced. Over half of the students were now able to demonstrate good, productive understanding of buoyant effects, incorporating differences in the pushes from the fluid from above and below the object. This is in contrast to the less than 4 percent of the students who

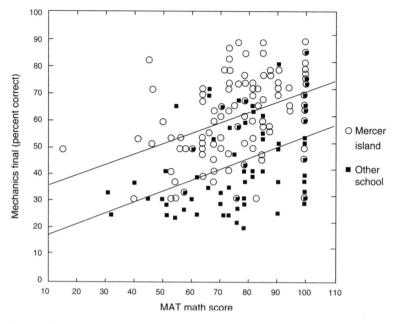

Figure 3.3
Mercer Island vs. comparable school

were able to articulate these ideas at the beginning of the unit. Given that this is a difficult topic conceptually, even for many physics teachers, we see these results as encouraging.

Moving away from this specific unit, we have considerable evidence showing that the method of instruction is beneficial over a variety of topics. Figure 3.3 compares the performance of Mercer Island High School students to the performance of students receiving more conventional physics instruction at a comparable high school in Washington State.[2] Performance on a national examination is compared, as a function of school and the student's score on a mathematics achievement test. We used this test as a covariate because mathematics has often been found to be a good predictor of physics achievement (as it is amongst our students) and because the comparison shows that the control school is, indeed, generally comparable in student quality. The performance of Mercer Island students is clearly better than that of students in the comparable school, even after allowing for the small difference in mathematics achievement, which favored the Mercer Island students.

Figure 3.3 in part compares conventional instruction methods to those delivered by Jim Minstrell (JM), who developed the instructional

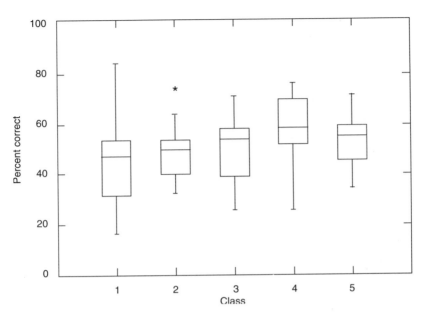

Figure 3.4
Mercer Island electricity final results divided by class

method himself. It is important to show that others can use the same method. Figure 3.4 shows the performance of five sections of the Mercer Island course; one taught by JM and the other four taught by teachers he coached. The sections are clearly comparable. The only section that stands out (which was not taught by JM) contained students who were also participating in a special mathematics course, and who were probably superior candidates for science instruction.

These results show that the teaching technique and its accompanying technology can be used to improve physics instruction, within an important limit. The teachers involved received intensive, on-site coaching by the method's originator. This is clearly not feasible for teachers in general. What we need to know next is whether the method can improve physics instruction in other schools, in situations in which teachers receive much less coaching. During the 1991–92 and 1992–93 school years the teaching method was tested in five other high schools, including the comparison school for which data was reported earlier. The results of this study will be crucial in determining how widely the teaching approach can be exported.

Finally, we close with a practical comment about the techniques described here. They take a great deal of time, compared to conventional didactic instruction. As a result, teachers using these methods simply do not get through what many regard as the appropriate curriculum for the year. This is clearly an administrative problem. In our defense, we point out that many critics of U.S. science teaching have said that the one-year physics curriculum is unrealistic. We agree with those who suggest that "covering less content well" is "more in the long run" (e.g., American Association for the Advancement of Science 2061, California Framework, National Science Teachers Association Scope, Sequence and Coordination Project). However, this issue is a matter for educational policy rather than cognitive research.

In psychological and educational terms, the methods described here provide a relatively unstructured setting in which the same physics ideas are presented using multiple, varied contexts. There is a great deal of research showing that when the same amount of information is presented in a structured or an unstructured manner low ability students do best learning from structured material, while high ability students do best learning from unstructured material (Snow and Yalow 1982). Our results (and particularly figure 3.3) show improvement throughout the range of ability in the classroom. This indicates that the redundancy of the multiple-context approach to teaching has overcome any disadvantage that the less able students suffer from the unstructured style of presentation. It might be that the more capable students could learn as much in less time by following a less redundant course of instruction. We have not systematically collected any data that could be used to address this issue.

Results Relevant to Cognitive Science

The relationship between the results we observe here and theory in cognitive science is complex. Before going into detail, we offer an analogy. Trying to develop basic theories of cognition by observing classroom behavior is a bit like trying to develop theories of aerodynamics by observing bird flight. There are simply too many variables covarying simultaneously to get the sort of precise picture essential to good theory development.

This does not mean that classroom observations are irrelevant to cognitive theory (or vice versa), any more than bird flight is irrelevant to aerodynamics. In each case, we would be disturbed about the status of a theory if observations seemed to contradict it. With that idea in mind, we may ask how well cognitive science concepts can account for our observations. Note that here we are somewhat in the same position as were the students weighing a block inside of a vacuum chamber. The students had to realize that the conclusions drawn from observations are always qualified by the accuracy of those observations. Sadly, in the psychological case, the scale is far from perfect.

There are two levels at which we relate cognitive theory to classroom observations. One is at the level of theories of thinking in general; the other is at the level of theories about the organization of knowledge of the physical world. We will proceed from the more abstract level to the concrete problem level.

Since the pioneering work of Newell and Simon (1972), cognitive theories have stressed the pattern-action organization of thought. Basic thought is a two-step process: (1) recognizing that a pattern is appropriate for some action, and (2) taking the action. In terms of problem solving, the action is often the execution of some fairly complex procedure, such as determining the net force acting on an object under the influence of several forces. Our approach has been to stress the pattern-recognition step. By systematically presenting applications of the same physical principles in different contexts, these teaching methods effectively stamp in the pattern recognition part of problem solving. The success of the method, compared to standard instruction, which stresses the problem solving actions to be taken, attests to the importance of pattern recognition in complex problem solving.

This project has at least a potential for answering interesting questions about the way in which knowledge is organized in the mind. As we pointed out earlier, everyone's mind has to incorporate some rules for dealing with the physical world. One of the interesting questions raised is the way in which these rules are organized. Various proposals have been made arguing that students' untutored conceptions may be similar to Aristotle's, to those of the medieval scholastics, or may simply be incoherent.

As indicated earlier, we take an intermediate view. We do not think that students' ideas form a logical system, as Aristotle's did, but we do not think that they are incoherent either. Rather, we see their ideas as generally being consistent within a recognizable context, and perhaps following some rules of thumb about the use of very general principles. Consider diSessa's (1983) example of Ohm's "phenomenological primitive" (p-prim), which diSessa described as follows: if an action is achieved by acting through a resisting channel, it is necessary to increase the push through the channel when the resistive force increases. This concept could apply anywhere from physics to politics. In either field, Ohm's p-prim could not be recognized directly, but an instantiation of it could be recognized, for example, if a resistor were to be placed between a motor and a power source the power source would have to be increased to keep the motor running. Such instantiations, in physics, would correspond to something like our facets.

If diSessa's ideas are correct, a person who believed strongly in a particular p-prim should use its various instantiations in a variety of different contexts. In our terms, this means that the use of facets derived from the same p-prim ought to be correlated over subjects tested in different contexts. We have, on occasion, made some observations that suggest that this is the case. An example is what we have called the "more means more" principle. This principle asserts that if a surface property of a problem appears to be correlated with a physical measurement, then increasing the surface property will always increase the quantity of the physical measurement.

To illustrate, students know that pulleys are used to obtain mechanical advantage (to be able to exert less force) when lifting weights. They also know that resistors increase the resistance of a circuit. The "more means more" principle asserts that given two pulley systems, one with X pulleys and one with $X + Y$ pulleys, the second system produces the greater mechanical advantage. Applied to electrical circuits, the "more means more" principle asserts that if two circuits have an unequal number of resistors, the circuit with the greater number of resistors has the greater resistance. Neither assertion is strictly correct, because the configuration of pulleys (or resistors) must also be considered.

We have found that students who rely on the "more means more" principle to solve problems in mechanics also use this principle to solve problems in circuit electricity. We are now trying to determine whether or not similar "rough and ready" heuristics will cause clustering of other facets. We are hindered in this endeavor by the constraints of the teaching environment. Since we are dealing with real students, the multiple-choice questions on examinations must be constructed to balance physics facets against each other. The limited time available makes it hard to construct examinations that also pit facets derived from more abstract p-prims against each other.

General Discussion

In this section we will discuss what we think we have learned, and what these findings imply both for cognitive science and for education. We first ask where cognitive science has made a difference in this project. We see two sorts of contributions. One is conceptual. While the cognitive science approach certainly did not create the teaching techniques, the cognitive science analysis has provided a systematic way of thinking about the sorts of conceptual organization with which students begin the course, and hopefully the sorts of conceptual changes that take place during the course.

We speculate that these changes are of three sorts. The first, which are easiest to document, simply have to do with the facets and concepts of physics. The examination results are prima facie evidence that students have acquired something akin to physics knowledge. The second change we hope to effect, but which is much harder to document, is student acquisition of well-organized problem-solving methods. What we do not know, though, is whether these problem-solving methods would transfer to areas outside of physics instruction.

Finally, we hope, but again cannot prove, that students have acquired an important concept about science: the concept that scientific authority rests on the ability to interpret or explain empirical evidence, and not upon the social authority of learned savants. Both the benchmark experience and the DIAGNOSER exercises are oriented toward interpreting and explaining observations. Students are reinforced for offering coherent explanations about why something happened. They are not rewarded, not even by the computer program, for predicting a correct answer without having an adequate explanation for it.

Cognitive science's (or more properly, cognitive psychology's) second contribution to this program has been in the application of technology. The development of computer presented questioning systems, such as DIAGNOSER, and the application of statistical techniques, such as clustering and multidimensional scaling (MDS), are quite routine in cognitive psychology laboratories. These technologies are not normally available to classroom teachers, nor do teachers often have the time or background to learn to use them when they are available. By integrating computer-driven procedures for data acquisition (DIAGNOSER) and analysis (MDS, clustering, and other methods not mentioned here), we hope to provide classroom teachers with technical tools for managing the mass of data that they can easily acquire during the course of a semester's instruction.

The teaching and technological methods developed during this project are almost completely independent of the subject matter of physics. The most extreme separation is the DIAGNOSER, where the physics questions are presented as data to a domain-independent program. Strictly speaking, the only requirements are that the instructor have a clear idea of the schema and facet structures that are the targets of instruction, that the instructor have some way of eliciting students' preinstruction understanding and reasoning about the topic, and that the instructor be sufficiently versed in the topic so that he or she can construct the appropriate benchmark experiences and DIAGNOSER questions. In fact, these restrictions are fairly severe if they are applied to individual instructors. On the other hand, we believe that groups of experienced teachers, working together, can develop courses along the lines that we have indicated here.

We are now exploring the possibility of constructing DIAGNOSER programs and concomitant teaching methods for introductory statistics. Some interesting suggestions have been made to us about using the methods for teaching elementary English composition and history, but these have not been developed in any detail.

We close on a cautionary note. While we are generally encouraged by our results, we have found, and are finding, certain problems with the method of instruction. We list them here, with a brief commentary on each problem.

1. The method takes a great deal of time. It is simply not possible to get through the High School standard physics curriculum in one year using this technique. An exploratory study revealed a similar problem with introductory psychological statistics. Of course, American education has been criticized for generally putting too much into the curriculum. The United States is one of the few industrialized countries in which high school physics is a one-year course. We would like to think that leaving students with a firm foundation in the basics of physics is better than leaving them with a fuzzy picture of more material. However, we cannot prove this. Perhaps a student who can handle the standard instructional methods can learn more, in the same amount of time, in a standard course.

2. The method assumes student (and social) acceptance of the technique. This has proven a problem, especially as we have tried to export the method to schools outside of its original home. It may be even a larger problem in university classes. Students in high school physics have already been exposed to ten or more years of the U.S. instructional system. A great deal of that system—and to an even greater extent, university education—relies on a social situation in which an instructor, acting on social authority, presents problems and solutions that students are supposed to comprehend. Students are used to this technique, and are quite sensitive to the instructor's skill in using it. There is a sort of social contract, in which a good instructor is one who tells the student, in a clear, unambiguous manner, what it is that the student is supposed to memorize.

The sort of instruction suggested in this paper violates that contract. Students and parents do not always accept the violation, and may even perceive a teacher's failure to give answers as evidence of a teacher's inability to do so. Indeed, we have anecdotes about students who have condemned the DIAGNOSER for its failure to unambiguously tell them when their answers are "right" and when they are "wrong."

3. If the technique is to be of general use, it has to be exportable to many schools. The easiest part of the technique to export is the DIAGNOSER, but even it is not easy. The problem is not "buying a computer"; many schools have computers. The problem is keeping the program compatible with the continual, asynchronous changes in operating systems, software and hardware updates, and even fighting student hackers' attempts to sabotage the program. Since the school system is decentralized, these problems are typically different at each site. As a result, we believe that the continued use of the technology, alone, would require a technical support staff far greater than that usually available to educational systems, outside of a few selected demonstration projects.

4. The method depends upon capturing teachers' experience with student conceptions, with appropriate benchmark experiences, and with asking DIAGNOSER sorts of questions. Our own work capitalized on the experience of one teacher (JM), integrated over more than twenty years. A more feasible method of capitalizing on experience is to aggregate the experience and ideas of several teachers. This implies a communication network among teachers within one school and/or in different schools, and provision of time for the teachers to communicate as they develop their courses. "In-service education days" hardly capture the level of commitment required.

We believe our demonstration studies have shown that substantial improvement in physics instruction is achievable. We are fairly confident that the methods can profitably be generalized to other fields, although field-specific modifications will certainly be needed. The educational techniques are limited by certain noncognitive aspects of education, as just outlined. We believe that these noncognitive limitations can be overcome, given sufficient commitment of resources to education on a continuing basis. Whether or not such commitment is likely is a topic beyond the scope of this chapter.

Notes

Although this project was initiated by the authors, the present effort, findings and implications are the results of efforts of many other teachers and staff members. Physics teachers in Mercer Island, Bellevue, Northshore, and Spokane School Districts are now coaching us and each other in curriculum revision and in teaching strategies. Colene McKee, Björn Levidow, and Dawn Aiken have contributed greatly to the programming of the DIAGNOSER. Emily van Zee, Dorothy Simpson, Virginia Stimpson, and Vicka Corey have contributed thoughtfully to the generalization of the teaching approach. The authors are thankful for the effort and ideas that all these people have shared.

1. The ideal student should also grasp another point about science itself. The currently believed principles of physics lead to inconsistent reasoning in some circumstances, for example, the distinction between wave and quantum explanations of radiation. The ideal student will realize that physicists (like all other scientists) claim not to have discovered truth, but rather to be developing successively more general, more consistent explanations.

2. Both Mercer Island and the comparable high school are in upper middle-class suburban school districts.

Chapter 4

Enhancing the Acquisition of Conceptual Structures through Hypermedia

Kathryn T. Spoehr

The goal of education is to ensure that students learn to think productively and flexibly in a number of subject areas fundamental to their ability to function in the world. Productive and flexible thinking implies that students can identify important problems, muster relevant information, and use that information in appropriate ways to solve problems or create new ideas. The problem for educators is, of course, *how* to help students learn and appropriately use these critical skills for thinking. But to teach such skills effectively requires a detailed understanding of the procedural and declarative knowledge needed to carry out each one. Assembling such detailed knowledge can be time-consuming and inexact for even the simplest skills, and the whole endeavor can be frustrating because the way in which each component skill works may well depend on the domain or subject matter in which it is applied.

The research and educational intervention project discussed in this chapter arose from the conviction that one of the most important functions basic research in cognitive science can fulfill for education is to describe thinking skills in ways that lead to effective classroom practice. More specifically, the work here demonstrates how general principles of knowledge representation in human memory derived from the experimental literature in cognitive science can be applied in educational settings. The project focuses on the kinds of knowledge representations that support reasoning in subject matters rarely studied in the laboratory, namely, history and literature. Understanding the nature of these representations, especially those associated with sophisticated reasoning in these fields, has motivated a particular, technology-based instructional intervention based on hypermedia. The intervention, in turn, has provided an additional resource for deepening the basic science of understanding how knowledge representations change with learning.

Expertise and How It Develops

To begin to understand the importance of knowledge representation to acquiring skill in thinking, it is instructive to review the findings on expertise in fields such as physics and mathematics, where considerable research has been done. When one looks for findings that are consistent across a wide range of subject-matter disciplines, the research literature suggests several ways in which experts differ from novices. Obviously, experts in a domain know more about the domain than novices. But there are several important points to be made about what it means to "know more." Certainly, experts have learned more pieces of information, the declarative knowledge base. Under normal circumstances, having a larger knowledge base might be a disadvantage. Anderson (1974) and others have demonstrated what has come to be known as the "fan effect," that the more individual facts someone knows about a single entity, the more difficult it is to retrieve any one of those facts from memory. The fan effect, however, appears only to occur when the set of facts associated with a given entity has no internal cohesiveness or integration (Smith, Adams, and Schorr 1978). Since experts do not exhibit fan-effect difficulties in their own domains of expertise, it is likely that they integrate individual pieces of knowledge into organized structures that aid retrieval. Chiesi, Spilich, and Voss (1979) have shown that experts, in fact, do better memorizing integrated sets of information in their chosen field than they do in memorizing many individual facts.

Because experts have a well-organized representation for information in their field, they can capitalize on that structure to help them learn and memorize new information. The knowledge provides a scaffold for acquiring new information—experts are consistently able to learn new pieces of information in their fields more thoroughly and with much less study than are novices (Adelson 1981; Chase and Simon 1973b; Dawson, Zeitz, and Wright 1989; Dee-Lucas and Larkin 1986; Hatano and Osawa 1983; Reitman 1976). The same set of studies demonstrates that people who become experts in various fields do not simply learn better because they have generally superior memory. The advantages experts enjoy extend only as far as their fields of expertise.

Many studies have made it clear that while novices may organize information in a domain according to surface similarities between facts, the expert's knowledge organization reflects deep, abstract principles. Chi, Feltovich, and Glaser (1981) conducted what is now the classic study of expert performance in physics problem solving. Subjects in this experiment were asked to sort problems in basic mechanics into meaningful categories. While the novices tended to sort on the basis of which problems contained mention of the same physical objects (e.g., all the problems having to do with springs in one pile, and all those having to do with inclined planes in another), experts sorted on the basis of which physical principles were required in the solution to the problem. This suggests that an expert's information about a domain is organized according to deep principles that are linked to or result from well-learned reasoning procedures. This means that the knowledge representation is set up in such a way that the identification of a particular set of facts or states of the world is tied directly to a set of reasoning procedures which make use of that information to solve problems.

A final component of expertise is that the more experienced one is in a domain, the more likely it is that one has developed fast, efficient procedures to retrieve and use information in the domain. Procedures become automatic through practice (Neves and Anderson 1981) and eventually can be carried out effortlessly. Moreover, procedures originally accomplished through a succession of component steps gradually become integrated wholes in which the individual steps lose their separate identities. Neves and Anderson call this process of compilation of problem-solving steps "proceduralization" and note that although it creates a repertoire of fast, accurate methods for reasoning in the domain, the resulting procedures are often immune to conscious manipulation or metacognitive inspection.

One particularly revealing set of experiments about how knowledge is organized by experts has been conducted by Chi and her associates (Chi and Koeske 1983; Gobbo and Chi 1986; Chi, Hutchinson, and Robin 1989). These studies focused entirely on expertise in children and found many of the same phenomena alluded to above with adult experts and novices. By testing children who had different levels of familiarity with dinosaurs, Chi was able to derive concept maps of the domain for each of her subjects. Such maps use a node/link structure where concepts, in this case dinosaur names, were the nodes, and the relationships between them were the links. Chi, Hutchinson, and Robin (1989) found that the more expert representations had a strongly hierarchical flavor and were locally coherent (i.e., had a great number of linkages between similar concepts) and globally differentiated (i.e., had relatively few links between clusters of quite different concepts).

Expertise in the Humanities

While concepts in the sciences and mathematics can usually be organized (at least by experts) according to lawful relationships and logical entailments, and can be verified by empirical observation, it is much more difficult to understand and define an appropriate conceptual structure for students to learn in the humanities and social sciences. In these disciplines the knowledge representation is multiply linked, such that the meaning of an abstract concept derives, at least in part, from the ways in which it relates to other abstractions, and specific pieces of information are associated with more than one abstraction. Moreover, in these disciplines categorical relationships between concepts are often amorphous. Thus it is not surprising that students, especially those in high school just beginning to acquire a systematic understanding of subjects like literature and history, have difficulty learning an appropriate conceptual organization for either of these two subjects.

There is some relatively recent research which indicates that at a general level, the characteristics of expertise in the sciences also apply to expertise in historical and literary thinking. Zeitz (1989) compared the performance of doctoral-level graduate students in literature with that of non-experts in literature (high-school students and graduate students in science) on a number of tasks that assessed comprehension and reasoning using literary materials. Like experts in many other domains, Zeitz found that literary experts demonstrate superior memory for new, domain-relevant information. The effect was particularly pronounced for abstractions and material which had more than one level of meaning from a symbolic point of view. Since these are the elements upon which literary analysis is based, it seems that the knowledge representation that supports new learning is one that is intimately tied to reasoning procedures in the field.

Two studies on historical thinking show analogous results. Spoehr and Katz (1989) tested history faculty members, history graduate students, and undergraduate students. The experts in this study were able to recall more of a novel text in the field, and showed organization in a sorting task that was based on abstract relationships rather than surface characteristics of the stimuli. Similarly, Wineburg (1991) collected protocols from trained historians and from high school students who were asked to think out loud as they conducted a limited historical investigation based on a set of primary-source historical documents. Wineburg found that the trained historians were much more likely to use three particular heuristics. First, they were more likely to check back and forth among documents to *corroborate* evidence. Thus, as they were constructing hypotheses, they were looking to find whether the information supporting them was correct and whether there might be contradictions. Second, historians were more likely to consider the *source* of a document in interpreting its contents. They often began reading an individual document by making sure they knew who wrote it and when. This reflected their implicit under-standing of the role of an individual's values and beliefs in describing and interpreting historical events. Finally, historians also tended to *contextualize* their interpretation of events in terms of when and where the events happened. By doing so, they could develop a clearer idea of cause and effect.

What emerges from this literature is a picture of expertise in history and literature in which the goal is to generate explanations at an abstract level by extracting patterns and commonalities from a collec-tion of data. The processes by which this happens in these fields does not follow strict rules of logic and is almost never based on universal laws. Instead, problem solving in history and literature requires look-ing for patterns of knowledge; in other words, it does not call for accumulation of declarative facts, but discrimination and informed judgment about the relationships between parts of that knowledge base. Landow (1989) characterizes this process in literature by stating that "the reader must investigate connections and how their relative value might be evaluated" (p. 6). According to Crabtree, Nash, Gag-non, and Waugh (in press), the historian's job is to ask the right questions, to draw appropriate inferences, to make careful judgments when possible (and speculations when necessary), and to arrive at considered conclusions about what it all means.

This is not to say that reasoning in the humanities is entirely differ-ent from reasoning in the sciences and mathematics. In almost every discipline, individual pieces of declarative knowledge have different facets that must be turned to respond appropriately to different lines of reasoning. In ecology, knowledge of a region's climatic temperature can be used as part of an explanation for rainfall; it can be used in a different way to explain vegetative growth. In history, the Kansas-Nebraska Act can be relevant to political history when investigating the causes of the Civil War. It may also be useful to someone trying to follow a line of investigation in economic history (such as the growth and development of American railroads), or to someone looking at the connections between attitudes on slavery and attitudes on race. In other words, in any field not only can facts in one category be affected by facts in another, but even a single fact can move from category to category, depending upon how it is viewed.

Conceptual Neighborhood Structure

A consistent picture of the knowledge representation needed to sup-port historical and literary thinking emerges from the scientific studies discussed so far. The knowledge representation must be richly linked, with the associations between related concepts labeled in a way that facilitates the retrieval of appropriate subsets of material in service of different lines of reasoning. Any one concept is likely to be related to many others, and may even be linked via many labeled associations to any one particular neighbor.

If we take seriously the findings of Chi and Koeske (1983), Spoehr and Katz (1989), and Zeitz (1989), we can be even more explicit about the structure of this linked knowledge representation. Since some concepts are more likely to have links among themselves, with relatively fewer links to other, less related concepts, the knowledge representation must have local coherence and global differentiation. It follows that a basic element to skilled knowledge representation in these domains is what might be termed a *conceptual neighborhood*. A conceptual neighborhood is a cluster of related facts and/or instances, and the relationships between them. The basic elements of such a conceptual neighborhood are most often organized in a roughly hierarchical way, and the neighborhoods themselves can be combined roughly hierarchically to form even larger neighborhoods, and so forth. Moreover, expert conceptual neighborhoods are likely to be organized using deep, abstract concepts. That is, more sophisticated knowledge representations tend to abandon neighborhoods built out of exemplars and information sharing surface characteristics, and move in favor of clustering based on deeper, abstract principles.

Figure 4.1 shows the structure of a relatively sophisticated neighborhood for the concept of "romanticism" in the form of a node/link map. Such concept maps can be generated either by asking people to draw them to reflect their understanding of a particular topic, or can be directly inferred from computer-based hypermedia databases, as we shall see below. Having students generate concept maps has been shown to be an effective instructional method by itself in that it encourages students to organize and systematize their knowledge, identify gaps in their knowledge, and it forces them to be explicit about the nature of relationships between ideas (Novak and Gowin 1984).

But concept maps can also be used to shed light on the nature of the knowledge representation held by its creator. The map in figure 4.1 illustrates some important characteristics of an expert's conceptual neighborhood. Although there is not enough space in the figure to legibly label all of the nodes and links, an important characteristic to know about this particular concept map is that it does not contain appreciably more information on romanticism than might be expected in the map of a student who had just completed an instructional unit on the topic in a high school English class. What is important about this map is the pattern of links. Clearly the number of patterns of links

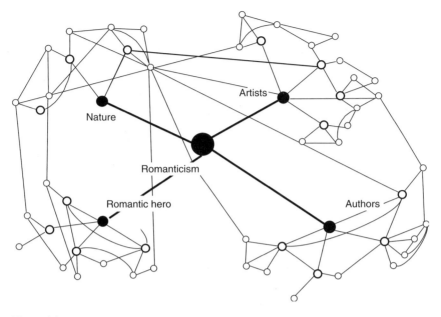

Figure 4.1
An illustration of the conceptual neighborhood for "Romanticism"

among any fixed set of nodes is potentially quite large, each pattern defining a different conceptual neighborhood structure. The conceptual neighborhood structures for experts should be governed by abstractions linked to thinking in the domain. Moreover, conceptual neighborhoods for large, abstract concepts typically have structures with multiple subneighborhoods within which there are many links (local coherence), and between which there are fewer links (global differentiation). Finally, we note that many nodes in an expert neighborhood structure are tied to more than one other node. This allows the expert to use that piece of information in multiple contexts (Spiro, Vispoel, Schmitz, Samarapungavan, and Boerger 1987). On the other hand, some nodes are more tightly bound to a given neighborhood than are others by virtue of having more connections to other nodes in that neighborhood.

Using Electronic Conceptual Neighborhoods to Teach History and Literature

In recent years computer-based hypermedia have begun to attract widespread attention as innovative instructional media (e.g., Beeman et al. 1987; Hammond 1989; Marchionini 1989). Hypermedia allow the user to explore a body of knowledge with multiple connections between any one piece of information and others related to it in some way. In hypermedia the basic units of information comprising the overall corpus may be static text, video, computer graphics, animation, sound, or any other technology that can be computer-controlled. By convention these basic units are referred to as "nodes," while the electronic pathways (often in the form of active screen "buttons") between them are called "links." Although different hypermedia interfaces support different types of user interactions, the attraction of hypermedia for instruction lies in their ability to actively engage the user (student) in the acquisition and use of information, to support multiple instructional uses (tutoring, research, etc.), to support different learning styles, and to promote the acquisition of multiple representations that underlie expert-level reasoning in complex, ill-structured domains (Spiro et al. 1987). From the point of view of a cognitive scientist concerned with helping students acquire expert-level knowledge representations, hypermedia provide one further advantage: they can provide students with examples of sound conceptual neighborhood structures in an environment where these can be used for authentic problem solving in the domain.

Despite hypermedia's many educational benefits, Hammond and Allinson (1989) point out a number of potential problems that must be addressed in order to have an effective hypermedia instructional system. First, users tend to get lost, especially when the corpus is large and/or the users are novices to the domain represented in the corpus. Second, when browsing, users may fail to get an overview of how all of the information fits together. They may thus fail to acquire as much information as they otherwise would from the parts of the corpus they do view, and may also miss entire sections of potentially relevant corpus material because of ignorance of how it relates to the remainder. And finally, in the absence of information that might help them formulate goals and find relevant material, learners may stumble through the corpus in a disorganized and instructionally inefficient manner.

Hammond and Allinson's criticisms are important because they point out why the otherwise powerful hypermedia technology may fail to live up to its full educational potential. An important reason why many (perhaps most) of the instructional hypermedia systems developed to date exhibit one or more of these difficulties is that the technology is so new most operating systems are not yet based on a cognitively based theory of effective hypermedia design. The design issue goes well beyond issues of navigation tools and screen layout.

For if cognitive science is correct about the characteristics of effective conceptual neighborhood structure, then hypermedia design must also incorporate an appropriate structure for the corpus itself. Although many conceptual neighborhood structures might support browsing and simple information storage and retrieval for users who already know the domain well, a smaller set of them are likely to be effective in teaching the important attributes and relationships to a student who has never seen them before.

Over the past few years researchers at Brown University, in collaboration with teachers and students at schools near the university, have been engaged in research that aims to use the insights provided by the above cognitive analysis of knowledge representation to build an effective hypermedia instructional system. The project is known as the ACCESS (American Culture in Context: Enrichment for Secondary Schools) Project, and deals with the subject matter commonly taught in United States history, American literature, and American studies courses. The development of the hypermedia corpus has been accompanied by an evaluation of its effectiveness on a number of dimensions of teaching and learning, and by research that has begun the process of developing a cognitively based theory of hypermedia design.

Design and Construction of the ACCESS Hypermedia Corpus
The ACCESS Project corpus has been constructed primarily by high school teachers, with Brown University staff providing software and other technical support. It now contains over 36.6 megabytes of textual, pictorial, audio, and video materials spanning the time period from 1607–1970. The material was chosen to supplement traditional materials and teaching methods rather than to reproduce or replace printed textbooks. The goals have been to provide students with (1) contextual information that will deepen and broaden their understanding of the two disciplines separately, (2) material that will help integrate history and literature to give students a broader perspective on American culture, and (3) a structure that will encourage the student to acquire sophisticated conceptual neighborhood structures while engaging in problem solving. The corpus runs under HyperCard 2.1 on Apple Macintosh computers and makes use of video disk and audio CD materials.

The initial corpus development and testing was begun by two teachers at Lincoln School (Providence, Rhode Island) in the summer before and during the 1988–89 academic year. These teachers carried forward their authoring activities during the summer of 1989 and during the 1989–90 academic year, completing materials on a schedule that allowed the corpus to be used regularly in both of their courses throughout the entire academic year. They further expanded the corpus during the summer of 1990 and have been using it regularly ever since.

In the summer of 1989 two teachers from the Essential School program at Hope High School (Providence, Rhode Island) were added to the project and began their own authoring effort. The Hope High School teachers felt that they would be able to use parts of the existing corpus, but that because of the different focus of their course (an integrated American culture course rather than coordinated English and history courses), the different set of reading materials they used in their course, and the different nature of the students at their school, they would need to create a significant new portion of the corpus for their own students. Authoring for them began in the summer of 1989 and continued throughout the 1989–90 and 1990–91 academic years. The Hope High School teachers had only enough material prepared for the corpus to be used sporadically during the 1989–90 school year, but continued their development efforts so that it could be used consistently subsequently. Although the ACCESS Project has since grown to include several additional schools, the sections below examine the experience of approximately 175 students at the two schools who used the corpus during the 1989–1991 time period.

From the outset it was clear to the teachers who developed the corpus that its structure would be critical. It needed to maximize the likelihood that students would both extract major conceptual frameworks from the corpus and find relevant material in the corpus without getting lost. Because the teacher-authors were not only experienced teachers, but also subject-matter experts (holding advanced degrees in their subjects), they instinctively settled upon a locally coherent and globally differentiated structure. The corpus superimposes a roughly hierarchical overview structure on the naturally occurring web of links between related nodes. The teachers further decided to explicitly annotate many of the links using the abstract conceptual terms they thought their students should acquire. Other labels were purposefully omitted so that students could learn to use contextual cues to work out the meaning of the links for themselves.

The corpus was built modularly, each teacher individually developing sections of the corpus on topics of interest to her or him, but consulting with other teachers on content and structure. Each module is what is called a "stack" in HyperCard parlance, but also instantiates a conceptual neighborhood containing many subneighborhoods, links between ideas and abstractions, and links to other neighborhoods. The stacks/neighborhoods are roughly of three types:

1. *Historical Period Stack.*   These stacks provide supplementary material on a specific historical period in American History (e.g., "The Colonial Period," "The Civil War," "The 1960s," etc.).

2. *Literary Movement/Individual Author Stack.*   Literary movement stacks provide background and context for a particular literary movement (e.g., "Romanticism," "Modernism," etc.), as well as links to material in stacks on individual authors associated with the movement. Individual author stacks provide in-depth information on a particular author and particular works of that author (both works covered in the course and other works).

3. *Themes in American Culture Stack.*   Themes stacks (e.g., "Popular Music," "Values in American Society," "War and Revolution") pull together similar conceptual material from many of the different literary and historical stacks. They generally contain overview and organizational material, plus a number of links to the relevant specific material in the other stacks.

Although the corpus is organized hierarchically the stack boundaries are not apparent to the user. The initial entry screen to the ACCESS corpus gives the user a choice of general historical periods, literary movements, and themes. Choosing one of these initial options moves the user either directly to information on the chosen topic or to a screen giving a finer-grain breakdown of the options associated with that choice. Once a choice has been made the user is moved to an overview screen showing the major conceptual themes and types of materials associated with the chosen topic. These overviews are often in a diagrammatic form that indicates relationships between the themes. Selecting one of these takes the user directly to the beginning of the chosen topic material. Very often there will be an intermediate layer, or suboverview, which sets forth a finer-grained organization of the theme.

After "descending" through one or more overviews the user comes to individual screens or screen sequences that comprise the bulk of the corpus materials. Screen contents vary and might include any combination of text, graphics, played music, and/or video buttons. These screens also contain buttons that can move the user quickly back "up" through the hierarchy or permit conceptual jumps to other related material distantly located either in the same stack or another stack.

Both the vertical and the horizontal links within the ACCESS corpus provide a computer-based, visual equivalent of the type of mental knowledge representation the student should be constructing. The vertical links are important because they "unpack" important abstractions and concepts into their most important parts, and provide examples and evidence. Thus they give the student an idea of the general layout of the conceptual neighborhood he or she is about to enter. For instance, a student consulting the stack on romanticism will find major headings that include the major nodes labeled in figure 4.1. Often, the headings (vertical links) on major overview screens will recur on overviews for other time periods and issues. The notion of "Political Culture," for example, appears as a major conceptual theme on the overviews for almost every historical time period covered in ACCESS. By exploring this concept multiple times in different contexts, the student develops a sense of the core meaning of the term, but also a sense of how it is applied differently in different contexts

The horizontal links give the fine structure of the conceptual neighborhoods. Some of these will move the student from topic to topic within a single time period—a student reading about Georgian architecture, for example, will be able to follow links to material on the Enlightenment, on William Byrd II and his education as a gentleman, on Thomas Jefferson's ideas about architecture, and so on. Some links will connect to essays about architecture in other time periods, such as the Gothic revival of the nineteenth century. And some links will carry the student across both time and categories, linking, say, some popular music of the 1960s to poetry from the 1920s. The linkage patterns provide the student with multiple examples and representations of an idea. The fact that a single document or idea may be linked to more than one other idea again demonstrates concretely that any fact or idea may be used for different purposes in different contexts.

The screen design and interface support a variety of browsing and information retrieval strategies. Text and pictorial material are placed into the stacks as successive screen images, with some texts requiring several screens. With a few exceptions, the maximum length of such a sequence is eight screens. The basic screen layout is shown in figure 4.2, which illustrates many of the basic functions incorporated into the system. These include: basic sequential navigation (the white arrows), user-specified searches (the FIND icon), printing information (the printer icon), taking notes (the writing hand icon), marking (using the bookmark) one or more locations in the corpus for fast future return, getting system help (the question mark), and jumping to the main system overview or the stack overview. There are also links between nonsequentially created materials, for creating "pop-up" fields for study and quiz information, for displaying additional bibliographic material, for displaying images in an attached video disk monitor, and for playing music using the Macintosh's audio synthesis capability (the

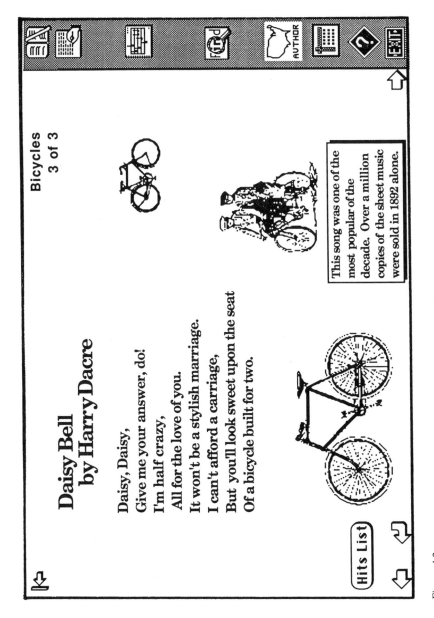

Figure 4.2
An example of the ACCESS corpus screen layout

musical clef) or audio CD. The example screen shown in figure 4.2 appears in the "Gilded Age" stack and provides the student some background on popular music of the era, and allows the student to hear the melody of a song and to read and analyze the lyrics.

The navigation buttons appearing in the upper left corner of each screen reflect the hierarchical organization of the material within each stack. The first screen of a sequence shows a white upwardly pointing arrow at this location. Clicking on this button immediately moves the user "up" one level in the hierarchy to the suboverview or overview sitting immediately "above" it in the information structure. This button also appears on suboverview screens, allowing for quick and easy branching to entry points for related materials. All screens in a multi-screen sequence other than the first have a left-bounded, left-facing arrow button at the top left of the card. This button takes the user directly to the first screen of that sequence. From the first screen the user can print the sequence, get bibliographic information, and/or jump up the hierarchy.

Using Hypermedia in High Schools

Teachers at the two schools used the corpus similarly, though with modifications based both on differences in curriculum and on the differences between the physical arrangements for the computers at the two schools. At Lincoln School, students used the corpus in carrying out two kinds of assignments. One quite regular assignment was for students to familiarize themselves with a teacher-designed portion of the corpus in order to prepare for a class meeting. Because of the nature of the classroom activities at Lincoln, using the corpus in this way encouraged students to look for patterns of information which could be tied to pieces of information in other assigned readings or to issues which might be raised by the teacher in class. The other type of assignment was to research and write an essay based wholly or in part on the materials in the corpus. The essay always required the students to engage in literary or historical analysis—that is, problem solving in one of the domains. Students were also frequently observed in the computer lab browsing the corpus out of their own general interest, and often used the corpus in conjunction with courses taken after their ACCESS year.

At Hope High School, browsing to prepare for class discussion was less frequent simply because the computers were situated in a room where "drop-in" use outside of class periods was difficult to arrange. These students tended to use the corpus during class periods dedicated to individual hypermedia research and exploration. ACCESS was used formally as the basis of two major literature-related projects

(Essential School "exhibitions of mastery") and two history-related projects where the goal was to encourage students to develop reasoning and explanation skills. Corpus browsing was perceived by many Hope High students to be sufficiently fun and interesting that they would request, and usually receive, permission to use the corpus during class time as a reward if they finished other assigned work.

Results

Over the years of using and refining ACCESS, the project staff has investigated several dimensions along with ACCESS has affected teaching and learning. The sections below discuss illustrative findings from each of these types of evaluative criteria.

Student Evaluations of the Corpus and How It Affected Their Learning

As part of the corpus evaluation procedure, a questionnaire was developed to be filled out voluntarily by students after using a portion of the corpus. The responses on the questionnaires were consistent with the comments provided in year-end interviews, and indicated that the corpus was both easy to use and informative. This coincided with computer-lab observations that most students became competent corpus users within ten minutes of starting to use it, and many took frequent advantage of the more advanced functions such as "Find" and "Bookmarking." The students were forthright in their suggestions for improvements and enhancements, especially with regard to the user interface, and many of their suggestions were incorporated into subsequent software revisions.

Since the majority of the responses on the student evaluation questionnaires dealt with the specifics of the material in a particular part of the corpus, those responses will not be detailed here. But at the end of each school year, students at both schools were given a more general survey about their overall experience with the corpus and how they thought it had affected their learning and performance in the relevant class. Table 4.1 shows the percentage of students whose responses fall into certain important categories.

It is clear that students at both schools enjoyed using the corpus despite occasional navigational confusions. Almost all of them found information of value there (though it is hard to imagine how we could have failed to obtain this result, given that successful completion of many assignments depended on the information in the corpus) and felt it helped them in their classes. One interesting aspect of these evaluation data is that many students felt they had missed important connections between the historical and the literary material in the

Table 4.1
Student evaluations of ACCESS

Question	% Agreeing (Lincoln)	% Agreeing (Hope)
Easy to use	94	78
Informative	95	70
I got lost in ACCESS sometimes.	96	100
I could find my way around ACCESS.	96	95
ACCESS made me more thoughtful about what I read.	48	42
Helped me do better in history.	92	63
Helped me do better in English.	86	79
Helped me relate my English and history courses.	47	32
Taught me important computer skills.	73	89
I would have liked to do more with ACCESS	100	84

corpus and thus felt they were unable to relate the two subjects conceptually. Although the students themselves may have thought they were missing connections between the two subjects, their teachers thought the ACCESS corpus was, in fact, significantly enhancing their students' cross-disciplinary thinking. Both teacher comments and classroom observation suggests that students were more likely to bring in information from "outside disciplines" in the ACCESS classes than were students who had not used hypermedia. It appears that because of the natural mixture of history and literary materials in the corpus itself, students were assimilating the interdisciplinary connections without being aware that they were doing so.

How ACCESS Affected the Teachers and Their Instructional Practices
The reactions of the four teachers who used the ACCESS corpus during the 1989–90 school year were assessed through three structured interviews conducted with each teacher at the beginning, middle, and end of the academic year. They were assessed again through a written project chronology and overall assessment at the end of the 1990–91 school year. Because of the small number of respondents it is impossible to quantify their responses in any meaningful way, and so we note that all four teachers felt that using the ACCESS corpus had benefited their students, though the reasons they gave for this opinion differed widely. All of them reported that they thought their students showed better ability to make conceptual connections in class discussions and tests than did students in previous years who had not used

hypermedia. One teacher characterized the difference that ACCESS had made as giving the students "license to make links between ideas," a license that generalized to all parts of their class performance.

One central concern for the teachers was how to fit hypermedia into the traditional set of instructional activities in their classes. The teachers did not think it prudent to significantly increase student workload by giving ACCESS assignments in addition to traditional reading and writing assignments, nor did they wish to use significant amounts of class time for computer-based activities, though this worry was more characteristic of Lincoln School than of Hope High. Over the course of the project the teachers began to worry less about how they could use ACCESS to more efficiently accomplish the same types of assignments they had given in the past, and began to think more about what new things they could do with the resources now available to them. This, in turn, affected their other instructional activities.

One interesting result of having students use ACCESS was observed in the classroom activities of the teachers. While the ACCESS corpus provided students with examples of links and relationships between different types of material in the corpus itself, an important element in many class sessions became finding the links between the corpus materials and other sources of information. Although all of our teachers had joined the project originally because they believed in the importance of students understanding patterns of connections between concepts, they found that the students' interest in and ability to do so was heightened by their hypermedia experience. Linking activities became more common in class, not always at the teachers' instigation, and discussions of issues were more likely to be accompanied by steadily growing concept-map diagrams on the blackboard.

How ACCESS Affected the Academic Performance of Students
One obvious question about the effectiveness of any instructional innovation is whether it makes any noticeable differences in general measures of student performance. In order to see whether ACCESS had any affect on "objective" measures of students' mastery over the subject matters represented in the corpus, we compared, at both schools, the performance of students in the classes of the participating teachers the year before ACCESS became a regular component of instruction with the performance of students the year ACCESS was regularly used. For Lincoln School the comparison was made between the 1988–89 and the 1989–90 school years. The equivalent comparison at Hope High was made between 1989–90 and 1990–91. Final grades in the students' history and English courses for the year (all computed with respect to a maximum score of 100) were analyzed for both

Table 4.2
Comparison of student performance preceding and following the introduction of ACCESS

| | Lincoln School | | | | Hope High | |
	English grade	History grade	U.S. history AP score	G.P.A.	English grade	History grade
Non-ACCESS	80.42	80.22	3.22	73.61	77.47	74.47
ACCESS	83.38	82.00	3.81	81.96	86.81	84.25
t	2.07**	0.931	1.799*	2.82***	2.08**	1.65

***$p < .01$ **$p < .05$ *$p = .05$

schools. At Lincoln the students' grades on the CEEB's Advanced Placement U.S. History examination (out of a maximum score of 5) were also analyzed, while at Hope the G.P.A. over all academic subjects was included. Table 4.2 shows the results of this comparison.

Students in the ACCESS groups show better academic performance at both schools on all of these measures, with the comparisons for the three English course grades and the AP history score showing significant differences. Unfortunately, the comparison across years at Lincoln School (though not at Hope High) is contaminated by the fact that the ACCESS group (1989–90) was generally an academically more able set of students, so the fact that they did better may have had nothing to do with ACCESS. In order to make the comparison as fair as possible, a G.P.A. in all academic courses taken at the school prior to participating in the ACCESS Project was taken as a measure of a student's general academic ability. Stepwise multiple regression analyses were performed to partial out the effects of general academic ability and see whether there were any remaining differences in student performance across years that might be attributable to ACCESS. The analysis for the English course grades showed that with prior G.P.A. partialed out, the residual variability on grades accounted for by the hypermedia intervention was only 2 percent, which was not statistically significant ($F < 1$). The analyses of the history course grades and the AP history exam scores showed that the differences between years did account for a significant portion of the variance, even with G.P.A. partialed out. The proportions were 9.98 percent ($F(2,27) = 10.69$) and 11.35 percent ($F(2,27) = 3.557$) for course grades and AP scores respectively. Student performance in ACCESS classes at both schools since has tended to remain at or above the pre-ACCESS levels.

While it is encouraging to find "tangible" improvements in student performance, it is important to keep these findings in perspective. As we saw earlier, the computer-based intervention brought with it a number of other changes in teaching practice: assignments were changed and classroom discussions were altered in subtle ways. Thus it is difficult to attribute the effects to the technology per se. But as we shall see below, looking for hypermedia effects alone may be taking too restrictive a view of how cognitive science can influence instruction. Instead, we should look at the effects of the total intervention of emphasizing relational thinking, which happens to include hypermedia as one of its parts.

Hypermedia's Effect on Students' Conceptual Understanding

Although it is reassuring that ACCESS apparently imparts some general educational benefits, there are also likely to be more specific effects it might have had on what students know about history and literature and how they use it. Therefore students have been asked to generate concept maps for the various abstract and not-so-abstract ideas introduced to them in the participating classes. This has been done for groups of students taking courses without hypermedia with the participating teachers (the non-ACCESS groups) and for students who used ACCESS while taking the same courses with the same teachers (the ACCESS groups).

The concept map task asks each student to generate diagrams that contain all of the aspects of the topic important to her or his understanding of it, including examples, and to indicate how the items in the map are related to one another. Although students vary in the type of notation they choose, students who have used ACCESS regularly tend to use a line-link notation much more often than non-ACCESS students, probably because it is the type of notation used on many ACCESS overview screens. Thus the comparison between ACCESS and non-ACCESS students must be tempered with the knowledge that the ACCESS students probably had a clearer notion of what a concept map might look like.

If using ACCESS hypermedia had an effect on how students thought about a concept, its effect should be in the direction of making their concept maps more expert-like. Thus the ACCESS maps were expected to have more information (items), to have fewer groupings of items based solely on surface characteristics, and to be more differentiated (Chi and Koeske 1983). The concept maps were therefore scored for number of nodes or items depicted, the percentage of all clusters that two judges rated as being based on surface characteristics, and the differentiation of the conceptual structure. Following Chi and Koeske

Table 4.3
Comparison of concept maps from ACCESS and non-ACCESS students

	Non-ACCESS students	ACCESS students
Total # items	12.3	26.1**
# Abstract concepts	7.2	12.8*
% Surface characteristic clusters (top-level)	89.0	35.4**
Average # links per node	1.7	3.4*
Differentiation	1.9	2.6

$*p < .05, **p < .01$

(1983), differentiation was assessed by taking the ratio of the number of "within" subgrouping links shown to the number of "between" subgrouping links shown, a measure that is expected to be high in more expert-like representations. The data in table 4.3 come from history students who generated maps of the Enlightenment.

Table 4.3 shows that, as expected, ACCESS students tended to generate significantly more items in their maps and to have a more differentiated, expert-like organization to the material. The percentage of surface characteristic clusters did not differ between the two groups. This was because it was often difficult to distinguish between surface-level groupings and groupings based on deeper principles, because deep and surface principles often lead to identical groups of items. Nevertheless, it is clear that those students who used the ACCESS corpus came away with a better structured, more complete conceptual representation of at least one concept they studied.

Individual Differences in Corpus-Browsing Strategies
Because the ACCESS system can collect records of each student's interactions with the corpus, it was also possible to discover whether different students displayed different patterns of corpus usage, and whether those individual differences in corpus usage led to different understandings of the material. One way to measure whether different students have different understandings of a set of hypermedia material is to analyze the content and argumentation structure of research papers based on use of the corpus. The data presented below come from two such assignments given in one of the ACCESS history classes, one near the beginning of the school year and one near the end. Thus the corpus usage patterns for the first assignment are more likely to reflect "natural tendencies" than to reflect the build-up of traversal habits acquired from extensive use of the corpus, while the patterns for the second assignment are more likely to reflect any

Table 4.4
Hypermedia traversal patterns for two history assignments

	Early in school year	Late in school year
Total cards seen	195.4	248.3
% Overview	24.4	15.2
% Linear moves	62.6	49.9
% Nonlinear moves	19.1	21.7
% "Pop-up" moves	13.9	28.5
% of Branches visited (L1)	29.0	55.1
% of Branches visited (L2)	30.8	53.1
% of Branches visited (L3)	37.2	42.8
% of Branches visited (L4)	—	11.2
% Cards visited in series	92.0	97.4

internalization of productive conceptual neighborhood structures and the ways in which they can be traversed in hypermedia.

Table 4.4 summarizes the students' corpus usage for the two assignments. In addition to the total number of cards (screens) viewed, the table shows the percentage of cards viewed that were overviews, the percentage of screen transitions that were linear (from one card to the next in an electronic page-turning mode), the percentage of pop-up moves in which the student moved from one level of the organizational hierarchy to the next higher one (an index of the extent to which the student was making use of the expert-level organization provided in the corpus), the percentage of nonlinear moves in which a student followed a link to some other part of the corpus, the percentage of all nodes at each level of the hierarchy in the relevant part of the corpus visited by the student, and the percentage of all screens in multiscreen sequences that were viewed (to make sure that students were reading to the end of the sequences).

Although the data from the first assignment are more revealing when compared to those of the second assignment, some characteristics of the first assignment data are important by themselves. The students viewed considerably more screens than necessary, and this number represented many, many repetitions of a much smaller set of relevant screens. The fact that only 24.4 percent of the overviews were viewed indicates that many students were able to isolate the relevant portions of the corpus and stay in that general vicinity. The preponderance of linear moves resulted from the fact that many of them were necessary in order to move across the many multicard sequences in the corpus. Students were also highly reliable in viewing all of the material associated with a node once they got to that node.

A finer-grained analysis of these data reveals interesting differences in traversal patterns between students who ended up with ostensibly different conceptual understandings of the material. A very rough measure of how good a neighborhood structure a student acquired is her or his grade on the associated essay. Although the analysis of traversal patterns revealed no consistent patterns across difference conceptual mastery levels for many of the measures, there was a reliable pattern of the better students making fewer linear moves (58.5% versus 69.8%) and making more use of the hierarchical structure via pop-up moves (16.2% vs. 10.2%) than poorer students. The better students also reliably visited a greater percentage of nodes at the deeper levels (L2 and L3) of the structure, which is to be expected if they made relatively more hierarchy-traversing moves. Since the evidence is correlational in nature, we cannot tell whether making use of the conceptual structure in the hypermedia corpus caused students to produce a better understanding, or whether higher ability students (who end up with better conceptual structures) are more likely to notice and make use of such structures in the corpus.

By the end of a full year of ACCESS corpus use, most students had become relatively proficient users of most features of the system, and were likely to show different patterns of corpus traversal. Of course a number of other things had changed about these students over the year: they were older, they had learned more American history and literature, and had presumably acquired more expert-like knowledge representations. The right column of table 4.4 shows data from a corpus-based assignment late in the school year that should reflect the combined effects of all of these changes. This assignment gave the students considerable more leeway in what they could write about, and thus an added dimension to their use of the corpus was in determining the focus of their essays. Because of this, a much larger segment of the corpus was potentially relevant to their endeavor.

Table 4.4 shows that the students, as a group, changed their traversal strategies. The fact that the number of cards seen is greater on this assignment than on the earlier one is indicative only of the fact that there was more potentially relevant material to be viewed for this assignment. Since there were more overview (and suboverview) screens in the part of the corpus essential to this assignment, the percentage of overviews seen is lower, though the absolute number is about the same. However, the students made fewer electronic page-turning (linear) transitions and, instead, were relying more on the links and the hierarchical traversal methods (pop-up moves). They also visited a greater percentage of nodes lower in the conceptual structure

(L2 and L3), and continued to be thorough in viewing all material at a node once it was reached.

When this second set of corpus traversal data was partitioned according to what level of mastery over the material each student ultimately achieved (as measured again by the grade on the associated written assignment), some interesting individual differences again emerged. The better students tended to view fewer screens (182 versus 447 for poorer students), which suggests that they not only repeated viewing screens less often, but they also focused their research more on a subset of the potentially relevant material. Interestingly, all students were equally likely to make linear page-turning moves, use the links, and move up and down the hierarchy. Apparently over the course of the year the lower-ability students had learned how to organize their thinking along the conceptual lines embodied in the overview structure of the corpus and thereby to make better use of that structure in locating information. However, better students showed a significant tendency to visit a smaller percentage of nodes at each level of the conceptual hierarchy than did poorer students, which reconfirms the impression that they were using the structure in the corpus to focus their attention on a reasonably small subset of the material.

These results underline the fact that there are consistent individual differences between users of a hypermedia system. To some extent these differences can be modified by having extensive experience using such a system. However, the ability of a user to make use of the browsing resources and functionality of a system depends on the user's own conceptual representation of the domain embodied in the hypermedia system. Having an adequate representation allows users to orient themselves and navigate efficiently to find information, and progressively enlarge their own representation by assimilating hypermedia-based associations.

Discussion

The ACCESS Project's development of a hypermedia teaching tool based on a cognitive analysis of appropriate knowledge representation has been successful in a number of ways. As the above summary indicates, the intervention has affected how students learn more than just in the sense of using computers and hypermedia rather than other learning tools. It has also promoted changes in how the teachers structure other learning activities for the students. As we noted earlier, because there were several instructional changes associated with the introduction of hypermedia, it is more appropriate to take a broad view of what the "cognitive intervention" was in this case. A more accurate characterization might be that the project has made the ideas of knowledge representation and conceptual relationships much more central and explicit to both the students and teachers involved. The focus on conceptual linkages became increasingly important to the teachers partly through their own interactions with cognitive scientists involved in the project, but mainly through the process of self-examination and reflective thought as they went about organizing and building the hypermedia corpus. The change in focus played itself out not only in the teachers' use of hypermedia as a teaching tool, but also subtly in changes in other aspects of their teaching repertoire. As a result, students began to assimilate the new focus, leading to the various learning outcomes summarized in the preceding pages.

It is worth considering, for a moment, whether the effects we have observed in both teaching and learning are robust and substantial. The robustness issue is particularly important because there is a distinct possibility that the introduction of hypermedia into a classroom, with all of its bells and whistles, may produce little more than a Hawthorne effect, which will disappear when the newness of the technology wears off. However, there is reason for cautious optimism that the improvements we observed above are more than temporary. For one thing, the project continues in both schools (as well as in others) and the outcomes for students in subsequent years seem to corroborate the initial data reported here. A second reason for optimism is that the intervention has generated a variety of results, rather than just one, all of which converge on the conclusion that ACCESS makes a difference. Thus there is reason to believe that the effects are substantial.

It is harder to estimate the importance of the changes observed in students who use hypermedia. If the ultimate goal of education is to produce better-informed citizens who can think productively and flexibly in the real world, then it is difficult to tell whether any of the changes we have observed will lead in that direction. A more modest goal might be to produce some permanent habits of reasoning and understanding of how knowledge is structured that will stay with the students well past the time they spend in the ACCESS classroom. In both of the ACCESS schools students are likely to have the same teachers two years in a row, and the teachers report that even if hypermedia are not used in the later courses, former ACCESS students spontaneously make connections between what they learned in the ACCESS classroom and what they learn later. It would be interesting, but probably impossible, to find out if they continue to be more likely to think in terms of conceptual relationships even farther into their educational careers.

Accepting the premise that the ACCESS Project has produced some positive results, can we then begin to generalize from its experience? As a beginning for such generalization, it is worth examining some of the project's difficulties that might have derailed it entirely had they not been satisfactorily resolved. One difficulty was that the project depended on coordinating the efforts of research scientists, computer programmers, and teachers, all of whom start with different assumptions about learning, education, and technology, and all of whom have different dialects of intellectual discourse. Although there was relatively little difficulty in getting effective communication going between the cognitive scientists and teachers (we will return to this point below), it was often difficult to translate the needs of the teachers into a form to which the programmers could respond. This was a particular problem at the beginning of the project, when the teachers had little familiarity with either the technology or how to use it, and was resolved only when cognitive scientists who had teaching experience began doing the programming.

A second potential pitfall in this project also stemmed from the teachers' initial unfamiliarity with the technology. The teachers were typical of the vast majority of educators today—they simply had no idea what computers were about or how to use them productively in schools. To make the teachers competent to build the corpus, and even to get them to the point where they could begin to imagine and plan for what the technology would allow them to do, required much patient tutoring and psychological support. By contrast, cognitive science is a computer-oriented field; it uses computers not only for conducting empirical science but also as the basic metaphor in its theoretical work. Computers and computer-based thinking are second nature to cognitive scientists. If cognitive science is to make broad-based contributions to education, it will have to develop ways of bridging the technology gap, even when the cognitive interventions are not themselves computer-based. To make use of the insights provided by cognitive science, teachers will have to have a functional knowledge of computers as educational tools and as analogies to thinking systems. This will require educating several generations of teachers and administrators already in the schools, as well as future educators in teacher-training programs.

And finally, once the technology and training issues were under control in the ACCESS Project and the teachers began to build their hypermedia conceptual structures, it became clear that there were as many expert-level representations of any one conceptual neighborhood as there were teachers working on the project. The technical interface that the ACCESS Project developed fortunately was flexible enough to accommodate multiple representations. An argument can even be made that the flexibility resulted from the obvious tension between conceptual representations. In the long run it was possible for each teacher-author to feel comfortable with the corpus that emerged, and there are now teachers at many other schools who had no hand in building it who also seem comfortable in using the corpus. The multiple-representations problem in ACCESS is a case study of what can happen if cognitive scientists attempt to be too prescriptive in designing educational interventions. To be successful, insights from cognitive science must be used to define and surround teaching practice, but they should not be used to prescribe exact methods.

Having discussed the general implications of the problems experienced by ACCESS, we can now turn to some general principles that can be derived from the positive experiences of this project. A key element to the success of the project was the prior existence of a systematic and reasonably complete body of laboratory data that supported a well-articulated cognitive theory, in this case a theory of expert knowledge representations. Although some of the basic research pieces were missing at the beginning of the project and were filled in through research within the auspices of the project, few basic science surprises were expected at the outset of the project. If the gaps had been too numerous, it would have been much more difficult to build an effective intervention.

Another point contributing to the project's success was that the gist of the scientific literature seemed intuitively correct to the teachers who played a crucial role the design and use of the educational intervention. This made it relatively easy to translate the terminology and findings from scientific lingo to language familiar to the teachers. In fact, it is not unreasonable to suggest that teachers possess "folk cognitive science" knowledge in the same way that philosophers and cognitive scientists speak of most people having an understanding of "folk psychology." Had the underlying cognitive theory seemed less intuitively correct to the teachers, the results might have been much different.

It is probably because folk cognitive science exists in the minds of good teachers that it is possible for cognitive science and education to support and strengthen each other. The ACCESS Project has served as an example of an important and productive symbiosis between the fields. When a theory and set of data are sufficiently developed in the laboratory, they become prime candidates for application in schools. Such applications can help determine how robust the laboratory findings are—if they stand up in the messy environment of a school then they are probably capturing real "truths." More often, attempting to apply the theory in practical settings exposes gaps in the basic science and provides insight on how to develop theory further. Classroom outcomes frequently also lead to empirical questions that no one thought of before, and these return to the laboratory in the form of new experiments. And as much as we wish to develop cognitive theories that deal with the messiness of real life, there is still an important role to be played in the development of those theories by careful, controlled laboratory study.

ACCESS is one of a growing number of demonstrations that cognitive science can be a powerful positive force in education. But if the ACCESS experience is any indication, the changes will come slowly, and only with the painstaking effort of those committed to seeing them come about. Broad educational reform based on a shared understanding of how thinking and learning occur from a cognitive point of view will require that all educators understand the basic insights cognitive science provides and that they practice applying them consistently. It will take some time, but it will be worth the effort.

Note

The author wishes to acknowledge the James S. McDonnell Foundation's program Cognitive Studies in Educational Practice, and the Center for Technology in Education, both of which provided grant support for the software development and research reported here. She is also indebted to Apple Computer for providing hardware for the project.

The ACCESS Project has been a collaborative effort of many teachers, researchers, and students, whose assistance has been invaluable. We are particularly indebted to the teachers who have participated in the project and helped in the software development: Sherry Hepp and Luther Spoehr at Lincoln School, and Kay Scheidler and John Zilboorg at Hope High School. Many programmers, students, and research assistants at Brown contributed to the collection and analysis of the data reported here. Chief among these have been Cynthia Romano, Cathy Fitta, Joseph Horvath, Amy Shapiro, Rebecca Smith, Colleen Zeitz, Karin Kalkstein, Donald Katz, and Rachel Westerman.

Portions of the data discussed here have been presented at the annual meetings of the American Educational Research Organization in 1991 and 1992.

PART II

Across-the-Curriculum Applications

Chapter 5

Intelligence in Context: Enhancing Students' Practical Intelligence for School

Howard Gardner, Mara Krechevsky, Robert J. Sternberg, and Lynn Okagaki

The Clash of Two Cultures

Nice Work is one of a series of highly amusing "campus novels" written by the contemporary British professor-turned-author David Lodge. The heroine is Robyn Penrose, temporary lecturer at the University of Rummidge. Penrose knows her field of English literature extremely well but has otherwise led a cloistered life. Unfortunately, academic life in Britain being what it is these days, Robyn does not figure to get a permanent position. Perhaps this uncertainty emboldens her to become involved in a scheme, in which she agrees to "shadow" a captain of industry one day a week.

Penrose's shadowee—and the novel's hero—is one Victor Wilcox, Managing Director of J. Pringle and Sons Casting and General Engineering, a company that turns out 937 different products. Wilcox is a competent, efficient, no-nonsense middle-level manager. At first, true to form, Penrose and Wilcox do not get along with one another; there is mutual wariness bordering on contempt for their respective lifestyles, values, and bases of knowledge.

But the enterprise of shadowing brings the two protagonists close together, at first geographically and, eventually, emotionally as well. In pursuing their joint endeavor, Penrose and Wilcox acquire a mutual respect for one another. Penrose notices that Wilcox is able to teach his employees by using a variant of the Socratic method and to help them develop skills they can use in the industrial context. Wilcox observes that Penrose is far more alert than he to words and to casual yet potentially revealing situations in the everyday world. Penrose stimulates Wilcox to read works of literature and then aids him in making sense of them, thus broadening his intellectual horizons. The novel's tension centers on whether the respective worlds of Penrose and Wilcox can merge. In fairness to David Lodge, we shall not divulge here how these two contrasting cultures and personalities sort themselves out in the final pages of *Nice Work*.

In literary garb, *Nice Work* introduces the problem with which we are concerned in this chapter. Contrary to what many psychological researchers have maintained, the term *intelligence* is not an unloaded one. What counts as intelligence differs significantly depending upon the context in which one finds oneself and the values that obtain there. In Robyn Penrose's case, her vision of an intelligent person is an academic or scholastic one: a person knowledgeable about literature (or some other discipline), able to discourse about it, to express herself fluently, and to score debating points qualifies as intelligent. In Victor Wilcox's universe, a quite different set of criteria applies: a person who can identify a promising product, decide how to market it, hire and fire employees efficiently, manage a factory, and turn a profit counts as intelligent. Only if their respective cultures happen to abut and to interact, as occurs in Lodge's novel, is there a likelihood that either individual will become aware of the parochialism of his or her conception of intelligence.

A Brief History of the Concept of Intelligence within Psychology

No doubt the term *intelligent* has functioned adequately enough "on the streets" for many centuries. Few would have quarreled if Cardinal Richelieu or Thomas Jefferson, Isaac Newton or Jane Austen, Nicolo Machiavelli or Florence Nightingale had been termed "smart." But it was less than a century ago that psychological researchers first undertook to operationalize "intelligence" and to attempt to measure it for scientific and practical purposes.

Research on intelligence has its roots in the British interest in individual differences (Galton 1892), the German interest in measuring intellectual processes (Wundt 1980), and the French interest in a more effective educational system (Resnick 1991). Credit for devising the first intelligence test is generally given to the French psychologist Alfred Binet (Binet and Simon 1905), who was asked to come up with a measure that could predict which students would be likely to encounter difficulties in the primary grades. Proceeding in a totally empirical manner, Binet tried out hundreds of deliberately disparate items, eventually selecting those that most effectively differentiated those students who succeeded in school from those students who did not. Within a few years, Stern (1912) had coined the term *intelligence quotient*; Goddard (1910) had imported the Binet test to the United States; Terman (1916) had developed the first norms for the Binet scales using a large group of American children; and Yerkes (1921) had accomplished the same feat for young adults. Within a quarter of century, thanks in no small measure to its widespread use in World War I and in testing immigrants to the United States, the intelligence test had become ensconced in American life. Moreover, in the opinion of certain observers (Brown and Herrnstein 1975), the concept of intelligence and the device of the IQ test represent psychology's most successful achievement to date.

In some ways, the intelligence effort was a victim of its own success. Having determined that, in E. G. Boring's (1923) famous quip, "Intelligence is what the tests test," psychologists and psychometricians turned their attention almost entirely to the question of which items to use and how to score them. The premium fell clearly on the production of more efficient and more reliable instruments. Probably the biggest "theoretical dispute," whether the structure of intelligence was unitary, pluralistic, or hierarchical (Spearman 1923; Thomson 1948; Thorndike 1924; Thurstone 1938), turned on the assumptions built into the factor analytic methods used to cluster scores on different subtests (Gould 1981; Guttmann 1992). By the 1970s, despite a huge expenditure of energy and funds in the area of intelligence, it was difficult to point to significant theoretical advances in the preceding decades.

Recent Theoretical Advances in the Study of Intelligence

The hegemony exerted over American psychology by the behaviorist and learning-theory traditions was finally broken in the 1960s and 1970s (Gardner 1985). This break from the past stemmed from several causes, including the rise of the computational/cognitive approach, interest in information-processing analyses, a lessening of the gulf between experimental and individual-differences approaches, renewed attention to cultural factors influencing psychological processes, and a fresh recognition of the relevance of neurological and neuropsychological approaches to the study of the mind. As part of the reconsideration of the mission of psychology, and its place within the cognitive and biological sciences, the study of intelligence once more took its place as a central concern of scientific investigations of the mind. Indeed, the very term *artificial intelligence* signaled an invigorated interest in the structure and operation of intelligence, whether embodied in the human body or in man-made machines (Minsky 1985; Newell and Simon 1972).

One indication of a marked increase in interest is the proliferation of publications and organizations. Such an explosion certainly took place in the case of intelligence. Since 1975, there have been innumerable symposia and conferences, dozens of monographs on intelligence, several monograph series, a major handbook, a peer-reviewed journal, lengthy chapters in several encyclopedic works, and even a forthcoming encyclopedia (Sternberg in press). Discussions of the nature of intelligence have occurred not only with regard to human and animal psychology but also with respect to computation, philosophical, and sociological considerations (see *Behavioral and Brain Sciences;* Block and Dworkin 1976; Premack 1976). More important, a number of new conceptualizations of intelligence have been put forth, and genuine debate has arisen between the adherents of the "old" and the "new" theories of intelligence, as well as among those who might be termed the "new" theoreticians (Anderson 1992; Anderson and Diskin 1987; Baron 1985; Ceci 1990; Gardner 1983, 1993b, 1993c; Laboratory of Comparative Human Cognition 1982; Olson 1974; Perkins et al. 1987; Scarr and Carter-Saltzman 1982; Sternberg 1985). The main points of this debate have been discussed in several review publications (e.g., Sternberg 1977, 1985, 1990a; Sternberg and Detterman 1986) and will not be further elaborated upon here.

Two of the more influential of the new positions have been put forth by two authors of this chapter. In the early 1980s, Robert Sternberg (1984, 1985) introduced his triarchic theory of intelligence. According to this comprehensive formulation, intelligence is best thought of in terms of three primary subtheories: (1) a componential subtheory, in which the operations of particular component processes are detailed; (2) a contextual subtheory, in which sensitivity to the particular surrounding contexts is probed; and (3) an experiential subtheory, which captures the capacity to deal with new situations.

Around the same time, Howard Gardner (1983) introduced his theory of multiple intelligences (hereafter MI theory). Rooted in both the neural sciences and in anthropological studies, the theory maintains that human beings as a species have evolved to be able to carry out at least seven relatively independent forms of information processing, each gauged to a particular environmental content. All normal individuals possess all seven intelligences, but the strength of each intelligence, and the ways in which the intelligences interact to solve problems or fashion products, can differ greatly across individuals, and across cultures as well.

Quite clearly, these theories derive from different intellectual traditions and put forth distinctive claims and analyses. Yet there is little, if anything, in either of the theories that stands in direct conflict with the major assertions and implications of the other. Indeed, both can be seen as part of a general dissatisfaction with the overly narrow or scholaristic definitions of intelligence embraced in earlier eras. Each is also an effort to frame a definition in terms that are theory-based and susceptible to empirical investigation. Moreover, as products of the scientific zeitgeist, both the triarchic theory and the theory of multiple intelligences reflect the themes of the cognitive revolution as well as the sensitivity to social and cultural contexts that has become increasingly prevalent in recent work in the behavioral sciences.

Points of Contact between Triarchic and MI Theory

In significant measure, MI theory and the triarchic theory are complementary. A major portion of attention in the triarchic theory falls on a delineation of the nature and operations of the particular components entailed in executing intelligent acts. In contrast, MI theory is largely descriptive and, while it assumes component processes, makes no attempt to delineate them. The major attention in MI theory falls on the descriptions of the particular contents with which individuals come into contact (music, language, spatial information, etc.) and the level of expertise that individuals bring to that encounter.

Both theories stand out from more traditional views of intelligence in their emphasis on the importance of different environments or contexts. The triarchic theory holds that an important facet of intelligence is the capacity to be sensitive to different environments, and to adjust to and/or to shape the contexts within which individuals find themselves. MI theory rejects the notion that any intelligence can develop in the absence of the stimulation and "messages" of different environments, and hence, the study of intelligence necessarily involves attention to the way in which intellectual potentials unfold in different social or cultural contexts.

In the work described here, we have sought the optimal ways in which to coordinate the principal constituents of our two theories. At a theoretical level, it is possible to impose (or superimpose) the three subtheories of the triarchic theory on each of the several intelligences. One such effort is depicted in figure 5.1. As shown here, each of the seven intelligences can be analyzed in terms of its components (some of which may be common, some distinct); each can be analyzed with respect to relative novelty or automatization, as befits the novice-to-expert continuum; and each intelligence or set of intelligences can be mobilized to deal with various contexts. It is also possible to apply an amalgam of the two theories to explicate specific instances of intelligent behavior. In the domain of computer programming, for example, a novice will activate different sets of intelligences in ways different from an expert. To take another kind of example, musical performance in India entails sensitivities to contexts and a combination

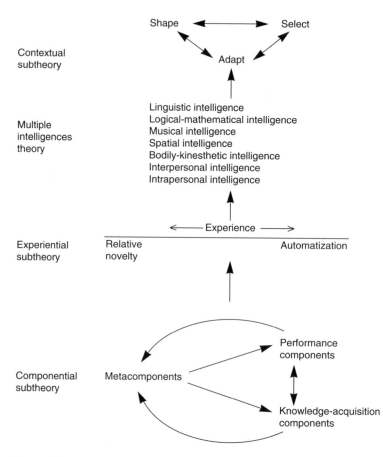

Figure 5.1
Integration of theory of multiple intelligences, which specifies domains of intelligences, with triarchic theory of intelligence, which specifies processes that occur in each of these domains

of intelligences that may be quite different from musical performance in Mexico, Austria, or Japan.

Though such examples can be multiplied, until recently neither theoretical effort has devoted much attention to the actual delineation of the varying contexts within and across different cultures. The discussion has taken place at a general level. And so, faced with the specific case of *Nice Work,* both theories would acknowledge the importance of the differences between the scholarly environment in which Penrose spends the bulk of her time, and the industrial context in which Wilcox is embedded. However, neither theory is as yet in a position to tease out the specific factors that make a crucial difference in these and in comparable environments.

The American Middle School: An Important Contemporary Context

For the purposes of theoretical advancement, any context or set of contexts might be examined by theorists of intelligence. And, indeed, in our own empirical work, we have each examined a variety of contexts (Sternberg and Wagner 1986; Gardner 1989). Within the contemporary American situation, however, one setting stands out, both in terms of its interest and its social importance. That is the American public school, and in particular, the period and the institution of middle school.

In one sense, of course, an interest in the school setting has always been important to theorists of intelligence. One might go so far as to maintain that intelligence theory has described, de facto, intelligence as it is deployed in the modern secular school. However, precisely because the school context has been assumed, it has remained essentially invisible in analyses of intelligence. Those students who have, for whatever reasons, been able to handle school tasks successfully have been deemed intelligent; while those who, for whatever reasons, have encountered difficulty in school have been judged less intelligent, if not stupid or even retarded.

In our collaborative work we have sought to convert the usual "ground" into "figure." Rather than assuming that scholastic intelligence is a given and/or a transparent entity, we have attempted to analyze its component parts. On the basis of such an analysis, it is possible to tease out the factors that may be required if one is to succeed in the very particular context of middle school, and then, as warranted, to help students master that context so they can perform more successfully—"more intelligently"—in school.

A word is in order about our decision to focus on middle school—on grades 5–8 and on the ages 10–14 (cf. Steinberg 1992; Lipsitz 1984). In all probability, some aspects of "school intelligence" will prove applicable to all years of school: the ability to focus on what the teacher is saying and doing is one such candidate skill. In contrast, other aspects of "school intelligence" may turn out to be geared to specific grades: learning to line up properly may be peculiar to kindergarten, while knowing how to curry favor with seniors may be the traditional lot of freshmen.

What characterizes the middle school years, however, is a unique transition from one kind of scholastic environment to another. In the primary grades, students tend to be placed in one class taught by a single teacher; curricula are often theme-based and subject matters are not sharply delineated one from another; there is relatively little homework, relatively modest social pressure, and a generally supportive milieu. Just a few years later, however, by the beginning of high school, the atmosphere changes dramatically. Students now are taught by a series of teachers, who are basically subject-matter experts; the students move on schedule from one classroom to another; there is considerable dependence upon textbooks, tests, and homework; much more tracking takes place; and most students feel subjected to an ensemble of psychosexual, social, and lifestyle pressures.

Under such circumstances, it is fortunate if a student possesses the kinds of intelligence that have traditionally been useful in school: the logical-mathematical and linguistic intelligences described by Gardner, and the componential and metacomponential facilities detailed by Sternberg. However, traditional academic intelligence is not totally necessary and in many cases it is clearly not sufficient. According to our analysis, success in school depends as much on the capacities to understand the demands made by the environment of middle school and to adjust to those demands as it does on any particular set of academic competences.

Practical Intelligence for School (PIFS): The Basic Concept

Combining our theoretical perspectives and analyses, the authors of this chapter began a collaborative project in 1987 called "Practical Intelligence for School," affectionately abbreviated PIFS. According to our analysis, rooted both in theoretical considerations and in long-term observations of the American educational scene, the student who is "practically intelligent" in the scholastic context exhibits an adequate appreciation of three distinct areas: (1) his or her own particular learning strengths or styles and how to draw upon them in the school context; (2) the nature and demands of the various tasks and requirements across disciplines within the school context; and (3) the human or interpersonal dimension of school, including relations to other peers and teachers, and more generally, the operation of the school as a social institution. In Gardner's terms, the first focus highlights intrapersonal intelligence; the second focus draws, as needed, on various content-specific intelligences; and the third focus highlights interpersonal intelligence. In Sternberg's terms, all three areas involve all three aspects of the theory, with an emphasis on the contextual part.

As an example, consider how a student during middle school years goes about choosing and carrying out a project for a class. To accomplish this task effectively in terms of MI theory, the practically intelligent student needs to choose a project appropriate to his or her own interests and strengths (intrapersonal intelligence); to develop a project appropriate for different kinds of subject matter (drawing upon logical-mathematical intelligence for a science project, or linguistic intelligence for an English project); and to address the expectations of each teacher (interpersonal intelligence). To accomplish this task effectively in terms of the triarchic theory, the practically intelligent student needs to carry out the steps required to realize his or her project (the componential part); to exhibit sensitivity to the requirements posed by each teacher and the awareness of available resources (the contextual part); and to apply what he or she has learned to plan new projects (the experiential part).

While such lines of analysis made reasonable sense as a starting point, it was important to determine whether they had any empirical validity. To secure information on this point, we interviewed fifty students, ranging in age from 10 to 12, on a number of topics having to do with school, including study habits and peer interactions, differences between subject matters, the demands of various academic tasks, and the operation of the school system (Goldman et al. 1988). On the basis of these interviews it proved possible to array students along the following continuum.

Those with a "high PIFS profile" readily gave elaborated responses to our questions; they showed an awareness of the existence and utility of a number of strategies and resources, and they had a keen and differentiated sense of themselves as learners. Conversely, those with a "low PIFS profile" tended to give brief and undifferentiated responses to our questions, repeated a number of student platitudes (e.g., they responded, "You have to study harder or work harder," to a host of questions, rather than picking up on the differing implications of particular queries), and had little sense of themselves as learners with options that *they* could pursue. A group with "middle PIFS" profiles fell in between the other two groups, either because they offered some "low" and some "high" responses, or because they showed awareness, albeit limited, of the issues that were apparent to those with a "high PIFS" profile. Interestingly, in terms of MI theory, all of the students indicated at least one area of school that excited them, yet none of the students evinced much appreciation of the different "demand characteristics" of the several subject disciplines.

The PIFS Curricula: Phase I

In phase I of the PIFS Project, we sought to design a set of curricula to help foster students' practical intelligence for school. We developed

Table 5.1
Table of contents, Practical Intelligence for School separate program

---

Introduction to teachers

Introduction to practical intelligence for school
Overview of topics
Transition planning with the students

Introduction to students

1. Introductory lesson

I. Managing yourself

A. Overview of managing yourself

2. Kinds of intelligence: Definitions and principles
3. Kinds of intelligence: Multiple intelligences
4. Kinds of intelligence: Academic or practical intelligence
5. Understanding test scores
6. Exploring what you may do

B. Learning styles

7. What's your learning style?
8. Taking in new information
9. Showing what you learned
10. Knowing how you work best
11. Recognizing the whole and the parts

C. Improving your own learning

12. Memory
13. Using what you already know
14. Making pictures in your mind
15. Using your eyes—A good way to learn
16. Listening for meaning
17. Learning by doing
18. Accepting responsibility
19. Collecting your thoughts and setting goals

II. Managing tasks

A. Overview of solving problems

20. Is there a problem?
21. What strategies are you using?
22. A process to help you solve problems
23. Planning a way to prevent problems
24. Breaking habits
25. Help with our problems

B. Specific school problems

26. Getting organized
27. Taking notes
28. Understanding questions
29. Following directions
30. Underlining—Finding the main idea
31. Noticing the way things are written
32. Choosing between mapping and outlining
33. Taking tests
34. Seeing likenesses and differences in subjects
35. Getting it done on time

Table 5.1 (continued)

III. Cooperating with others

A. Communication

36. Class discussions
37. What to say
38. Tuning your conversation
39. Putting yourself in another's place
40. Solving problems in communication

B. Fitting into school

41. Making choices—Adapting, shaping, selecting
42. Seeing the school as a social system
43. What does school mean to you?
44. Seeing the relationship between now and later

---

two sets of materials: a stand-alone and an infused curriculum. The goals of the two curricula were similar: to enable students to take responsibility for their own learning by helping them think critically about themselves, the learning process, and the general school environment. The stand-alone curriculum taught students PIFS skills in the context of a separate course, while the infused curriculum infused PIFS concepts into existing school curricula.

The Stand-Alone Curriculum
The PIFS stand-alone curriculum is organized around three kinds of tacit or practical knowledge critical to adaptation in any environment: managing oneself, managing tasks, and working with or managing others (Wagner and Sternberg 1985). The curriculum includes both a student text and a teacher's manual that describes in detail how to teach the course. (See table 5.1 for course outline.)

The course opens with a unit on how students can effectively manage themselves. The goal of this unit is to help students identify their own strengths and weaknesses and their individual learning styles. It also presents various strategies for students to capitalize on and improve their abilities. The unit begins with a discussion of different kinds of intelligence and styles of thinking. It also addresses crucial aspects of adaptation to school, such as taking in new information, showing what you have learned, using what you know, and implementing what you have learned.

The second unit focuses on managing tasks. It is designed to provide students with a general process for identifying and solving problems: defining the problem, analyzing the parts, and locating strategies. This unit also addresses such topics as getting organized, breaking bad habits, seeking help with problems, and thinking about time

Table 5.2
Basic statistics

Survey of study habits and attitudes (SSHA)

	Experimental group		Control group	
Subtest	Pretest	Posttest	Pretest	Posttest
Delay avoidance	40.73	48.90	34.05	25.71
Work methods	50.01	61.92	44.61	32.66
Teacher approval	42.34	55.63	36.02	23.76
Education acceptance	39.81	51.71	31.54	19.29

Learning and study skills inventory (LASSI)

	Experimental group		Control group	
Subtest	Pretest	Posttest	Pretest	Posttest
Attitude	50.23	56.64	50.13	34.49
Motivation	52.43	61.23	47.30	32.88
Time management	55.52	65.25	45.75	44.90
Anxiety	58.73	68.72	52.97	43.51
Concentration	53.68	63.72	45.25	39.02
Information processing	46.90	59.25	46.15	39.39
Selecting main ideas	55.72	65.08	54.25	40.15
Study aids	42.15	62.33	33.67	42.51
Self-testing	48.03	62.46	42.67	43.46
Test strategies	61.47	65.70	60.70	41.02

Sternberg triarchic abilities test (STAT)

	Experimental group		Control group	
Subtest	Pretest	Posttest	Pretest	Posttest
Practical inference (verbal)	4.78	5.29	5.10	4.64
Practical data (quantitative)	5.21	4.94	4.58	5.49
Route planning (figural)	5.49	5.34	5.84	4.85

management. Chapters on understanding questions, taking notes, following directions, and taking tests are included as well.

The third unit, on cooperating with others, addresses topics such as how to handle yourself in class discussions, knowing what to say when, putting yourself in another's place, and solving communication problems. It suggests that the same problem-solving strategies introduced in the previous unit can be applied to social problems. The unit concludes by suggesting that students take a long-term perspective in dealing with other people, and by asking them to reflect on future choices for themselves.

The stand-alone curriculum was implemented in the spring of 1989 in Newtown, Connecticut, a middle-income suburb (Sternberg, Oka-

Table 5.3
Multivariate analyses of variance

Test	F	p
SSHA	F (4,95) = 5.85	< .001
LASSI	F(10,78) = 2.92	< .01
STAT	F(3,86) = 6.48	< .001

T-tests of subtest difference scores (Posttest minus pretest scores)

Experimental vs. control group

SSHA subtests	t	STAT subtests	t
Delay avoidance	3.56**	Practical inference (verbal)	2.47*
Work methods	4.64**	Practical data (quantitative)	−2.36*
Teacher approval	4.54**	Route planning (figural)	2.32*
Education acceptance	4.78**		

LASSI subtests	t
Attitude	3.71***
Motivation	3.43***
Time management	1.29
Anxiety	2.66**
Concentration	2.08*
Information processing	2.64**
Selecting main ideas	3.22**
Study aids	1.27
Self-testing	2.37*
Test strategies	3.38**

*$p < .05$, **$p < .01$, ***$p < .001$

gaki, and Jackson 1990). One hundred seventh grade students participated in the study. Three mixed-ability reading classes served as the
experimental group, and another two classes as the control. The
experimental students received the PIFS course materials, while the
controls received the standard basal reader. The program was administered three days per week over a semester. A second implementation
was carried out in Danbury, Connecticut during the 1989–90 academic
year; however, in the latter site, teachers taught the stand-alone curriculum in a year-long course that met once a week.

The evaluation measures used to determine the effectiveness of the
implementations included the Survey of Study Habits and Attitudes
(SSHA) (Brown and Holtzman 1967); the Learning and Study Skills
Inventory (LASSI) (Weinstein and Palmer 1988); and the Practical Intelligence section of the Sternberg Triarchic Abilities Test (STAT). In the
Newtown site, the results suggest that the PIFS curriculum units were
successful in improving practical intellectual skills as measured by two

tests of study skills and one of practical intelligence. Based on an analysis of the seventeen subscales in the three measures, significant differences in favor of the experimental groups were found on fourteen of those scales. (See table 5.2 for pre- and posttest scores for experimental and control groups, and table 5.3 for multivariate analyses of variance and T-Tests of subtest difference scores.) In the Danbury site, qualitative data (observations in classes and conversations with teachers) indicated that the students and teachers were very satisfied with the program. However, the statistical data revealed no pattern of significant gains on the pre- and posttest measures. Hence, we do not provide the statistics for this part of the study.

The contrasting results in the two communities merit brief comment. In Newtown, the teacher trainer was highly demanding; this led to a cadre of teachers who were mildly disconcerted by the intervention but who secured higher performances on the posttests. In Danbury, a more interpersonally effective but less demanding trainer worked with the teachers. This trainer won the affection of the teachers, but was less successful in enabling them to depart from their usual way of teaching. In general, we believe that much more intensive training and preparation will be needed if teachers are to feel positive about the program and if reliable gains are to be secured in student learning, as measured by performance on the appropriate evaluations.

The Infused Approach

In the infused approach, we taught ten different units to students, six of which target problems in particular subject matter. (See table 5.4 for the list of units.) Two of the units address issues relating to social studies, such as using a variety of resources or considering alternative report formats. Two of the units address issues in mathematics, such as solving word problems and using math resources. And the two reading-and-writing units tackle such issues as understanding symbolism in fiction and choosing a topic for a project.

The other four units address more general, cross-disciplinary skills, which are nonetheless infused whenever possible into the context of regular classroom assignments. The first two units seek to foster students' note-taking and organizational skills, while the last two units are designed to present conceptually difficult, but crucial, issues for the student in school. In "Discovering Your Learning Profile," students discuss the concept of "intelligence," exploring their own strengths and weaknesses in light of more pluralistic notions of intelligence. The "Why Go To School" unit encourages students to examine their own personal short- and long-term goals, and how school relates to those goals.

Table 5.4
Practical intelligence for school infused units

Reading and writing units

Choosing a project—helps students to choose and plan school projects which are well-suited to both class requirements and their personal interests.

Understanding fiction: Reading between the lines—focuses on strategies for discerning the deeper, symbolic meanings in stories.

Mathematics units

Word Problems—helps students to focus on the process of solving math problems, the variety of potential problem-solving strategies, and their own most effective problem-solving techniques.

Finding the right math tools—leads students to become familiar with a range of math resources and to develop strategies for using them efficiently.

Social studies units

Using a variety of resources—fosters students' awareness of the diversity of available resources, as well as of their own personal resources.

Making research reports your own—helps students to consider alternative report formats that both discourage copying and promote a deeper understanding of new information.

General units

Organizing and presenting your work—helps students to develop personally appropriate ways of organizing and presenting their work.

Taking Notes—fosters the development of more efficient note-taking skills.

Why go to school—leads students to consider the connections between school and their personal lives, both in the short and long runs.

Discovering your learning profile—encourages students to identify their own special array of abilities, particularly nonacademic abilities, and to draw on them when confronting difficult situations.

All of the infused PIFS units emphasize the purposes that underlie school activities. They encourage students to consider these purposes, to investigate various methods of carrying out assignments, and to explore alternative resources. They also reduce the emphasis on producing a final product in favor of increasing attention to process. The infused units also give students the opportunity to incorporate their own experiences and interests into their schoolwork, and to reflect on and monitor their own work.

Nine teachers in six Boston-area schools taught subsets of the infused units to students in grades six to eight during the spring of 1990. Unlike the stand-alone curriculum, no special time was allotted to the presentation of the PIFS units; rather, they were slotted into regular class subject matter and projects.

To assess students' ability-in-context, we developed and piloted evaluation measures for each of the infused units. Each measure in-

Table 5.5
Examples of test items

Understanding questions

For "Choosing a project": student is asked to read a list of school and extracurricular activities, to identify the one she think is the most project-like, and to explain her answer.

For "Making research reports your own": student is asked to imagine that she is a teacher, and that one of her students has just handed in a report which is copied directly from the text books; student writes dialogue between herself and the student in which she convinces the student not to copy.

Task-oriented questions

For "Organizing and presenting your work": student is given a stack of unorganized school papers and asked to put them in order, paper-clipping the ones that belong together, and giving each paper-clipped stack a category label.

For "Understanding fiction: Reading between the lines": student is asked to choose a character or an object from a familiar story and to explain why she thinks that element is symbolic, and what it means.

Reflection questions

For "Why go to school": student is presented with another student's suggestions for altering the school curriculum; student is asked to write down the advantages and disadvantages to making such changes.

For "Math tools": student reads about how a hypothetical student handles his difficulties in solving a math problem; student is asked to suggest other resources the hypothetical student might have used, and how they might be better than the ones already used.

---

cludes three types of items: definitional, task-oriented, and meta-task. The "definitional" items assess students' understanding of the issues addressed by the PIFS unit and why these are important. The "task" component samples the actual skills targeted in the unit. Finally, the "meta-task" component requires students to step back and reflect on the nature of the process or skills involved in a particular task. (See table 5.5 for sample items for two of the units.) Data on the effectiveness of the infused units were gathered from a variety of sources, including classroom observations, teacher observations, interviews with teachers and students, and results on pre- and posttests administered to experimental and control groups. On both quantitative and qualitative measures, the infused units proved successful. On all units, the experimental groups' scores improved from pre- to posttest. Table 5.6 presents the results of the Mann-Whitney U Test and Fisher Exact Probability Test. The results show that all of the units producing significant gains were linked to specific disciplines. In contrast, significant differences between experimental and control groups were

Table 5.6
Results of Mann-Whitney U test

All Units Combined:	z = 6.35	p < .001
Domain-specific units	*z value*	*Significance*
UF: reading between the lines	3.10/2.58	p < .001/.005*
Choosing a project	3.06	p < .01
Word problems	3.44	p < .001
Math tools	1.17	n.s.
Using a variety of resources	3.17	p < .001
Making reports your own	3.60	p < .001
Domain-Specific Units Combined	6.57	*p < .001*
General units		
Organizing and presenting work	0.29	n.s.
Taking notes	0.35/1.15	n.s.*
Why go to school	1.10	n.s.
Discovering your learning profile	1.45	n.s.
General Units Combined	1.91	*p < .05*
Results of Fisher Exact Probability Test		
Why go to school	p = 0.10	
Discovering your learning profile	p = 0.07	

*The two scores are for the two different classes in which the unit was implemented.

generally not obtained for those units which sought to cut across subject matter.

Experimental groups also showed significant gains in the three categories of test items, with the strongest effect in the "task" component and the weakest effect in the "meta-task" category (see table 5.7). Those questions which tapped students' understanding of process and appreciation of pluralism also yielded significant gains. More generally, those units which exploited extracurricular interests and those which were implemented in conjunction with other units proved most successful.

The greater success of the discipline-specific units, as compared to the general units, is noteworthy. In our view, the general units more closely duplicated materials already taught by teachers as part of their ordinary "study skills" concerns; thus, they contained less novel information. In addition, it may be more difficult for students to know when to invoke the skills conveyed by the general units, since these have not been tied to a particular disciplinary demand.

Table 5.7
Chi square analysis by item

	Understanding items			
	Up	Same	Down	
Experimental	112	85	53	250
Control	109	54	77	240
	221	139	130	490

chi square = 11.18574
p < .01

	Task items			
	Up	Same	Down	
Experimental	146	46	58	250
Control	64	65	111	240
	210	111	169	490

chi square = 51.71006
p < .001

	Reflection items			
	Up	Same	Down	
Experimental	103	88	59	250
Control	80	77	83	240
	183	165	142	490

chi square = 7.479415
p < .05

	Pluralism items			
	Up	Same	Down	
Experimental	141	45	54	240
Control	92	53	91	236
	233	98	145	476

chi square = 20.36699
p < .001

Table 5.7 (continued)

	Process items			
	Up	Same	Down	
Experimental	75	31	19	125
Control	50	39	31	120
	125	70	50	245

chi square = 8.695867
p < .05

Summary

In terms of the goals set for each of the programs, phase I of the PIFS program was successful. Students in each of the two programs surpassed students in control classrooms in their performances on the principal measures. In addition, both students and teachers indicated satisfaction with their involvement in the program; it proved to be fun as well as instructive. Considerable interest in PIFS-I has also been exhibited by educators throughout the country and by our colleagues in research.

Despite our own positive feelings about the first phase of the PIFS program, we felt it was important to strengthen and extend the program in various ways. To begin with, while the PIFS program was successful in terms of its principal indices, it still seemed relatively remote from daily classroom practice. It would be possible to succeed on the PIFS measures without significant improvement in class performance, papers, homework, tests, projects, and the like. Hence, one emerging goal was to tie a PIFS curriculum more closely to the kinds of performances that students ought to be exhibiting in their daily and yearly schoolwork.

A second concern had to do with vast differences observed among teachers, classrooms, and school districts. Put simply, PIFS proved far more successful in some settings than in others. For example, an extension of the stand-alone curriculum to a more challenging school context proved unsuccessful, and some of the classes involved in the infused program were much less affected than others. These results suggested the need for more careful examination of the factors that contribute to success or failure, as well as more extended efforts for staff development in designated sites.

A third area of concern centered on the frankly "accommodative" nature of the program. As initially devised, PIFS accepts the curricular objectives of traditional schools and seeks to train students to conform to conventional scholastic expectations. Our own analyses of cognition, however, place at least as great importance on the creation of novel products and on learning how to use the context productively in order to achieve one's own ends (Gardner 1988, 1993a; Sternberg 1988; Sternberg and Lubart 1991). To complement the PIFS perspective, we felt the need for a companion program, Creative Intelligence for School (CIFS).

Finally, while we recognized certain advantages of having two specimen programs, we thought it optimal to combine the strengths of the two programs. Accordingly, we elected to create an amalgamated PIFS that would feature both stand-alone and infused components.

The PIFS Curriculum: Phase II

In the second phase of the PIFS program, we are pursuing each of the aforementioned considerations. Specifically, we have designed a single, coordinated curriculum. The curriculum has four disciplinary foci (reading, writing, testing, and homework) and explores five recurrent themes (understanding the purposes of schoolwork, understanding one's own strengths and weaknesses, understanding the processes involved in carrying out school tasks, understanding the differences across subject areas, and being able to review and revise one's work). Consistent with the stand-alone approach, each of the organizing themes is introduced explicitly in units at the beginning of the year. Thereafter, consistent with the infused approach, the themes are introduced as part of the regular schoolwork.

To our battery of measures that look directly at the acquisition of PIFS knowledge, we have added an examination of actual student work in the areas of curricular focus. We are also studying different classroom contexts in an ethnographic fashion. Finally, we plan to supplement the amalgamated PIFS curriculum with a separate, optional emphasis on creative work, thereby ending up with a combined PIFS–CIFS curriculum. PIFS-II is still in its formative phases; the first results of our research indicate that students are able to master the curriculum and that their classroom performance improves as a consequence of participation in this program. By the completion of phase II, we expect to have ascertained the power of this new approach to PIFS, as well as its susceptibility to combination with a program oriented explicitly toward more creative uses of mind within a school context.

Discussion of the PIFS Program

Our work thus far indicates that it is possible to create theory-based curricula that can aid middle school students to become "practically intelligent for school." To be sure, some of the procedures we have developed have already been used for many years by skilled teachers; moreover, our programs share many features with "study-skill programs" that are based on other theories or that lack theoretical grounding altogether. We must note as well that it remains to be seen whether our program, in its various forms, can affect student performances across the curriculum, even when PIFS virtues are not inculcated directly.

What, then, are the advantages of educational interventions undertaken by researchers in the cognitive sciences? We see at least three. First, because there is a basis in research for the recommended procedures, it should be possible to analyze an intervention into its component parts and ascertain which features are effective and which are not. For example, in the present program, we discovered that the more effective infused PIFS units were those that were discipline-specific and that built on the students' extracurricular interests and experiences. We also learned that students improved on their ability to use the skills targeted in the infused units and to understand why these were important; however, their ability to reflect on their own and others' work did not significantly increase.

Second, the existence of a research basis provides a rationale for making important procedural decisions. Having carried out both stand-alone and infused versions of the original PIFS program, and having identified the strengths and weaknesses of each through qualitative and quantitative analyses, we have now created a new PIFS-II combining the strengths of both while eliminating the more problematic aspects of each. Thus, in PIFS-II, we are able to include those aspects of the "stand-alone program" which worked well, such as techniques for addressing skills useful in several domains like homework and testing. At the same time, we have incorporated the most successful aspects of the "infused program," such as the focus on individual differences in students, and the merging of the PIFS concepts into material the teacher was already teaching.

Third, and perhaps most important, the participation of cognitive researchers in the actual design and implementation of educational interventions can help bring about important and needed realignments in educational reform. Little progress can be expected if researchers simply "use" the schools to prove their own theories correct, ignoring evidence to the contrary. If, however, researchers attend carefully to the findings obtained in these naturalistic sites, then their own theories may be revised and improved as a consequence. In our own cases, for example, the difficulties observed in certain sites affected our own analyses of contextual effects on intelligence. We now recognize that there is a difference between contexts where individuals claim a

willingness to change, contexts where individuals are deeply committed to change, and contexts where individuals actually prove capable
of inducing change. Unless investigators are attuned to these critical
differences, they may erroneously treat these contexts as equally fertile
(or equally fallow).

Moreover, it is both possible and desirable for researchers and educators to form significant partnerships in work of this sort. To be sure,
not all educators are cut out to be researchers, no more than all
researchers can be effective educators. However, to the extent that each
group can learn to think in terms of the considerations relevant to the
other, their practices are likely to improve. And, in the happiest cases,
some role reversals do occur. Both Gardner and Sternberg have themselves tried out in their own classes some of the practices recommended to teachers in the middle school. By the same token, some
teachers have become valued contributors to the research, pointing out
problems with our materials and approaches, and making apt suggestions for improvements. When such results in the PIFS program are
combined with similar productive alliances across other laboratories
(such as those represented in this volume), one has the beginning of
a quite powerful leverage for educational reform (Bruer 1993).

Conclusion: Intelligences for All Contexts

When we began our respective programs in the area of intelligence
some fifteen years ago, both research teams were concerned principally with making a contribution to the discussion of the nature of
intelligence—an issue that had been relatively dormant in psychological theorizing for the preceding few decades. Clearly, silence
about intelligence is no longer a problem in the academy, and we are
pleased to have contributed to this reinvigoration of a topic of classical
importance.

Remote from our own thinking was the possibility that new work
on intelligence might also contribute to efforts in educational reform.
And indeed, despite the publication of the influential *A Nation at Risk*
(National Commission on Excellence in Education 1983), most discussions of reform have not concerned themselves with altered conceptions of intelligence nor with the need for approaches that would
equip students to deal with the increased demands of school.

Nonetheless, like a large number of researchers trained in cognitive
and developmental studies, we found ourselves directing an increasing amount of our attention to the nation's schools—and not only as
sites for research-as-usual. We were therefore delighted to have twin
opportunities: on the one hand, to combine our approaches to the

study of intellect, and on the other, to determine whether such a combined program might actually prove of help to students of middle school age.

At least provisionally, we can conclude that the work described in this chapter has had some educational utility. Yet, like most work inspired by research, it raises many new and vexing questions. Clearly, the attention thus far directed toward intelligence "in the head" needs to be directed equally toward intelligence "in the world." We need to pay attention as well to the distinctive contents of different domains—history, music, physics, the arts—and to the particular contexts of the world—middle school, Rummidge University, Wilcox's foundry. Fortunately, many researchers are now turning their attention to these contextual issues (Lave and Wenger 1991; Resnick et al. 1991; Rogoff 1990; Salomon in press; Stigler, Schweder, and Herdt 1990), and while the emerging picture of cognition will undoubtedly be more complex as a result, it should be clearer as well.

A theory of intelligence sensitive to nuances of context is desirable, but it is also clear that, for scientific purposes, one does not want a theory for every content and for every context. Urgently needed is a research program that can tease out factors that remain constant from among those factors which vary with context. Detailed case studies must be undertaken in different countries and contexts, but at the same time, the search for generalization will require both focused empirical investigations and powerful efforts at synthesis.

One good test for a theory-based approach like ours, in the end, is whether it actually can inspire enhanced practical intelligence in one or more contexts. In that sense, our efforts represent exploration of new territory. Even if there is nothing as practical as a good theory, sometimes good practice can inform a theory—and perhaps particularly when the theory is about practical matters.

Note

Support for this research has come principally from two grants generously provided by the James S. McDonnell Foundations. Lynn Okagaki is now at Cornell University. The authors are grateful to Drs. John Bruer, Dana Kay, Jill Larkin, and Kate McGilly for their support and flexibility. For collaboration on the various phases of the PIFS project, the authors thank their colleagues Tina Blythe, Alice Jackson, Jin Li, Lenora Manzella, Noel White, and Wendy Williams, as well as the many teachers, administrators, and students who have aided with their research in various ways. The authors are especially grateful to Tina Blythe and Susan Papa, who gave many helpful comments on earlier drafts.

Chapter 6

Classroom Applications of Cognitive Science: Teaching Poor Readers How to Learn, Think, and Problem Solve

Irene W. Gaskins

The goal of schooling is understanding (Gardner 1991; Perkins 1992)—understanding that will lead to a lifetime of meaningful application. Yet too often what goes on in schools, especially for students with poor literacy skills, does not achieve that goal (Allington and McGill-Franzen 1989). We know, for example, that teaching poor readers to read better does not necessarily lead to reading with understanding, nor, for that matter, does teaching content knowledge lead to understanding the content (Scardamalia and Bereiter 1985). This suggests that for students to achieve understanding and to make applications, another kind of knowledge is necessary—knowledge about how the mind works and how to control that process.

Instruction, particularly for poor readers, needs to guide students to an awareness of, and control over, mental processes and dispositions for constructing understanding *and* to a motivated commitment to employ those processes and dispositions in all subject areas throughout their school years (Paris, Lipson, and Wixson 1983). Creating such an instructional program and training teachers to teach it were the challenges that faced Benchmark School, a school attended each year by 165 poor readers (ages 6–14) with average or above average intelligence. This chapter tells of a three-year adventure in program development and professional growth. The goal was to produce students who were knowledgeable both about factors affecting their own learning, thinking, and problem solving and about how to control those factors. The outcome we sought was motivated students who understood and applied what they were learning.

To achieve our goal we had to overcome the traditional view that the teacher's job, particularly in content-area instruction, is to dispense facts. We felt instead that what students really needed to know was *how* to learn. The knowledge explosion in the last several decades has made it impossible for children to learn in school everything they will need to know to be productive and successful adults. Thus, it is imperative that schools teach students how to search for and think about information, rather than focusing primarily on the static subject matter of the curriculum. Although learning is a knowledge-based process, it is one that depends on knowing how to think well and in a variety of ways about knowledge. Knowledge that is merely memorized is inert, unusable (Resnick and Klopfer 1989). To be of value, knowledge must be deeply processed (Nickerson 1988). This requires that learners be willing to immerse themselves in the subject matter, to react to it personally, and to be satisfied that covering less material may, in fact, result in greater retention and more usable knowledge (Gardner 1991). Knowing how to learn gives individuals the power to take control of their education and personal destinies by thinking well and processing information deeply. The result is understanding. When knowledge is understood, it becomes generative (Wittrock 1986). It can be used to think, learn, and problem solve.

Unlike most reports of research and development projects, this chapter provides detailed information about how the project staff was trained. Our project also was notable in terms of its longevity, and the complexity of its goal—the integration of instruction about metacognitive awareness and control into all academic activities across the curriculum and throughout the school. In addition, the project was conducted by school staff members within the context of the day-to-day exigencies of a school's complex social organization—management of groups, creation of a learning climate, special events, and so on. Further, we evaluated the project over three years, longer than most projects measuring the effects of instruction.

We begin by defining the student need that was the focus of the research and development project, and we examine the role of cognitive theory in creating a program to meet that need. Next, we discuss the process of program development and professional growth at Benchmark. Finally, we describe the strategies-across-the-curriculum program, the reactions of teachers and students to that program, and the results of both quantitative and qualitative analysis regarding students' performance.

The Problem and Insights from Cognitive Theory

It had been our hope that teaching our bright, poor readers to decode effectively would be the key to their overcoming school difficulties, for comprehension was usually not a problem with these students. Thus experts were consulted, research conducted, and a formal word identification program was developed (Gaskins, Downer, Anderson, Cunningham, Gaskins, Schommer, and the Teachers of Benchmark School 1988; Gaskins, Gaskins, and Gaskins 1991). Unfortunately, better decoding did not produce better students, although it did produce better readers. Follow-up of students who left the school suggested that while Benchmark graduates maintained above-the-mean standardized test scores in reading, there were not nearly as many excellent students (judging by teacher comments and report card grades) as native ability would suggest there should have been. We were faced with the question of why teaching bright, poor readers to read well had not assured school success commensurate with ability.

Sternberg's (1990b) theory of "mental self-government" regarding thinking styles and studies by Gaskins (1984) and by Gaskins and Baron (1985) shed light on this dilemma. A thinking style, according to Sternberg (1990b), is the "way of directing the intellect that an individual finds comfortable" (p. 366). The study by Gaskins (1984) suggested that a number of nonacademic factors often coexist with poor reading. Included among these factors were disorganization, inattention, passivity, and cognitive-style characteristics that negatively affect school achievement. Gaskins and Baron (1985) conducted a year-long, cognitive training study of dysfunctional learner characteristics and found that the students who received training in how to cope with maladaptive cognitive styles (impulsivity, inflexibility, and nonpersistence) scored significantly higher than the controls on measures of reflectivity, flexibility, and persistence at the conclusion of the study.

The success of the cognitive training project made us wonder if the missing ingredient in our overall program for poor readers might be teaching students *how* to manage factors affecting learning. There was certainly other research support for the fact that students like ours "frequently use different processing routes and mental patterns" (Meltzer 1991) and display inefficient and inflexible strategies for approaching tasks, and thus perform at a level below that which they might be expected to perform based on intellect (Swanson 1989; Torgesen 1978).

Our question became: Can immersing poor readers in a program of cognitive and metacognitive strategy instruction reverse the downward spiral of school performance usually associated with poor reading? Our objective was to produce goal-directed, planful, self-assessing, strategic students who were motivated to understand and apply what they were learning.

Why Teach Poor Readers Strategies for Awareness and Control?
There are at least three excellent reasons to teach poor readers, at as early an age as possible, the metacognitive awareness and control

concepts of how to learn. First, poor readers do not tend to exhibit awareness and control strategies unless these concepts are directly taught (Chan and Cole 1986; Torgesen 1980; Wong 1985). Good readers are aware of factors that affect comprehension and learning, know how to implement an array of strategies, and actively manage the strategies that are needed to succeed (Pressley, Goodchild, Fleet, Zajchowski, and Evans 1989). Poor readers do not demonstrate these traits; however, they do profit from explicit training regarding awareness and control (Garner 1987; Wixsno and Lipson 1991).

Second, instruction that stresses the what, why, how, and where of awareness and control increases motivation to apply thinking strategies in real learning situations (Swanson 1990; Zimmerman 1990). One key factor in creating motivation appears to be informing students of the practical benefits of each strategy taught (Paris, Lipson, and Wixson 1983). Explicit training that fosters the beliefs that strategies are important, worth some extra effort, and instrumental in enhancing performance has been shown to motivate students to apply these strategies independently (Paris and Oka 1986). In addition to directly explaining why specific strategies are beneficial, teachers who initiate miniexperiments (Gaskins 1988), in which students compare their usual strategies to ones the teacher recommended, have found that students are motivated by the discovery that specific strategies are of value.

Third, students need to be informed about awareness and control concepts in the early school years so that the disposition to apply awareness and control strategies has time to reach the level of automaticity that results from having applied these concepts and strategies throughout their years in school. While training studies suggest that teaching and scaffolding specific learning strategies are relatively easy to accomplish, the executive control mechanism that assesses, combines, and regulates learning strategies is not as amenable to training (Duffy, Roehler, Sivan, Rackliffe, Book, Meloth, Vavrus, Wesselman, Putnam, and Bassiri 1987). Johnston (1985) also believes that considerable repeated exposure is necessary, during which time the teacher gradually releases responsibility for control to the student. Executive control and the disposition to apply it need to be developed gradually over an extended period of time (Resnick and Klopfer 1989). (See Derry and Murphy 1986 for a review of this literature.) Experience more than maturation determines cognitive proficiency (Glaser 1989).

When and Where Should Awareness and Control Strategies Be Taught?
Once a decision is made to teach metacognitive awareness and control strategies, then the school or teacher comes face to face with decisions

that affect curriculum design. With respect to when and where to teach these strategies, there is a choice whether to teach metacognitive strategies as an isolated, stand-alone course or to embed (or infuse) the teaching of these strategies in one or more courses or in all areas of the curriculum. Nickerson (1988) argues for combining stand-alone and infused (or embedded) courses, feeling both can coexist. Derry and Murphy (1986) conclude from their review of the research that stand-alone courses cannot adequately develop executive learning skills and recommend that learning strategies instruction be incorporated into standard subject-matter courses. This conclusion is echoed by Bereiter (1984), Brown (1985b), Duffy and Roehler (1987b), Garner (1987), and Winograd and Paris (1988). Weinstein and her colleagues suggest that the two important variables involved in strategy acquisition are "opportunities to *practice* as well as to *receive feedback* about both the new strategies and the kinds of self-monitoring activities necessary for selecting, modifying, and evaluating strategy use" (Weinstein and Underwood 1985, 252). They suggest a "metacurriculum," a program for teaching students how to learn and process knowledge that is part of all content-area courses. Thus, current evidence suggests that the best time to teach metacognitive awareness and control is in the context of real subject-matter teaching. That does not rule out, however, the benefits of combining stand-alone and embedded courses.

How Should Awareness and Control Strategies Be Taught?
Like many learning theorists (Bakhtin 1986; Vygotsky 1978; Wertsch 1991), we are convinced that it is how individuals communicate and how they appropriate what they hear that give rise to intellectual development. How one learns, thinks, and problem solves is constructed and situated socioculturally, and mediational means such as language learned in the home and school shape how well one will process information. Further, verbal mediation needs to be coupled with meaningful activities structured around important concepts. Thus a program of mediated strategy instruction embedded in the regular curriculum seems an excellent way of guiding students to become learners, thinkers, and problem solvers.

To be successful in mediating and/or teaching strategies for metacognitive awareness and control, teachers must themselves understand cognition and metacognition, including learning theory, be aware of a variety of cognitive and metacognitive strategies, and be able to analyze the strategies they plan to teach into their component parts (Gardner 1985; Joyce 1985). Teachers need to be explicit in their explanations regarding the mental acts of strategy use (Duffy et al.

1987; Perkins 1992) and to know as much about the influence of prior knowledge, strategies, task, and situation as they know about the text itself (Pearson 1985). The research is clear—the main determinant of a teacher's ability to teach is his or her understanding of the process to be taught (Beck and McKeown 1987; Bereiter and Scardamalia 1985; Bruner 1985; Shulman 1986).

The advocates of direct, explicit, informed instruction believe that teachers should inform students of *what* is to be learned, *why* it is worth learning, *when* it can be used, and *how* to learn it, followed by modeling and by gradually releasing responsibility (Duffy and Roehler 1987a; Paris, Lipson, and Wixson 1983; Pearson 1985). During modeling, the teacher reasons out loud "to make visible the essentially invisible acts involved" (Duffy and Roehler 1987a). The goal of instruction is to move "from teacher-centered responsibility for learning to student-centered responsibility" (Marzano and Arredondo 1986)—a goal that can only be accomplished if students are aware of what affects learning and if they have the skill and will to take charge of the learning process.

In summary, the "how" of teaching awareness and control strategies requires that a number of pieces be in place. First, teachers need to acquire substantial background knowledge about the awareness and control factors affecting learning and thinking. Second, teachers need to break this information into teachable components. With this preparation, teachers will then be ready not only to directly teach cognitive and metacognitive strategies, but to mediate how to learn and think during instructional conversations throughout each school day. The goal is for teachers gradually to hand over the responsibility for applying the strategies to students, while giving students support in the form of feedback and reexplanations. The result should be students who have the skills and the will to handle learning tasks successfully, with understanding and application.

Program and Staff Development

As stated earlier, *acquiring content-area knowledge,* rather than *knowing how to learn* often is seen as the primary goal of schooling. Yet research and reviews of research (e.g., Chan and Cole 1986; Kletzein 1991; and Wong 1985) consistently have demonstrated that the difference between good and poor students of similar aptitude is not in the amount of content-area knowledge they possess, but in their ability and disposition to learn. Thus we believe that teachers should see their role as learning coaches rather than as knowledge tellers. It was our hypothesis that if teachers had a better knowledge base regarding cognition and metacognition and were well grounded in both content (declarative) and procedural knowledge (Nickerson 1988), they would become learning coaches. Acquiring this background of procedural knowledge became the focus of Benchmark's many vehicles for program and staff development.

Since the inception of Benchmark School in 1970, program development has been research-based and staff development has been collaborative and collegial. Vehicles in place for program and staff development include a large professional library of journals and books, weekly research seminars, monthly in-service meetings, conference attendance, collaboration for professional writing, weekly individual and team meetings for teachers and supervisors, and curriculum updates by curriculum-area coordinators. With the advent of the strategies-across-the-curriculum project, other innovative means of program and staff development evolved, including coteaching, retreats, and interactive journals.

To explore teaching students how to learn the staff decided to study metacognition. We read and discussed articles and chapters in professional journals and books about cognitive science, consulted with experts, and made metacognition a frequent topic of our weekly research seminars. At the same time, the teachers experimented with some of the ideas suggested in the readings, and by the visiting experts, and reported to the seminar each week about their attempts to apply concepts from cognitive science to classroom instruction. Weekend retreats were held to discuss instruction and to write strategy units. Teachers and supervisors collaborated in teaching instructional units, often communicating daily about their lessons in an interactive journal. This frequent staff interaction on applying cognitive science to instruction provided the common foundation upon which we built an across-the-curriculum strategies program. Instruction stressed the what, why, when, and how of awareness and control as soon as children entered the school. This section describes the program and staff development milieu in which the strategies-across-the-curriculum program was constructed.

Professional Library. To support research-based program development, the school maintains an ever-growing professional library with a librarian who, upon request, compiles references for staff members on topics of interest. The school subscribes to approximately thirty-five professional journals a year that are routinely circulated among the staff. In addition, each year 20–30 professional books related to cognition and instruction are added to the professional library.

Research Seminar. Another support for the development of research-based instructional programs is the research seminar, a weekly, after-school meeting where staff members discuss their professional reading. Each hour-and-a-half seminar is devoted to a specific topic. Staff members present a brief summary of what they have read, then there is a discussion of possible classroom applications of the ideas presented. Everyone seems to enjoy the discussions and there are times when the room seems electrified with enthusiasm about the ideas that are generated.

In-service.   A third support for research-based program development is monthly in-service. Once a month school is dismissed early and teachers gather for two hours of in-service presented by a well-known expert in cognition and instruction. Guests who have helped us develop our strategies program include Richard Allington, Donna Alvermann, Richard Anderson, Isabel Beck, Gerald Duffy, Linnea Ehri, John Guthrie, Marjorie Lipson, Donna Ogle, Annemarie Palincsar, Scott Paris, David Pearson, Charles Perfetti, Michael Pressley, Taffy Raphael, Laura Roehler, Peter Winograd, and Karen Wixson. In addition to interacting with the speakers during the formal afternoon in-service presentations, the staff is given an opportunity to chat informally with the speakers during morning roundtable sessions. This is a time when they are able to elicit ideas for dealing with specific classroom concerns. These in-service days generate much excitement. Clearly, the staff enjoys getting to know the experts whose research has influenced their practice.

Conferences.   Further support for developing research-based instruction is provided at conferences and workshops. Each year staff members attend national and local conferences, including the International Reading Association Conference and the National Reading Conference, where they seek out experts with whom to discuss specific issues related to applying research findings to classroom instruction. Those who attend conferences write summary notes, which are distributed to the staff. Implications for practice are discussed at meetings with other staff members, and ideas are tried out in classrooms.

Staff members also grow professionally from the experience of making presentations at conferences and workshops. Preparing for such occasions provides opportunities for theoretical as well as practical discussions among the staff as they support the presenter in his or her preparation and preconference presentation to the staff.

Professional Writing.   In addition, staff members collaborate in writing chapters and articles, as well as books. Prepublication drafts are distributed to the staff and Benchmark authors receive a great deal of rich input for consideration. The readers feel they learn as much from this process as the writers do.

Weekly Individual and Team Meetings.   Program and staff development is further enhanced by individual weekly collaborative meetings between teachers and supervisors, supervisors and the director, and teachers and the director. In addition, the middle school team composed of eleven teachers, seven psychological service staff members, and one supervisor meets weekly to coordinate the instructional program for the fifty middle school students. For the most part, the topic of discussion during both individual and team meetings is how to best meet the needs of Benchmark students. These discussions inevitably include conversations about what teachers can do to provide students with the best possible program.

Curriculum-Area Coordinators.   As a means of nurturing recent innovations at Benchmark, coordinators are appointed to keep the staff abreast of happenings and publications in the areas they coordinate. At the time the strategies-across-the-curriculum program was begun, we had coordinators for written composition, decoding, metacognition, social studies, computer education, and spelling. Coordinators are responsible for maintaining the quality of the programs developed at Benchmark, as well as for staff development and program improvement, as related to their assigned areas of responsibility. They publish memos, present in-service meetings, write lesson and/or curriculum guides, consult with teachers, and share relevant professional articles and chapters with the staff.

Coteaching and Collegiality.   As a result of our study and discussions of the research literature, the staff became increasingly convinced that we needed to develop an across-the-curriculum program to help students become aware of and take control over factors that affect learning, thinking, and problem solving. However, in the mid-eighties there were few models for how to do this. Based on the input of several Benchmark teachers who were beginning to include strategy teaching in their reading instruction, a pilot program was begun in social studies. This first attempt with strategies across the curriculum was initiated by my coteaching with Jim Benedict, a middle school social studies teacher. (See Gaskins and Elliot 1991 for the story of that pilot year of strategy instruction.) Originally, Jim was to teach the content of social studies and I was to teach the students how to learn the social studies. Although Jim loved his subject matter, he proved to be a fast learner with respect to providing strategy instruction. With each passing day he incorporated more and more explicit teaching of awareness and control strategies into his lessons. By spring I was no longer needed. Jim had integrated explicit strategy instruction into his teaching of social studies. Throughout the year, Jim and I had been sharing our successes with process teaching with the research seminar participants. More teachers began employing a process approach and sharing their ideas and successes with us. The development of a process approach to teaching became increasingly synergistic.

About the same time, we received a grant from the James S. McDonnell Foundation to support the development of a strategies-across-the-curriculum program. As a result, interest in strategy teaching among the staff increased. Teachers who had experimented with teaching awareness and control strategies in earlier years began to develop definite routines for including strategy instruction as part of all their lessons and they shared these routines with their teaching assistants, coteachers, and supervisors, who in turn, observing the successful response of students to being told explicitly how to learn, shared these instructional routines with others. During each of the three years of the grant, Jim and I taught, or cotaught with, new-to-Benchmark teachers to develop a program that integrated content and process instruction. For example, each year Jim taught social studies in the classes of three teachers, and I cotaught with at least one other teacher. Teachers of the classes to whom Jim and I taught social studies began making explicit strategy teaching part of their instructional repertoire across the curriculum. Thus, a great deal of cross-fertilization took place with respect to strategy teaching.

Retreats.   With the advent of the three-year research and development grant, teachers were asked to volunteer to be McDonnell teachers, their task being to help develop the strategies-across-the-curriculum program. Weekend retreats were held where these teachers, who were beginning to meet with success in developing classroom strategies programs, shared their ideas and collaborated with other McDonnell teachers to develop a consistent, coherent school-wide program. In addition to discussions, the retreats featured times when teachers worked alone developing written lesson plans, as well as times when they met with a supervisor to gain feedback about their developing plans. Teachers usually left these weekend retreats with a written plan for a unit of instruction featuring a specific strategy such as summarizing, clarifying, or task analysis, to be taught in reading, social studies, health, or science classes. They also left with renewed enthusiasm for the promise that strategy instruction held for their students' academic success.

Interactive Dialogue Journals.   Realizing that a great deal of excellent process instruction was being developed in our classrooms, we were anxious to document what this instruction looked like and how students reacted. (See Gaskins, Anderson, Pressley, Cunicelli, and Satlow

1993 for an analysis of instruction in six Benchmark classrooms.) Research assistants, who also had other part-time teaching responsibilities at Benchmark, were assigned to observe, take field notes, and audio tape the lessons of the McDonnell teachers, all of whom had volunteered to take part in the strategies project. Supervisors also became part of the corps who observed and recorded strategy lessons.

Notes about the lessons were recorded in what came to be known as "interactive journals." The journals were interactive because, from the first day of observations by the researchers and supervisors in September 1988, the contents of the journals were shared with teachers. Teachers were encouraged to communicate with the observer by recording explanations, concerns, questions, and insights. Over time, these journals became a dynamic force in instructional change. For example, teachers might express their concern about a specific aspect of lessons and request the observer's input about how lessons might be improved. When the observer was the teacher's supervisor, the supervisor would often volunteer to teach a lesson, so that the teacher could be the observer and analyze what seemed to work and not work with respect to strategy teaching.

In several cases, the researcher observers were also part-time teachers of the same students they observed. As a result of their observations, they often incorporated the language of the teachers they observed into their own process teaching, helping students make across-subject connections. Other researchers were teaching assistants in language arts classes. They also were able to bring into their classrooms what they were learning as researcher observers.

The Strategies-across-the-Curriculum Program

Over the course of three years Benchmark developed a three-pronged program: (1) teaching strategy units as an embedded/infused part of all instruction, (2) teaching courses about how the mind works, and (3) mentoring students who were at high risk for failure. This strategies-across-the-curriculum program did not develop overnight, nor is it static. What is described here reflects our current program, a program that is continually evolving as a result of ongoing program evaluation.

The Embedded/Infused Strategies Program

Informed by our study of the research and by piloting units of strategy instruction in classrooms, plus the knowledge we gained from visiting experts, Benchmark teachers developed a model of strategy instruction. Information about how the thirty-two Benchmark teachers

Explain Process Object

WHAT: (When first introduced) "Today we are going to learn...."
                                         "What this means is..."
                 (After introduced)   "What strategy have we been using to..."

WHY: (When first introduced) "This is an important strategy because..."
                 (After introduced)   "Why is .... an important strategy?" "How will it
                                          help you understand and remember?"

WHEN: (When first introduced) "You can use this strategy when..."
                                          "Tomorrow I want you to tell me a time during your
                                          studies that you applied the strategy we are
                                          learning."
                 (After introduced)   "When did you use the strategy?"

HOW: (When first introduced) Tell students how to do the strategy.
                                          Be very explicit about the self-talk (what students
                                          should say to themselves as they employ the
                                          strategy).

                                          Illustrate the strategy with a personal experience.

                 (After introduced)   "Can someone tell me how to do the strategy we are
                                          learning?"
                                          "What do you say to yourself to guide yourself in
                                          using the strategy?"

MODEL: (When first introduced) Model the process objective using real text.
                 (After introduced)   Teacher continues to model and occasionally asks a
                                          student to model.

GRADUAL RELEASE OF RESPONSIBILITY: Walk students through the process of
                                       of implementing the strategy taught, scaffolding
                                       (providing support as necessary).
                                       Re-explain/elaborate where students exhibit difficulty.
                                       As students demonstrate readiness to take over
                                       control of strategu use, provide only the amount of
                                       support needed for success.

Figure 6.1
Explicit teaching outline

responded to the strategies project is presented in an interview study of the entire academic-content-area faculty (Pressley, Gaskins, Cunicelli, Burdick, Schaub-Matt, Lee, and Powell 1991) and in a chapter about change at Benchmark (Gaskins, Cunicelli, and Satlow 1992). Examples of how the program was carried out can be found in a series of case studies (see Gaskins and Elliot 1991; Pressley, Gaskins, Wile, Cunicelli, and Sheridan 1991), as well as in a research report describing the moves and cycles of six strategy teachers (Gaskins, Anderson, Pressley, Cunicelli, and Satlow 1993).

The strategies program developed by the Benchmark staff is described in detail in *Implementing Cognitive Strategy Instruction across the School* (Gaskins and Elliot 1991). Figure 6.1 outlines the format used for lessons within a strategy unit. The strategy lesson model outlined in figure 6.1 provides a flexible framework within which teachers may individually implement the process and content objectives of the curriculum, as well as meet the needs of particular students. The staff implements the strategy program at all grade levels and in teaching all subject matter. Classroom activities are accompanied by conversations about how to think one's way through each task. The strategies that receive the most attention are determining importance, summarizing information, drawing inferences, generating questions, and monitoring comprehension (Dole et al. 1991).

Courses about How the Mind Works
The second prong of the strategies-across-the-curriculum program is composed of two stand-alone courses. The purpose of both is to further develop student and teacher understanding of the way the mind works. Psych 101 is a fifteen-minute-a-day course taught each year to the four middle school classes (grades 6–8). The course introduces the students to concepts about learning theory and intelligence and provides a rationale for why they should be actively involved as goal-directed, planful, self-assessing, strategic students. (See Gaskins and Elliot 1991 for a description of the course.) A simplified, ten-lesson version of Psych 101 called "Learning and Thinking" (LAT) is presented each year to all but the youngest lower school classes. Regular classroom teachers and assistants are active participants in the classes, and as a result, these two courses contribute to the development of a common language to describe metacognitive processes during instruction in all areas of the curriculum.

The Mentor Program
The mentor program is designed to support automatizing the disposition to process information strategically. Students who take part in

this program are those identified by their teachers as most at risk for academic failure. Mentors (volunteer staff members) meet with students individually for a minimum of fifteen minutes per week. The primary role of the mentor is to be an adult friend and an academic coach. This approach is based on the premise that cognitive development involves someone mediating or assisting students to perceive and interpret their environment. Mentors guide students in filtering and organizing the school happenings by giving cognitive assistance that directs, focuses attention, clarifies, and illuminates. They also mediate the process of changing, challenging, or discounting erroneous beliefs, as well as help students see the possibilities for growth and development of their unique capabilities and skills. Each year approximately 30–40 students in grades 2–8 are assigned mentors. (See R. W. Gaskins 1992 for a more detailed description of the Benchmark mentor program.)

Student Response to the Program

Data gathered from performance-based assessments and a standardized achievement test confirmed the student growth reported by staff members and parents during the three year project. The formal evidence regarding student growth is presented below, followed by anecdotal snapshots of student progress in awareness and control.

Quantitative Data

Just as the authors of chapter 5 (Gardner, Krechevsky, Sternberg, and Okagaki) chose to study middle school students, so did we. However, in the Benchmark project, the strategies-across-the-curriculum program was taught each year to all 165 students in the school, grades 1–8; thus, all students who entered the middle school after the fall of 1988 had experienced a year or two of strategy instruction in the lower school.

Our rationale for studying middle school students was similar to that of the Gardner-Sternberg group. We, too were interested in how middle school students adjust to the demands of a school environment that is different from that traditionally encountered in elementary school. In the case of poor readers, the transition from elementary to middle school can be particularly problematic because middle school courses tend to be much more text-driven than do elementary school programs. Middle school students who are below grade level in reading often find their content-area texts difficult to read, yet these texts contain the concepts these students should be learning.

The question we wanted to answer was, can immersing poor readers in a program of cognitive and metacognitive strategy instruction reverse the downward spiral of school performance usually associated with poor reading? It is well documented that, even with intervention programs such as "Chapter 1" and special education, poor readers usually become poorer students with each passing year (Allington and McGill-Franzen 1989; Stanovich 1986). Might the missing ingredients in these programs be (a) instruction that makes students *aware* of how to adjust to the demands of a school environment and (b) instruction about *how* to implement the strategies they need to take control of those demands?

To examine our middle school students' application of strategies taught in the school-wide strategies program, a performance-based assessment for middle school students was developed and conducted. The assessment was a six-day social studies unit (complete with homework assignments). (See Gaskins, Guthrie, Anderson, Satlow, Boehnlein, Cunicelli, and Benedict, in preparation, for detailed information about the components of this assessment.) The assessment included four homework assignments, each requiring students to read independently several pages of middle school text about the Cherokee Indians and to respond to the assigned passages using a different strategy for each assignment: summarize each paragraph in a sentence ("Summarizing Paragraph"), outline the passage ("Outlining"), summarize each of the two sections of the assigned reading in a paragraph ("Integrating Text"), and take notes using a method of choice ("Taking Notes"). On the fifth day of the Cherokee unit, the students completed two assessments that comprised the unit test: (1) "Memory for Text Information" composed of ten true/false questions and five vocabulary words to match with five of nine possible meanings and (2) "Interpretation of Text Information" composed of six interpretative questions calling for an answer of several sentences for each question and one major essay question asking students to interpret "lack of clarity" regarding Cherokee policies before and during Jackson's presidency. This six-day assessment attempted to represent the kind of tasks that middle school students in schools throughout the United States are asked to perform on a daily basis (including the recall, interpretation, and written integration of text-based content material). We were interested in how our students would cope with typical middle school demands (completing homework, handing in assignments on time, asking for clarification about confusing concepts, studying for tests).

In addition to the performance-based assessments, we also included a standardized measure of reading comprehension in our analysis, the "Reading" subtest of the Metropolitan Achievement Test (Prescott,

Balow, Hogan, and Farr 1978). We wanted to test our belief (and that of others: Hiebert and Hutchison 1991; Kirst 1991; Paris, Wasik, and Turner 1991; Winograd and Gaskins 1992) that standardized tests are inadequate measures of cognitive and metacognitive strategy use, although they may measure gains in low-level comprehension (e.g., recognition of information found in short passages).

The performance-based assessment was administered to all middle school students in each of four school years. Full data sets were gathered for 118 students who attended the middle school between fall 1987 and spring 1991. These students with a few exceptions were between the ages of 11 and 14 and in sixth through eighth grades. During each year of the study there were between 48 and 50 students in the middle school, with 23–29 of these graduating each year. The mean IQ (Full Scale WISC-R) for the 118 participating students was 111.7.

In order to assess the effects of strategy instruction, students were divided into two groups: those who had not received strategy instruction in the middle school (baseline group) and those who had strategy instruction. The baseline group ($N = 47$) was comprised of the students in the middle school during school year 1987–88, one year prior to the implementation of the strategies-across-the-curriculum project, who were present for the six days of baseline assessment. The strategy-instruction group was established by pooling students who were new to the middle school in the fall of 1988, 1989, and 1990 ($N = 71$). In each of these years assessments were administered after nine months of instruction. In addition, students entering the middle school in the fall of 1988 ($N = 27$) received an assessment prior to any middle school instruction. Despite their additional assessment experience, analysis of covariance (which adjusted for age and IQ) suggested no significant differences in mean performance between those students receiving a second assessment after nine months of instruction (those entering in the fall of 1988) and those receiving their first assessment after nine months of instruction (those entering in the fall of 1989 and 1990). Therefore, students with the same amount of instruction were grouped together, regardless of experience with the assessment. An additional set of assessment data was collected in May a year later for those students who remained in the middle school strategy program for a second year ($N = 39$).

Analysis of covariance, which adjusted for IQ and age, was employed to identify differences in mean performance between middle school students who received strategy instruction and middle school students who had received no strategy instruction (baseline group). The mean scores of the strategy group after one year of strategy

Table 6.1
Performance of students with and without strategy instruction

| Measure | Baseline group | | | Strategy instruction group | | | | | |
| | | | | After 1 yr. instruction | | | After 2 yrs. instruction | | |
	N	M	SD	N	M	SD	N	M	SD
MAT (reading)	47	751.9	60.2	64	778.3	59.2	36	802.2**	56.4
Memory for text information	46	46.5	10.9	71	50.3	9.6	39	55.3**	8.4
Interpretation of text information	46	47.0	7.7	71	48.3	9.7	39	55.9**	11.4
Summarizing paragraphs	42	45.5	8.2	67	50.4*	10.2	35	51.2*	10.4
Outlining	39	46.7	9.4	68	51.3*	10.5	35	52.3*	9.6
Integrating text	41	47.7	9.7	67	49.5	10.5	35	54.0	9.1
Taking notes	38	48.6	9.9	62	47.7	10.2	35	53.4*	7.9
WISC-R (full scale)	47	110.2	11.0	71	112.7	13.4	39	113.7	13.0
Age	47	12.9	0.8	71	12.5	0.6	39	12.4	0.6

Note: All scores are standardized using the Benchmark Middle School population raw scores between spring 1988 and spring 1991. MAT and WISC-R scores are the nationally normed standard scores.
*Significantly different from comparison group at $p < .05$ after covariance adjustment for IQ and age.
**Significantly different from comparison group at $p < .01$ after covariance adjustment for IQ and age.

instruction were significantly higher than those of the baseline group on two of the seven measures ($p < .05$). After two years of strategy instruction, the mean performance for the strategy group exceeded that of the baseline group on six of the seven measures ($p < .05$). These results are presented in table 6.1. (For ease of comparison, scores for the performance-based assessments have been converted to a common scale where the mean and standard deviation for all scores are 50 and 10, respectively.)

In order to confirm the between-group findings, within-groups contrasts were made. We were interested in determining how well students would perform after one or two years of strategy instruction as compared with their initial performance prior to any instruction. Data for the two groups of students who had completed the assessments prior to the implementation of strategy instruction in school year 1988–89 were subjected to analysis of variance for repeated measures. The first group consisted of students in the baseline group who remained in the middle school for an additional year after their first

Table 6.2
Performance of baseline group

Measure	N	Prior to strategy instruction		After 1 yr. strategy instruction	
		M	SD	M	SD
MAT (reading)	21	739.5	49.6	794.2*	62.4
Memory for text information	20	46.7	12.1	48.1	9.7
Interpretation of text information	20	46.8	5.7	51.3	8.8
Summarizing paragraphs	20	43.4	8.2	52.8*	9.9
Outlining	16	46.4	11.0	54.4*	11.2
Integrating text	16	46.4	10.5	49.8	10.2
Taking notes	16	50.8	8.5	55.1	10.8
WISC-R (full-scale)	21	111.0	12.4	—	—
Age	21	12.7	0.5	—	—

Note: All scores are standardized using the Benchmark Middle School population raw scores between spring 1988 and spring 1991. MAT scores are the nationally normed standard scores.
*Significantly different from scores prior to strategy instruction at $p < .01$.

Table 6.3
Performance of strategy instruction group

Measure	N	Prior to strategy instruction		After 1 yr. strategy instruction		After 2 yrs. strategy instruction	
		M	SD	M	SD	M	SD
MAT (reading)	19	752.1	45.5	789.9*	63.2	794.4**	48.9
Memory for text information	19	47.8	9.4	51.0	9.4	53.9*	9.6
Interpretation of text information	19	46.4	8.6	51.9**	8.6	59.0**	8.9
Summarizing paragraphs	11	50.5	8.2	51.4	10.5	53.4	11.4
Outlining	16	43.4	8.2	55.1**	8.7	55.2**	11.0
Integrating text	15	46.8	6.2	49.7	12.2	57.7**	10.3
Taking notes	11	45.8	7.6	42.4	8.3	53.7**	8.4
WISC-R (full-scale)	19	114.6	11.9	—	—	—	—
Age	19	12.3	0.5	—	—	—	—

Note: All scores are standardized using the Benchmark Middle School population raw scores between spring 1988 and spring 1991. MAT scores are the nationally normed standard scores.
*Significantly different from scores prior to strategy instruction at $p < .05$.
**Significantly different from scores prior to strategy instruction at $p < .01$.

assessment ($N = 21$). The second group consisted of students who entered the middle school in the fall of 1988 and remained for two years, through the spring of 1991 ($N = 19$). It was thus possible to compare the before-strategy-instruction performance of these students to their performance after one and two years of strategy instruction.

Results of the within-group contrasts are presented in tables 6.2 and 6.3. After one year of strategy instruction, students in both baseline and strategy-instruction groups improved significantly on three of the seven measures ($p < .025$). After two years, students in the strategy-instruction group exceeded their initial performance on six of the seven measures ($p < .025$). These results are consistent with the between-group contrasts, which showed significant differences for two measures after one year of strategy instruction and differences for six measures after two years of strategy instruction.

An unexpected finding, in view of the fact that standardized tests are generally regarded as poor measures of strategy use, was that the strategy group outperformed the baseline group on the MAT in the second year (see table 6.1) and both groups made significant within-group gains on the MAT. For the most part, however, the ability to complete school tasks did not change significantly after one year of strategy instruction, while changes after the second year were more dramatic. These findings support the notion that strategy instruction needs to take place over an extended period of time if students are to develop the disposition, motivation, and automaticity to apply strategies independently and at increasingly higher levels of comprehension.

Our middle school students made exciting progress during the three-year, strategies-across-the-curriculum project, both with respect to progress on assessment measures and as reported by classroom teachers. The downward spiral of school performance usually associated with poor reading was not observed in our population. We used a range of assessments that tapped metacognitive and cognitive features of strategy instruction designed to develop motivated and planful learning of subject matter, and we showed significant gains over two years. Of course, we cannot rule out that there may have been some benefit from taking the set of assessments more than once, although it is doubtful that students would become more facile at writing imperative essays merely by being asked to write them again a year later without intervening instruction. A concurrent control group would have been a more satisfactory research design; however, it certainly would not have been in the best interests of our students. We also should note that in addition to the strategies program, there were many factors operating within the school that undoubtedly affected the students' performance (e.g., the exceptional amount of reading and writing expected of students, the weekly class meetings conducted by psychological service staff members, and a high level of parent support, to name only a few). However, these were all part of the program experienced by the baseline group. The strategies-across-the-curriculum program was the only new and different aspect of the middle school program during the three-year strategies-across-the-curriculum project.

Qualitative Evidence
As teachers began implementing cognitive and metacognitive strategy instruction in their classrooms, stories of students' responses to being taught explicitly how to learn and problem solve circulated among the staff and parents. This anecdotal evidence suggested success in applying a variety of awareness and control strategies. A number of these anecdotes are recounted here in order to illustrate the multifaceted approach to strategy instruction that was taking place in the school. It should not be inferred from these anecdotes that all of our students learned and applied these strategies, or that students successfully mastered and applied strategies in all possible academic situations. Most students, however, did seem to improve with respect to at least some aspects of awareness and control.

Awareness of Task. When Sarah complained that she was having difficulty understanding the reading assigned for homework because her social studies book had too many hard words in it and was poorly organized, her teacher shared with her the technique she used for coping with hard books, "I ask the librarian to help me find an easy-reading book on the subject." Later the teacher was pleased to hear that Sarah not only tried the suggestion, but that she shared with her classmates how much easier it was to read the social studies text after she had read an easy-reading book on the topic they were studying.

In a follow-up interview with the teacher of a former student, Betty, we discovered that, as a result of awareness instruction, Betty had learned the importance of analyzing a task before she began it. One of Betty's teachers commented to Benchmark's placement counselor that Betty had provided her with a "first" in her teaching career. After the teacher had assigned a number of pages to be read for homework, Betty raised her hand and asked, "What will we be expected to do with the information? I need to know because that will affect how I read the assignment." All those years of encouraging Betty to analyze the components of a task before plunging ahead seemed to have paid off.

Awareness of Person. Paul was notorious for his inflexibility. Both teachers and aides were reluctant to go near his desk to give him feedback regarding his written work, for such an interaction was sure to result in an argument from Paul. Paul did not willingly accept input about the quality of his written work unless it was that the work was totally satisfactory. No matter how gently an adult tried to guide him to see a better way of doing something, Paul seemed to be satisfied with his way. Unfortunately, this inflexibility often stood in the way of Paul's responding to instruction. Finally, the teacher gained Paul's agreement to respond to adult input by saying, "Thank you very much, I'll consider it." At the same time she made it clear that she was not forcing him to agree to change anything he had written. Using an adaptation of Meichenbaum's (1977) program of self-talk and cognitive-behavior modification, the teacher or teaching assistant marked a square on a card each time Paul responded that he would consider the input. Apparently Paul enjoyed seeing the card fill with check marks, for he became much more pleasant to work with and, seemingly without realizing it, he also became more flexible about receiving *and acting on* adult input. When Paul was followed up in his new school the next year, his teacher completed a questionnaire on Paul's learning characteristics, checking "flexibility" as one of Paul's strengths. Benchmark's placement counselor showed Paul the questionnaire and asked him how he accounted for the teacher viewing him as flexible. Paul's answer was candid and revealed his understanding of his own cognitive style. "Teachers don't like working with kids who are rigid, and I want her to help me and like me. I'm still rigid with my mom, though. She'll like me even if I am rigid." Paul certainly was aware of his learner characteristics, and when it was propitious to adapt them to enhance school success, he did so.

Awareness of Strategies. A few years ago one of our students, George, approached me about a wasteful practice that was going on in the school. He held up a stack of about fifty note cards and showed me the notes he had written on them. When I saw nothing unusual, he pointed out that only one idea was written on each card, and that, had he been allowed, he could have written much more on each card and not wasted so many of the school's cards. That was the last time I heard of George's concern about one of the strategies his teacher was teaching him for writing a report until one day when an excellent report written by George was brought to my attention. I asked George to tell me his procedure for writing such a well-organized report and was surprised and amused to hear him say that one of his secrets for success was writing only one idea on each card. That practice, he told me, allowed him to experiment with the organization of the report by sequencing the cards. When asked what other strategies he needed to use to write a report, George told me how he had to be selective when reading information about his topic and only collect data that were related to his topic. Before he wrote information on a card, he tried to put what he had read in his own words as a test of whether or not he really understood it. If he did not understand what he had read, he would reread it, and, if he still did not understand and needed the information, he would either discuss the passage with someone or look for an easier book. George was so enthusiastic about the strategies he was using to attain academic success that he would have been happy to share more, but he had already convinced me that he was aware of the strategies he needed to produce a well-researched and well-written report.

Awareness of Environmental Factors.   When James complained that he could not complete his seatwork because his seat was too near the reading-group table and the group distracted him, the teacher praised him for being aware of what interfered with his completion of the task and challenged him to come up with a solution to his problem. James said that if he could move his desk to the back row, he was sure he could complete his work. His desk was moved and he proceeded to fulfill his prophecy.

Richard attributed his poor test grades to the fact that his class had gym before dismissal, thus he never had time to gather the proper materials for studying before his bus was called. His teacher helped Richard develop a strategy for organizing his materials before his class left for gym and found that, as a result, Richard's awareness of how to organize his environment improved.

Control—Making a Plan.   Anne had difficulty completing assignments on time and/or appropriately, as did some of her classmates, so her teacher developed a planning sheet to help the students keep in mind factors they needed to consider when completing an assignment. On the planning sheet the students would write the exact assignment and answers to these questions: What do I know about the topic? What strategies can I use in completing the assignment? What do I know about myself that will help me complete the assignment and what do I know about myself that might get in the way—the factor I must take charge of? What environmental factors must I control?

First, the teacher guided the students through the planning sheet step by step, then she gradually released responsibility to the students, with the end result that the planning process, at least for Anne and some of the other students, began to become internalized and more automatic. According to Anne, one advantage of the teacher's walking students through the planning sheet was it provided an opportunity for students to work together. Anne liked hearing the variety of strategies her classmates proposed for completing assignments. This activity also provided both teacher and students with an opportunity to give and receive feedback about the strategies they were planning to use.

Control—Monitoring.   Carl is a student who these days at Benchmark can be heard blurting out in reading group, "This doesn't make sense." This phrase is music to at least one teacher's ears. When Carl entered Benchmark School, he silently made his way through pages of text and just as silently sat through the discussion of the text. Individual conferences with Carl revealed that he thought admitting he did not understand something was tantamount to admitting he was dumb. The teacher decided to teach self-monitoring and, in the process, to make the point that admitting something does not make sense is what all intelligent readers do. To introduce students to the concept of monitoring, the teacher explained the what, why, how, and when of monitoring, then modeled the process. Special emphasis was placed on the *why* of monitoring. Because monitoring often appeared to be a new concept for our poor readers and because it required extra effort, students needed to be convinced of its value. Monitoring was modeled by the teacher, using self-talk as she read or solved a problem, or wrote an essay, to show students how successful learners and problem solvers, as if by split mind, deploy strategies and make meaning. Some of the sentences the teacher used in modeling self-talk were

- "Wait a minute, what I just read doesn't agree with what we read in the last chapter. I'd better reread that sentence to see if I read it right."
- "There is an awful lot of information in that last paragraph. I'm not really sure I understood it. I'd better see if I can paraphrase it in my own words."
- "What I'm reading agrees with my prediction. I guess I knew more about energy than I thought. There is some new information, though, that I want to remember."
- "I'm going to have to revise my purpose for reading this section. It is about something entirely different than what I guessed it would be about."

Initially, the teacher provided students with a great deal of support as they monitored their performance in completing a task. The scaffolding, or gradual-release-of-responsibility, stage challenged the teacher to devise activities that provided a glimpse of what students were thinking as they processed text. Having students write in process journals as they read (Fulwiler 1980; Nist and Simpson 1987) was one way to do this. Working in dyads, where one partner explained to the other what was being read, was another form of monitoring (Dansereau 1987), as was the use of the reading-thinking strategy K-W-L Plus (Carr and Ogle 1987). In K-W-L Plus, students recalled what was *known*, determined what they *wanted* to learn, and identified what was *learned*. The "plus" included mapping and summarizing information. Encouraging mental imagery, as outlined by Gambrell, Kapinus, and Wilson (1987), was another way the teacher guided students' monitoring.

Control—Evaluating/Revising.   On the first day of school Jill requested that her social studies teacher allow the class ten minutes each morning for a self-assessment and discussion of concepts about which they might be confused. Jill explained that at the start of each class she liked to write a summary of what she thought she understood about her homework assignment and previous classwork. Then she liked to discuss that summary with a classmate to see if it made sense; and if it did not, she wanted to have the opportunity to ask questions about any misconceptions or confusions. Jill's new-to-Benchmark teacher was surprised at Jill's level of awareness of the need to self-evaluate and, if necessary, revise what one thinks. The teacher later learned that the previous year one of Jill's teachers had placed a great deal of emphasis on the goal of self-assessing. Jill obviously had found the instruction helpful. The new teacher wondered about the previous instruction and was told, for example, that if the content goal had been "to find out why the chapter was called 'Jacksonian Democracy,'" students might have been expected to write or to recite to themselves a summary about Jacksonian democracy to check whether they had achieved their goal. They might also have assessed the subgoals of noting the differences in democracy before and since Jackson, and the factors that needed to be present in a government to call it a democracy. If the students encountered difficulty with any of these tasks, they found they had either to revise the purpose questions to fit the material or to revise their plan for acquiring the information and begin the task again. For in-class tasks, teachers sometimes used an adaptation of reciprocal teaching (Palincsar and Brown 1984) in which the students and teacher read the text silently and after each segment privately wrote a summary, question, clarification, and prediction. If they had difficulty with the writing, they reread. Then the students as a group debated the merits of what they had written, frequently rereading to clarify a point, until they reached a degree of consensus on the most appropriate version.

Conclusions

Cognitive science research translated into educational practice has the power to create students who know how to find, analyze, integrate, interpret, and apply the vast amounts of information resulting from the information boom. At Benchmark School there is a tradition of integrating research findings into classroom instruction. This practice has intensified during the past several years, and both the formal and anecdotal data cited above suggest that the results have been positive for both staff and students.

The exciting results of our strategies-across-the-curriculum project were possible because a great deal of time and energy was invested in the professional growth of the staff. Professional growth opportunities were numerous and ongoing, and focused on the application of research from cognitive science to classroom instruction (Gaskins, Cunicelli, and Satlow 1992). This model of change also moved in the opposite direction—research conducted in our classrooms informed and improved our model of instruction (Gaskins, Anderson, et al. 1993; Gaskins, Guthrie, et al., in preparation).

Continuous conversation and collaboration occur as a staff seeks to develop and perfect its model of instruction. It is through this process that the staff comes to "own" the cognitive science principles that undergird informed classroom practices. Without this ownership, and faced with the complexities of everyday classroom life, teachers are likely to fall back on the tapes that have played in their heads since their first encounter with schooling. Unfortunately, the voices on these mental tapes, for the majority of teachers, speak of instructional approaches that have little research support. Ongoing staff-development support is, therefore, crucial if an innovative approach to instruction is to be fully integrated into a teacher's instructional repertoire.

Based on the current knowledge-base of cognitive science, enough is known to create improved learners, thinkers, and problem solvers, even among students who have experienced difficulties in learning. At Benchmark we have begun to develop an effective model for enhancing change in teachers' understanding and instruction, with positive outcomes for our students. However, challenges remain. The staff is presently seeking to address issues such as student maintenance of strategy use over time, independent and consistent transfer of strategy employment across domains, and motivational factors that will encourage students to higher levels of strategy use. These and other instructional problems will not be resolved, however, until teachers and administrators are convinced of the value of cognitive science research and are willing and able to become immersed in reading, discussing, and applying current research findings. If the gap between research and practice is to be bridged, schools will need to cultivate environments where professional growth is valued, continuous, high-quality staff development is provided, teacher input into the change process is encouraged, and adequate time is allowed for change to take place.

In light of the current problems in our nation's schools, a realistic (but discouraging and often ignored) finding of cognitive science research is that lasting and meaningful change takes time. Lasting change evolves as teachers and administrators grow in their understanding of the theoretical underpinnings of an innovation. Revolutions in instruction can be accomplished more quickly, but usually the changes are not lasting. Although lasting and meaningful change is admittedly a slow process, the Benchmark staff has come to value being a creative part of program development that is ever-evolving, research-based, and anchored by a staff-development model in which "each one teaches one." Administrative and supervisory staff are in classrooms daily, sometimes to observe, but more often to teach and collaborate. This on-line staff development is supplemented by monthly in-service and weekly meetings (team meetings, teacher-supervisor conferences, and research seminars). Ideas from these meetings are regularly shared with the entire staff through position papers and by word of mouth. An environment such as this, where professional growth is valued, teachers have input into the change process, and change evolves over time, seems to provide the best opportunity for research in cognitive science to make the impact it should and can have.

Note

The author is grateful to the James S. McDonnell Foundation, which funded the research and development project described here; to Richard C. Anderson and John T. Guthrie for support and advice regarding the analysis of the data; to Eric Satlow, who analyzed the quantitative data; to the many cognitive strategy researchers whose wise counsel and research reports, as well as classroom modeling and workshops at Benchmark, have greatly influenced our model of teaching; to the Benchmark teachers who generously gave of their time and expertise to develop the strategies-across-the-curriculum program; to Elizabeth Cunicelli, who coordinated the project; and to the following colleagues, who read and responded to several drafts of this chapter: Thorne Elliot, Mildred Ellison, Eleanor Gensemer, Sharon Rauch, and Eric Satlow.

PART III

Classrooms as Learning Communities

Chapter 7

From Visual Word Problems to Learning Communities: Changing Conceptions of Cognitive Research

The Cognition and Technology Group at Vanderbilt

Our goal in this chapter is to explore some changing conceptions of cognitive research that have emerged during the past five and a half years as we pursued our research through the James S. McDonnell Foundation's program "Cognitive Studies for Educational Practice" (CSEP). Although we focus on changes that have occurred within our own research team, we believe that our experiences are relevant to others, too. The changes we discuss involve different models of the role of cognitive research in attempting to understand and improve educational practice. For us, the models were initially implicit. They became explicit only after we looked back over our experiences and began to articulate the changes in thinking that occurred.

We discuss three models of the role of cognitive research in understanding and improving educational practice: (1) the curricular elaboration model, where one changes some aspect of the curriculum but leaves all other aspects of educational practice intact; (2) the classroom restructuring model, where one attempts to change the overall nature of the teaching and learning process that occurs in classrooms; and (3) the learning communities model, where the goal is to create a dynamic system that breaks the isolation of classrooms and provides a basis for continual adaption to changing conditions.

The Curricular Elaboration Model

The request for proposals for the McDonnell Foundation's new CSEP program arrived in our mailboxes in September 1987, when we were working with middle school students who were having difficulties in school, especially in areas such as mathematics and reading. One area of our work involved helping fifth and sixth grade students learn to solve word problems such as the following:

> Tony rides the bus to camp every summer. There are 8 other children who ride with him. The bus travels 9 miles an hour. It takes 4 hours to get there. How far away is the camp?

Nearly every student with whom we worked used a mechanical approach to solving word problems rather than one based on an attempt to understand the problem. For example, a typical answer for the word problem noted above was 8 + 9 + 4 = 21. The following explanation about solution strategies was also quite typical:

> *Interviewer:* Why did you decide to add the numbers?
>
> *Student:* Because it said, like, "How far away is the camp?" "How" is to add.

Working with Raiders of the Lost Ark

In an attempt to facilitate problem comprehension rather than encourage the mechanical "key word" approach our students were using, we began to investigate the use of video-based scenarios to promote problem comprehension. In several studies we used the first twelve minutes of the film *Raiders of the Lost Ark,* where Indiana Jones travels to South America to capture the golden idol (see, for example, Barron, Bransford, Kulewicz, and Hasselbring 1989; Bransford, Hasselbring, Barron, Kulewicz, Littlefield, and Goin 1988). We asked students to imagine they wanted to return to the jungle to obtain some of the gold artifacts Indiana left behind. If so, it could be important to know dimensions of obstacles such as the width of the pit they would have to jump, the height of the cave, the width of the river and its relationship to the size of the seaplane, and so forth.

The goal of learning more about important dimensions of potential obstacles and events guided the selection of mathematically based problems derived from scenes in the movie segment. The idea was to use known standards (e.g., Indiana Jones) to estimate sizes and distances that were important to know. For example, the width of the pit could be estimated by finding another, earlier scene where Indiana used his bullwhip to swing over the pit. Through the use of freeze frame we were able to show a scene of Indiana swinging with his outstretched body extending halfway across the pit. Measurement on the screen (either by hand or through the use of computer graphics) allowed students to see that the pit was approximately two Indianas wide. Students were also encouraged to create visual and symbolic representations of problems, and they received individualized feedback about the strengths and weaknesses of their approach to each problem. All instruction was one-on-one.

Effects of learning in the video context were compared to the effects of learning in a control condition, outside the video context, where students received one-on-one instruction in solving and representing written problems. The results indicated strong benefits of the video context on students' abilities to solve analogous transfer problems that occurred both within and outside the context of Indiana Jones (see Bransford, Hasselbring, et al. 1988). Our explanation of these benefits was that instruction presented in the context of the video made it clear to students what they were trying to do and why. They were therefore more likely to use this understanding to represent the problem appropriately and to monitor the reasonableness of their answers.

Problems with the Raiders Context.   As we continued to work in the context of *Raiders of the Lost Ark,* we encountered several problems that eventually prompted us to create our own videos. First, it was difficult to expand the range of mathematical problems that could be posed in the context of *Raiders* because the film was not designed from this perspective (see Bransford, Hasselbring, et al. 1988). Second, discussions of the importance of identifying and defining problems (e.g., Bransford and Stein 1984) convinced us of the need to move away from presenting students with well-defined word problems; instead, we wanted to help them begin with a general goal and learn to generate relevant subgoals on their own. Third, we discovered that many people, including those sitting on the review boards of granting agencies, did not take our work seriously because it was presented in the context of a movie. As one reviewer wrote: "You can't teach reality with fantasy." (We're still not sure what that means.)

The River Adventure
To address the problems encountered in working with *Raiders* we produced a prototype videodisc, "The River Adventure." As discussed earlier, one of our goals was to create a context for studying how people identify and define important problems as well as solve them. Thus, in "The River Adventure," the viewer is told that he or she has won a one-week trip on a houseboat and must do all the planning for food, gas, water, docking the boat, and so forth. Data concerning the boat (its length, width, height, cruising speed, fuel consumption and capacity), the route, marinas along the route, and so forth were all embedded in the video. The students watching the video had to determine when and why to use various sets of data to help them achieve particular goals. For example, one important consideration in planning for the houseboat trip was to reserve an appropriate-sized dock at a certain marina. The houseboat's dimensions were not explicitly given

in the video; instead, students saw scenes of a 6-foot person on the boat and could use them to estimate its length, width, and height (analogous to using Indiana Jones as a standard in our earlier work). Similarly, data from maps, speedometers, fill times for the water tank, etc., could be used to estimate other information that one needed to plan for the trip.

Initial Research with "The River Adventure."   We began our work with "The River Adventure" by collecting baseline data on people's abilities to plan for the houseboat trip. Members of our research team worked with three groups of individuals: college undergraduates, academically successful fifth graders, and fifth graders who exhibited delays in their mathematics development and were receiving special services. After watching the video, students were given a structured interview consisting of several levels of questions. The initial questions were general and open-ended and were designed to assess students' abilities to articulate and elaborate important categories to consider in planning the trip (fuel, estimated time of arrival, food, water, etc.). Subsequent questions were designed to tap students' abilities to collect relevant data and formulate mathematical solutions for specific aspects of the plan (e.g., "How might you estimate the dimensions of the houseboat?").

The results of the planning questions suggested that most college students were relatively good at identifying and elaborating the important categories to consider to adequately plan for the trip (this was not surprising since the categories were mentioned at the beginning of the video). In contrast, fifth grade students, both academically successful and mathematics-delayed, were much less likely to mention key categories. When a category was mentioned, the responses of the students tended to be quite general (e.g., "You need to bring enough water"). Students' responses almost never involved quantitative thinking such as systematic attempts to estimate how much water would be needed for a one-week trip. In addition, nearly all the fifth graders had a difficult time identifying the relevant mathematical data needed to solve the problems associated with their plans, such as determining the boat's dimensions or estimating arrival time. Not surprisingly, mathematics-delayed students had even greater difficulty in these areas than their academically more successful peers (Furman, Barron, Montavon, Vye, Bransford, and Shah 1989; Montavon, Furman, Barron, Bransford, and Hasselbring 1989).

Overall, our initial work with "The River Adventure" suggested that even students who were relatively successful in mathematics (as judged by their performance on traditional achievement tests) experienced serious difficulties when asked to identify and formulate complex mathematics problems prior to solving them. These findings convinced us of the importance of creating contexts like "The River Adventure" that could be used for instruction on planning, problem formulation, and problem solving. We especially wanted to study how different approaches to instruction would affect the development of these abilities. It was at this point that the request for proposals for the McDonnell CSEP program appeared in our mail.

Proposal to the McDonnell Foundation CSEP Program
Our proposal included a discussion of our experiences with *Raiders*, plus an analysis of the added advantages of being able to extend our work by using "The River Adventure." We also proposed another component to our work that turned out to be extremely important: To bring a more multidisciplinary perspective to our research, we would form a "McDonnell group," composed of representatives from cognitive psychology; content specialists in mathematics, science, literacy, and special education; and professionals from the surrounding school systems. In retrospect, it was the opportunity to work in this multidisciplinary context that began our transition from a model of curricular elaboration to one of classroom restructuring and, eventually, to an emphasis on learning communities. We discuss the classroom restructuring model below.

The Classroom Restructuring Model: Designing Materials That Help
Change the Nature of Teaching and Learning Practices in the Classroom

Early meetings of our McDonnell group were spent developing a common ground for conversations among people with diverse backgrounds. One procedure that turned out to be helpful was to videotape particular situations (e.g., a mathematics lesson) and have people from different areas (e.g., cognitive psychology, sociology of the classroom, mathematics education) independently comment on what they noticed in front of a video camera. These different clips were then played back to the McDonnell group. There were marked differences in what different people noticed, yet each had valuable information to add to the collective wisdom of the group. This diversity of perspectives helped build a genuine respect for one another's expertise (see, for example, Bransford, Sherwood, Hasselbring, Kinzer, and Williams 1990).

Several members of our group (Elizabeth Goldman, Linda Barron, and Bob Sherwood) had received a National Science Foundation grant in mathematics teacher preparation that brought them in contact with some of the most experienced middle school mathematics teachers in our area. These teachers proved to be extremely helpful to our work. For example, when we discussed how they wanted to improve the curriculum, a major concern centered around word problems. The teachers were very enthusiastic about the possibility of videodisc-based problem settings like our "River Adventure," but they were not at all enthusiastic about the production values of our prototype. They helped us see that, as researchers, we could get by with such a proto-type because we were a special event that got children out of their scheduled classes. For regular instruction, however, the teachers wanted the video to be visually compelling to the students. Since we needed the teachers to help us study the effects of different types of instruction, we paid close attention to their ideas and concerns. Our collaboration with the teachers eventually led to three types of activi-ties: (1) theory-based development of the Jasper Problem Solving Se-ries; (2) cognitive research on processes of learning and transfer in the Jasper context; (3) a large-scale implementation project of the Jasper series that involved nine states. We discuss each of these below.

Theory-based Development of the Jasper Series

Because of the teachers' concerns about our "River Adventure" proto-type, a major challenge for our group became finding a way to take the ideas in our prototype and produce a video that teachers would want to use in their classes. Bill Hawley, Dean of Peabody College at that time, listened to the enthusiasm of the teachers and made a bold decision: He would find Peabody College money to help fund a pro-fessional-quality video. We hired a talented script writer, Tom Stur-devant, to take the best features of "The River Adventure" and turn them into a more interesting video. As we worked on the script for this new adventure, we attempted to explicitly define the design prin-ciples we wanted it to contain.

We wanted to produce a video that supported the kinds of teaching and learning activities emphasized by constructivist approaches to learning (e.g., Cobb and Merkel 1989; Resnick and Klopfer 1989; Scar-damalia and Bereiter 1991). We have described these activities and contrasted them to the types of learning activities promoted by other types of materials elsewhere (CTGV 1991, 1992a). For example, tradi-tional word problems typically provide the goal and only those num-bers needed to solve the problem; hence they afford little more than computational selection (e.g., CTGV 1992b; Porter 1989). In contrast, we wanted our Jasper adventures to afford students opportunities to create problem structure as they solve the problem, potentially leading to more opportunities for group interactions that support generative learning. Overall, the kinds of teaching and learning activities we envisioned were consistent with those emphasized by the National Council of Teachers of Mathematics (1989a).

Design Principles for the Series.   Our discussions resulted in six design principles we wanted to build into our initial Jasper script: video-based format; stories with realistic problems (rather than a lecture on video); problem complexity (i.e., each story involves a problem of at least fifteen steps, and in most of the stories, multiple solutions are possible); generative format (i.e., students must generate and formulate the subproblems comprising the major problem posed at the end of each story); embedded data design (i.e., all the data needed to solve the problems are in the video); and links across the curriculum. A seventh design principle was added after we decided to create a second adventure in the Jasper series. This principle emphasized the use of pairs of related adventures in order to allow students to experience and discuss issues of transfer from one environment to the next. These design principles are discussed in more detail elsewhere (CTGV 1991, 1992b; McLarty, Goodman, Risko, Kinzer, Vye, Rowe, and Carson 1990).

Our design principles are assumed to mutually influence one another and operate as a gestalt rather than as a set of independent features of the materials (CTGV 1992a). For example, the narrative format, the generative design of the stories, and the fact that the adventures include embedded data make it possible for students to learn to generate subproblems, find relevant information, and engage in reasoned decision making. The complexity of the video problems helps students deal with this important aspect of problem solving, and the video format helps make that complexity manageable. The video format also makes it easier to embed the kinds of information that provide opportunities for links across the curriculum. Video brings the world into the classroom in a manner that motivates students, and makes complex mathematical problem solving accessible to students who have difficulties imagining complex situations by reading.

The Initial Jasper Adventure.   The first Jasper adventure was entitled "Journey to Cedar Creek." It is a 17-minute, commercial-quality video (on videodisc) that provides a real-world context for teaching mathematical problem solving. In the video, a person named Jasper Woodbury takes a river trip to see an old cabin cruiser he is considering purchasing. Jasper and the cruiser's owner, a woman named Sal, test-run the cruiser, after which Jasper decides to purchase the boat. Because the boat's running lights are inoperative, Jasper must determine if he can get the boat to his home dock before sunset. Two major questions that form the basis of Jasper's decision are presented at the end of the disc: When should Jasper leave for home, and is there enough fuel in the boat's gas tank for the return trip?

As students work through the problems, they discover that this seemingly simple decision involves a great deal of thinking. For example, they have to determine how much time it will take to get home, whether they have enough fuel (they don't, because the boat has a small temporary tank), where and when they can get extra fuel, and whether they have enough money to pay for the fuel.

Collaborations with Teachers.   As soon as "Journey to Cedar Creek" was finished, we put it in the hands of experienced teachers and observed how they used it in the classroom. Our first observation was that students seemed to enjoy the video, and especially the challenge of attempting to solve it. Our second observation was that many different models of teaching with the adventure emerged. This helped us realize that the design principles of our videos did not dictate specific types of teaching and learning activities. We have come to view our design principles from the perspective of Gibson's (1977) notion of "affordances." Gibson noted that different features of the environment afford activities for particular organisms such as "walk-onable," "climbable," "swimmable," and so forth. Similarly, different types of instructional materials afford different kinds of learning activities (Jenkins 1979; Shaw, Turvey, and Mace 1982; Greeno, Smith, and Moore 1993). An important point about affordances is that, like instructional materials, they make various activities possible but do not guarantee them. The teaching and learning activities that accompany our anchors can be tailored to different needs and are not automatic consequences of their design. (Different models of teaching with the Jasper series, and an analysis of their strengths and weaknesses, are discussed in CTGV 1992a).

Additional Jasper Adventures.   Studies of learning and transfer that utilize "Journey to Cedar Creek" (JCC) will be summarized shortly. For present purposes, we note that the adventure was very well received by students and teachers, and the data on student learning and transfer were very encouraging. These experiences allowed us to receive funding to produce additional Jaspers. In the second adventure, "Rescue at Boone's Meadow," Jasper finds a wounded eagle while on a camping trip. He radios for help from his friend Emily Johnson; students help Emily find the best way to rescue the eagle. The problem involves consideration of a number of means of transportation (by car, by foot, or by ultralight), routes, and pilots. Having determined that the ultralight is the best way to get to the eagle, students need to consider fuel capacity, fuel consumption, payload limitations, and

┌─The Jasper Series─────────────────────────

Complex Trip Planning
Journey to Cedar Creek - 1
Rescue at Boone's Meadow - 2

Uses of Statistics
The Big Splash - 3
A Capital Idea - 4

Geometry
The Right Angle - 5
The Great Circle Race - 6

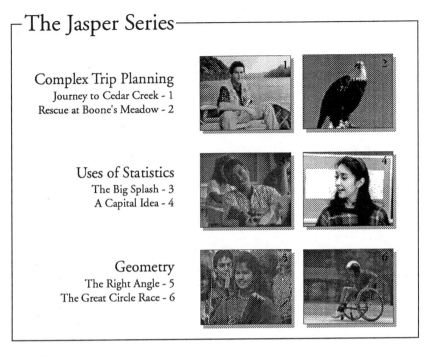

Figure 7.1
The Jasper series

other factors in order to determine the best way to use it. However, once the ultralight gets to Hilda's (shown on the map in the video), the best solution is to use a car, since it can go 60 miles per hour and the ultralight only goes 30 miles per hour.

Research with our first two Jasper adventures made it possible to receive funding from the National Science Foundation (NSF) to make four additional adventures.[1] The total set of six Jasper adventures is illustrated in figure 7.1. Thanks to new funding by the NSF[2], over the next three years we will create an additional six episodes for the series. Pairs of adventures will become triplets, with one episode being added to each of the trip-planning, statistics, and geometry pairs. We will also create a new triplet involving prealgebra and algebra concepts.

Analogs and Extensions of the Adventures. Each of our present and planned Jasper adventures also includes analogous problems that are formed by altering one or more of the parameters of the original Jasper problem. For example, after students have solved Emily's rescue problem in "Rescue at Boone's Meadow" (RBM), which took place on a calm day, they can be asked to reconsider whether her solution would work if there were a 6-mile-per-hour headwind while she flew from Cumberland City to Boone's Meadow (it wouldn't). Similarly, students can be asked to imagine that Emily used a different ultralight that had different fuel consumption, speed, etc. We are also designing computer tools that allow students to create their own analog adventures given specific constraints. For example, students might be asked to choose among a set of values that would allow Emily to rescue the eagle if she were using an ultralight with a 4-gallon rather than 5-gallon fuel tank (Crews and Biswas, in press).

Additional kinds of analog problems are specifically designed to help students explore important concepts in mathematics. For example, students can be asked to imagine that the old cruiser in "Journey to Cedar Creek" had a gas tank with length, width, and height dimensions such as $2n \times 2n \times 2n$ rather than $n \times n \times n$. Would the new tank hold twice as much gasoline? Problems such as these can help students explore concepts such as scaling factors and their effects on perimeter versus area versus volume.

Extension problems are designed to help students integrate their knowledge across the curriculum; for example, to see how the planning involved in the Jasper adventures relates to historical and current events. An excellent extension problem for RBM involves consideration of the planning that Charles Lindbergh had to do in order to prepare for his flight from New York to Paris. Extensions such as these also provide opportunities for further exploration of mathematical concepts.

Cognitive Analyses of Learning and Transfer

We noted earlier that our work on the Jasper series involved three major components: (1) theory-based materials development (discussed above), (2) cognitive analyses of learning and transfer, and (3) studies of the implementation of the Jasper series in nine states. In this section we discuss our findings regarding cognitive analyses of learning and transfer. We focus only on the first two Jasper adventures and do not attempt to discuss either the effects of group versus individual attempts to solve Jasper problems (see Barron 1991; Lamon 1992; Rewey and CTGV 1991) or the nature of student-generated argument that leads to effective problem solving (Voss and Means 1992). Instead, we consider the extent to which:

1. Our schools are preparing students to solve complex, real-world problems like those found in the Jasper series.
2. The ability to transfer to new, complex problems is influenced by instruction that focuses on complex problems such as those in the Jasper adventures, versus instruction that involves the

same concepts as Jasper problems (e.g., distance, rate, and time) yet is organized around the typical one- and two-step word problems found in most mathematics curricula.

3. Transfer from one Jasper adventure to another is based on general principles of problem solving versus more specific similarities in problem spaces and ways to navigate through them.

4. The ability to solve a Jasper problem and transfer to an analogous problem guarantees that students have developed a deep understanding of the problem spaces that characterize the Jasper and transfer problems.

5. Students spontaneously make connections between their classroom work on Jasper and other real-world problems encountered out of school.

Planning Net Analyses of the Jasper Problems.   Investigations of the issues discussed above require detailed analyses of students' and teachers' mental representations of the solutions to different Jasper problems. Our approach to describing how people mentally represent these problems has been first to construct a representation describing the plans, goals, and decisions that would need to be considered to solve each Jasper episode and then to describe people's problem solving relative to this solution structure. These representations are similar to planning net representations discussed by VanLehn and Brown (1980).

To illustrate, consider the planning net for the first Jasper episode, "Journey to Cedar Creek" (JCC) (see figure 7.2). As indicated above, in JCC the main character, Jasper Woodbury, buys an old cabin cruiser. The cruiser's lights do not work and it has a small, temporary gas tank. As depicted in figure 7.2, the major plan that students need to evaluate is whether Jasper can drive his new cruiser home. Time and fuel are the constraints that must be tested to decide if this plan is feasible. To determine if Jasper has enough time and fuel to make it home, students must first determine the distance to Jasper's dock. Information about the distance to be traveled and the cruiser's average speed are used to determine an estimate of trip time. Once trip time is established, students can compare it to their estimate of the time available for the trip. Furthermore, they can combine the estimate of trip time with information about the cruiser's average fuel consumption rate to determine the amount of fuel that will be used during the trip. Students compare this to the amount of fuel that is available in the cruiser's tank to determine if Jasper has a sufficient amount to make it home.

Jasper does have enough time, but does not have enough fuel to get home. The latter problem suggests a new plan, that of getting gas

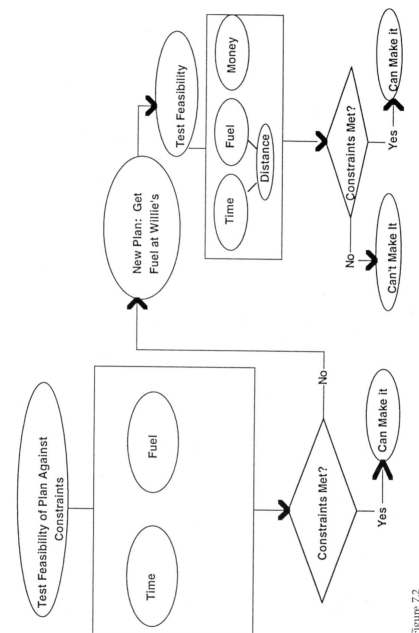

Figure 7.2
Planning net for journey to Cedar Creek (Challenge: Can Jasper make it home before sunset?)

along the way. From the video, students know that gas is available at Willie's. Evaluating the feasibility of the plan involves determining whether Jasper has enough time and fuel to reach Willie's and whether he has enough money to purchase the gas he needs to make it home. Because the procedures for determining time and fuel to Willie's are essentially the same as those used previously to determine time and fuel home, the planning net has iterative elements.

Baseline Studies of Problem Solving.   As mentioned earlier, one of our goals has been to assess the degree to which typical school instruction prepares students to solve complex problems such as those found in Jasper. Therefore, we have conducted a series of what we call "baseline studies" that assess people's abilities to solve Jasper problems prior to any experience with these problems. Two types of students have participated in these baseline studies: (1) high-achieving sixth graders (who scored in stanines of 8 and 9 on mathematics achievement tests) and (2) college undergraduates. Our assumption was that even though the high-achieving sixth graders did well on typical mathematics tests, they would not do well on Jasper problems because traditional curricula provide few experiences with complex geometry problems. We thought that college students would find Jasper problems easy to solve.

We used the idealized planning nets illustrated in figure 7.2 as a comparison with actual planning nets generated by people during problem solving. Our goal was to describe problem solving in terms of (1) the accuracy with which a given subproblem is evaluated mathematically, (2) the scope of the solution space addressed by the problem solver (i.e., the number of plans and problem constraints considered), and where relevant, (3) the degree to which problem solvers attempt to optimize their solutions.

In our baseline studies, students first viewed the Jasper episode, after which they were individually interviewed. The initial question was general; the experimenter restated the challenge from the video. For JCC, students were asked, "Can Jasper get his boat home? Tell me as much as you can about all the problems he had to think about in order to make his decision, and solve these problems if you can." The remaining questions cued students to consider specific subproblems. For JCC, the second level of questions asked students to determine if Jasper had enough time, fuel, and money to make the trip home. JCC also included a third level, consisting of questions on how to solve each subproblem comprising the challenge. In all our studies, students were asked to talk aloud as they answered the questions. They were provided with paper and a pencil, and a summary of the Jasper story

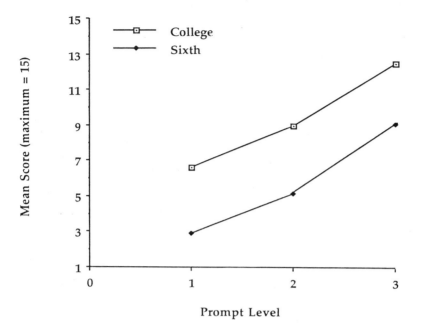

Figure 7.3
Mean scores on solution space elements in JCC

containing all of the data from the video. Interviews were audiotaped and subsequently transcribed for analysis.

Students' problem-solving protocols for JCC were examined for evidence that students had mentioned, attempted, or solved the major subgoals of the challenge (time to home, fuel to home, time to Willie's, fuel to Willie's, and money for gas). We computed a total score, where 1 point was awarded for mentioning, attempting, and correctly solving each of these subgoals, for a maximum of 15 points.

Analysis of the total scores indicated that both college students and sixth graders did relatively poorly, although college students had significantly higher scores than sixth graders. Figure 7.3 shows that scores increased at each level of questioning (i.e., levels 1–3) for both groups. Elsewhere, we explore this further by looking at the percentage of students who mentioned, attempted, and solved each of the five subgoals. When these percentages for level 1 are summarized across top-level versus embedded-level subgoals, the data indicate that roughly equal numbers of college and sixth graders *mention* the top-level subgoals (i.e., mention either the time home or fuel home goals), but more college students *attempt* and correctly *solve* these problems. (More detailed analyses of these data are presented in CTGV, in press a, and Goldman, Vye, Williams, Rewey, and Pellegrino 1991).

Overall, data from the baseline studies indicate that students are much more likely to solve the subproblems when subgoals are made explicit for them (level 3) than when they are left implicit (levels 1 and 2). This suggests that, even though students may have the mathematical knowledge necessary to solve particular problems, they also need skills for representing complex problems—especially skills that require them to *generate* and coordinate the solving of their own subgoals.

Effects of Different Types of Instruction.   An important issue raised by the baseline research is the extent to which students' problem-solving performance can be improved with instruction anchored in the Jasper videos–instruction that emphasizes the generation and definition of plans and goals, as well as mathematical skill. As discussed earlier in this paper (see also CTGV 1992a), Jasper instruction as we envision it is generative in nature. Under the guidance of the instructor, students generate the solution plans and subgoals, search for relevant data, and work cooperatively in small groups to find solutions. We have conducted several studies contrasting the effects of this form of instruction with a method derived from the work of Polya (1957), in which traditional word problems of the type needed for the JCC solution served as the instructional context.

In our first study, participants were fifth graders from a high-achieving mathematics class. Students were assigned within class to Jasper instruction or word problem instruction groups. Before and after their respective instruction (instruction took place in four one-hour sessions), groups were given several tests to assess learning and transfer. One test was designed to tap students' mastery of the solution to JCC, and consisted of items in which students had to match subgoals with their more superordinate goals, and subgoals with the data that were relevant for solving them. Not surprisingly, students in the Jasper group scored much better on the mastery test. For present purposes we focus on the results of a near-transfer test administered to students after the instruction because they relate directly to the results of the baseline studies discussed earlier. (For a discussion of the complete results, we refer the reader to Goldman, Vye, Williams, Rewey, and Pellegrino 1991; Goldman, Vye, Williams, Rewey, Pellegrino, and CTGV 1991; and Van Haneghan, Barron, Young, Williams, Vye, and Bransford 1992).

The transfer test was designed to assess transfer from JCC to a highly similar problem. The transfer problem was video-based and its solution was isomorphic to the JCC challenge. It told the story of a character named Nancy who buys a houseboat and must then decide if she can get the boat home before sunset without running out of fuel.

The boat has the same problems as Jasper's cruiser in JCC—it has a small temporary fuel tank and its running lights do not work. The solution has the same structure as JCC although the data are different; it involves consideration of the same subproblems and has the same outcomes. Students watched the transfer video and then solved the problem while talking aloud. The interview procedures were the same as those used in the baseline studies. The initial question was general and asked students to decide if Nancy could make it home (i.e., level 1); subsequent level 2 questions prompted them to consider three of the subgoals (time to home, fuel to home, and money).

As in the JCC baseline study, students' problem-solving protocols were scored in terms of the types of planning net elements contained in figure 7.2. Once again we examined the protocols for evidence that students had mentioned, attempted, or solved the major subproblems of the challenge (time to home, fuel to home, time to Tom's, fuel to Tom's and money for gas). Results indicated large differences between the Jasper group and the word problem group. Over 75 percent of the Jasper group solved at least one of the top-level goals, compared to less than 20 percent of the word problem group (see CTGV, in press a, and Goldman, Vye, Williams, Rewey, Pellegrino, and CTGV 1991 for more details). Overall, the performance after instruction of the fifth graders in the Jasper group was as good as the college students in the JCC baseline study who had not received Jasper-based instruction. Furthermore, the word problem group showed an uncanny resemblance to the performance of the sixth grade baseline students.

It is also important to note that we gave all our students posttests on one- and two-step word problems similar to those practiced by the word problem group—word problems that involved the same basic distance-rate-time concepts as the Jasper problem. Both groups did very well on these problems; however, a number of the students in both groups were at ceiling on the test, making it difficult to draw firm conclusions about how much the groups had learned.

We used the preceding instructional design (i.e., Jasper-based instruction versus word problem instruction) in a second study that involved a different test of transfer. The transfer problem was the Jasper video RBM. In contrast to the Nancy transfer problem, RBM does not share specific mathematical procedures or the same goal organization as JCC, but RBM and JCC do share elements of a general trip-planning schema. For example, several of the constant-testing elements from JCC, specifically, time and fuel considerations, are relevant to RBM. We predicted positive transfer on those elements of the schema that overlap from the first to the second trip-planning adventure. On the other hand, optimization elements of RBM are not present in the JCC adventure. For this aspect of problem solving, we did not expect to see positive transfer from JCC to RBM.

As in transfer study 1, high-achieving fifth graders were randomly assigned to either a Jasper or a word problem instruction group. The lesson plans used in transfer study 1 were used for each group, respectively. Again, prior to and following instruction, students were administered a series of tests designed to test mastery of JCC and transfer. For present purposes, we focus on the transfer results.

Results indicated that, compared to students who received word problem instruction, Jasper students showed positive transfer from JCC to RBM on the time and range subproblems (the subproblems present in both adventures). Data also indicated that a greater number of Jasper-instructed students mentioned, attempted, and solved the payload problem. Because issues of payload were unique to RBM, these data suggest that Jasper-instructed students may have learned a general heuristic from JCC, i.e., generate possible constraints on plans and test against them.

We also analyzed the extent to which students attempted to optimize their solution. We did not expect to see group differences in this aspect of problem solving because JCC instruction does not focus on generating and evaluating multiple plans for purposes of optimization. The results confirmed this expectation; 33 percent of the Jasper students and 41 percent of the word problem students generated only one plan for rescuing the eagle. Furthermore, although most students in both groups tried to determine how much time their plan or plans would take, in both groups, less than half of the students who generated more than one plan compared the time estimates associated with their plans to decide which was fastest (Goldman, Vye, Williams, Rewey, Pellegrino, and CTGV 1991).

Transfer to "What If" Perturbations of the Original Problem. We have also begun to explore an aspect of transfer that has received little attention in the experimental literature. It involves the ability to envision the effects of changes in particular elements of an overall problem structure. For example, we have asked students who have solved JCC to respond to "what if" questions such as "What if everything about Jasper's trip remained constant except that his cruiser had cruised at a speed of 9 rather than 8 miles per hour?" or "What if the temporary fuel tank held 10 rather than 12 gallons?" In cases such as these, declarative knowledge about the products of previous computations can set the stage for effective qualitative reasoning as well as for quantitative shortcuts. For example, if one knows that Jasper made the trip home in three hours when cruising at 8 miles per hour, it is clear that he can make it home in less than three hours at a cruising speed of 9 miles per hour. Other types of "what if" questions allow clear quantitative shortcuts. Thus, if the cruiser cruised at 16 rather than 8 miles per hour, Jasper should make it home in half the time, or one and a half hours.

Our studies indicate that, prior to any instruction on "what if" thinking, fifth and sixth grade Jasper students spontaneously attempt to make use of previous declarative knowledge when attempting to solve "what if" problems. However, they often have difficulty knowing which aspects of their previous knowledge should remain intact and which need to be changed (see Williams, Bransford, Vye, Goldman, and Carlson 1992; CTGV, in press a, 1993a).

A study conducted by Williams, Bransford, Vye, Goldman, and Hmelo (1993) compared the effects of working on "what if" software that was tied to JCC with those of working on word-problem-solving software that provided additional practice on the Jasper problem. Students who worked on "what if" problems were better able to explain their answers to subsequent transfer problems that asked them to consider the effects of changing particular values in trip-planning problems. This effect occurred both for transfer problems that involved the JCC context and for problems that involved new contexts. In general, "what if" thinking seems to help students develop more flexible representations of knowledge that facilitate qualitative thinking (see also Hmelo, Williams, Vye, Goldman & Bransford, and CTGV 1993). This deeper understanding should help students think of ways to optimize solutions, and help them monitor the quantitative aspects of their work.

Transfer Outside the Classroom.   An important aspect of transfer involves the degree to which students spontaneously make connections between activities in a particular class and those in other classes or outside of school. In some of our earlier research (Bransford, Hasselbring, et al. 1988) we worked with students in a summer mathematics program held on the Vanderbilt campus. We noticed a number of instances where students spontaneously made use of information from the classroom in their everyday activities. Most notably, as indicated earlier, we had students work with the videodisc anchor *Raiders of the Lost Ark*, prompting them to use standards (e.g., the height of Indiana Jones) to measure other objects (e.g., the width of the pit in the cave or the length of the airplane). These students spontaneously attempted to use similar techniques to estimate the height of objects on the campus such as the height of buildings, flagpoles, and trees.

Statements from the teachers using Jasper-based instruction frequently mention reports from parents who note that their children make connections between everyday activities and Jasper problems (CTGV 1992b). For example, several parents noted that their children began asking questions about the fuel capacity and efficiency of their car when they stopped at a gas station; others noted that children became interested in different units of measurement. And teachers noted that students often referred to Jasper problems in other settings. A commonplace event was to label complex, everyday problems that arose as "Jasper problems." One example of a "Jasper problem" involved the failure of a substitute lunchroom staff to correctly anticipate the meals it needed to prepare. When something was labeled as a Jasper problem, students understood that it was complex and would probably take time to figure out, but that was okay (CTGV 1992b).

We recently conducted a "spontaneous connection-making" study that was designed to assess the degree to which students would spontaneously think about Jasper-related ideas when presented with new problem contexts. In the study, we showed Jasper and non-Jasper students a series of videos and print materials and asked the students to evaluate the videos as possible instructional materials for other students. For example, one video followed a novice pilot taking his first solo flight. Data embedded in the video about the range and other properties of the plane and trip were similar to data available in "Rescue at Boone's Meadow," so there were opportunities to notice similarities between this Jasper adventure and the pilot's solo flight.

We told students that we wanted to have them help us evaluate various sets of educational materials, and we asked them to tell us what came to mind as they saw the materials. The results indicated that students who received Jasper instruction were no more likely to spontaneously make connections between the materials and their Jasper experiences than students who had watched, but not solved, Jasper adventures. In contrast, both groups were able to make connections when explicitly prompted to do so.

It is interesting to contrast the results of our spontaneous "connection-making" studies with comments of parents who remarked that their children were frequently reminded of Jasper. One difference in the situations is that our studies explicitly instilled a set to "think about teaching the information we are going to show you on video to younger students." There was no suggestion that these younger students would have seen Jasper. In contrast, both the parents and the children who participated in our Jasper implementation were well acquainted with Jasper. As Buhler (cf. Blumenthal 1970) might emphasize, parents and their children knew that they shared a common "semantic field." This may play an important role in increasing the probability of connection making. People's conversations suggest that they are quite good at remembering the kinds of knowledge they share and have discussed in the past (see Bransford and Nitsch 1978).

Our "connections-making" data suggest the need for more research. For example, we suspect that particular types of classroom-based activities can help students develop knowledge representations and habits of mind that facilitate the degree to which they make connections between in-class and out-of-class activities. As an illustration, Bransford and Vye (cf. Bransford, Sherwood, Vye, and Rieser 1986) were able to increase the degree to which college students spontaneously thought about concepts taught in the classroom after they had left the classroom. They did this by explicitly priming students to imagine concept-relevant situations they were likely to encounter in other aspects of their college life (e.g., other classes, their dormitory, the lunchroom, or talking on the phone to family and friends).

Transfer as Efficient Learning.   An important index of transfer is the degree to which one set of experiences helps one learn to learn in new settings (Brown, Bransford, Ferrara, and Campione 1993; Greeno, Smith, and Moore 1993). The ability to learn efficiently is different from the ability to solve a new set of problems without any opportunity to learn. Thus, person *A* may perform no better than person *B* when asked to solve a new set of problems that are presented in a typical static test of transfer. However, when given appropriate resources to consult, Person *A* may be more efficient at *learning* to solve these problems than person *B*.

We are just beginning to assess the degree to which students in anchored curricula are able to learn new information more efficiently. In a study we have conducted but are still in the processes of analyzing, Jasper students and comparison students both worked with one of the Jasper business plan adventures. The Jasper students had worked previously with our two trip-planning adventures, but these are quite different in content from the business-planning adventure. We are attempting to assess the efficiency of learning of the Jasper group in comparison to the group that had not worked on the trip-planning adventures. To the extent that Jasper students have learned to work cooperatively and to set and achieve learning goals, we expect to find evidence of transfer in the efficiency of learning about the new business-planning domain.

Nine-State Implementation of the Jasper Project
During the 1990–91 academic year we had an opportunity to carry out a project not anticipated in our CSEP proposal. Thanks to the leadership of Chancellor Joe B. Wyatt of Vanderbilt University, three-way

partnerships among Vanderbilt, corporations, and schools were created in order to implement the Jasper series in 28 middle school classes. Ten corporations sponsored the implementation in 11 school districts distributed over 9 states. Sixteen different schools participated: 5 inner-city schools, 5 suburban, and 6 in rural or small town locations. Eleven corporate representatives and 28 teachers (largely volunteers) attended a two-week summer training institute at Vanderbilt. The corporate representatives brought varied backgrounds, although all had information technology and computer expertise. Teaching experience of the teachers varied widely (from 4 to 25 years), as did their certifications and degrees (mathematics and nonmathematics). Some taught where classrooms were self-contained and others where instruction was departmentalized. In all, approximately 1,300 students in 52 classes solved Jasper adventures as part of the implementation project, with many teachers teaching more classes than initially required for the study. The sample was by no means homogeneous. The classes using the Jasper series were predominantly fifth and sixth grade, although two fourth grade classrooms also participated. Intellectual abilities of the children ranged from mildly retarded to gifted, as described by the teachers. A subset of these students participated in the formal assessment study that we conducted.[3]

The Jasper implementation project brought us face to face with a number of issues. One of the most important was professional development. A second was assessment, because our research group was held accountable to the corporations and school systems who implemented the Jasper program. Issues of professional development and assessment are discussed below.

Issues of Professional Development.   One of the goals of the school-corporation partnership was to provide teachers with the kind of ongoing support they needed to carry out the Jasper program. The model of corporate support implemented was as follows:

> 1. Participation by two teachers from one school or district and a corporate representative at a two-week Summer Institute held at Vanderbilt and conducted by the Learning Technology Center.
> 2. Fifty-percent release time for the corporate representative during the year for purposes of supporting the teachers in the implementation activities.
> 3. Purchase of three complete multimedia systems, consisting of the Jasper videodiscs, print materials, and multimedia software; a videodisc player and video monitor; a Macintosh computer, including the ScanMan Scanner, a Smart Modem, and MacRecorder; a projection pad for displaying computer screens; and a printer.

4. Telecommunications (America Online) capabilities for the teachers including telephones in the classrooms.
5. A reunion at the end of the academic year.

The Summer Institute was conducted during two weeks in August 1990 on the Vanderbilt campus. Approximately one-third of the Summer Institute time was devoted to solving Jasper adventures and brainstorming teaching ideas and lesson plans, one-third to computer skills, and one-third to multimedia-related competencies (i.e., using ScanMan, MacRecorder, and software for making presentations). To the degree possible, we anchored the computer and technology skills in the Jasper macrocontext (CTGV 1990). For example, we had participants practice word processing on lesson plans for a Jasper adventure; they used spread sheets in solving the adventures. (Additional details of the activities are found in CTGV, in press b, and in Pellegrino et al. 1991).

Learning from the Professionals.   One of the most important lessons we learned was that it was easier to talk about a generative approach to teaching than to actually do it. We began the institute with the idea that all the participants would work in groups to solve a Jasper adventure, so that part of our instruction was generative. Nevertheless, after the initial session we inadvertently shifted to telling teachers about theory, about teaching suggestions, and so forth. Luckily we had built an extensive daily feedback session into the institute and we paid attention to the feedback we received. The teachers pointed out the inconsistency between our theory and our method and helped us move from the "telling" approach we had implicitly adopted to one that was much more audience-centered and generative. As an illustration, our first attempts to help teachers create lesson plans for an adventure involved showing them how other teachers taught Jasper. Later we learned to first ask the participants to generate their own lesson plans and then showed video clips of others teaching Jasper as discussion starters. These images gave teachers "contrast sets" (to their own, self-generated images) that were quite useful in generating lively discussions. We also brought in local teachers who had taught Jasper to fifth and sixth graders. The teachers outlined what they had done and then answered questions. These sessions were very interactive and quite well liked.

We carried the generative model into the multimedia training included in institute activities. As an institute "challenge," we asked each group of participants to prepare a Jasper-related multimedia project; on the last day of the institute each team presented theirs to the group. We also set up a staffed computer lab available in the evenings so those

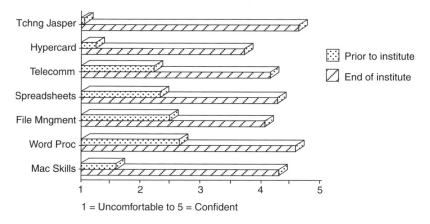

Figure 7.4
Skill evaluation data

who wanted to could do additional work with the materials and technology.

Teachers made frequent positive comments about our responsiveness to their daily feedback during the Summer Institute. Most indicated that, in other settings, they were rarely listened to, by academics. Each team left the institute with Jasper materials, a time line for teaching each of four adventures and administering assessment instruments that we devised, and the expectation of receiving their equipment (which they had worked with at the institute) within two weeks.

Skill Development.   Figure 7.4 shows the results of participants' evaluations of their own professional development during the two-week workshop. Participants clearly indicated significant improvement in skills related to technology as well as to their teaching Jasper. Teachers also expressed concern about what would happen when they got back "home" and had all their regular responsibilities plus Jasper. It was this very concern that had led to the "teaming" of a corporate representative with a pair of teachers. We also hoped that the pairs of teachers would be able to provide support for each other when they returned to their school campuses. We planned to bring teachers back together at the conclusion of the implementation year.

Assessment Data
We noted earlier that the school systems and corporations held us accountable for demonstrating the value of the Jasper materials. We assessed three aspects of our implementation: classroom instructional activities, student outcomes, and teachers' reactions to the

implementation. These are briefly discussed below (additional details are provided in CTGV, in press b).

Classroom Instructional Activities.   Our data regarding how the Jasper series was implemented in the classrooms are based on teacher self-report, artifacts we received (newspaper articles, letters, etc.), and a very small number of on-site observations of actual Jasper classes. There was wide variation in how teachers implemented the instructional model, especially regarding the use of large- and small-group generative activity. In some classes, problem solving was mostly teacher-driven and students' activities were mostly focused on fact finding. In others, problem solving was more consistent with the generative model we discussed above.

For the most part, teachers concentrated on implementing the mathematics problem-solving aspects of the program. All classes completed two trip-planning adventures; most also completed one of the business plan/statistics adventures, while five classes completed both of the business plan/statistics adventures. In general, students spent approximately one week's worth of class time watching and solving each adventure. For most classes, these activities took the place of time that would normally be devoted to word problems. Generally, teachers did not stress extensions in mathematics or other curriculum areas, and with a few exceptions, the multimedia publishing software was underutilized (teachers cited a lack of time and difficulties using the software). This area was one in which the technical support offered by the corporate representative was particularly important. In three of the corporate-teacher teams, the corporate person's tasks included directly helping the students work with the software. In another case, the corporate person took teacher-generated lessons on measurement and time and put them into the multimedia publishing environment so the students would have access to them.

There were a number of innovative activities implemented by the teachers we did not anticipate but from which we learned. For example, a number of classes planned field trips around the topics and events in the trip-planning episodes. Two classes in Arkansas went on a field trip to a small airport, where they watched a pilot flying an ultralight. It turned out to be a different model from the one in "Rescue at Boone's Meadow" and the students immediately barraged the pilot with questions about payload, fuel capacity, and so forth. Several classes took the business plan model depicted in one of the Jasper adventures ("The Big Splash") and devised their own plan to raise money for their school by selling snacks to other students. The students made enough money to finance a trip to a Civil War site in a neighboring state.

Other unanticipated activities included strategies for informing the community about Jasper. These provided important models for our own dissemination efforts and played a key role in the evolution of our thinking regarding learning communities. For example, a number of the teams made presentations to various groups in their local communities, including parents and parents' groups, other teachers, school and district administrators, local media, local and state government officials, and members of the corporations supporting the implementation. The teams frequently used the technology to make their presentations. One presentation that particularly impressed us was initiated to help parents understand what their children were doing with Jasper. Parents were invited to school to solve a Jasper episode; the children were the Jasper experts who assisted them. Thus the parents not only experienced the instructional activities in which their children were participating but they got a live demonstration of the competencies the children had developed through the activities.

The electronic network (America Online) was generally underutilized. About seven teachers and three corporate representatives used it regularly; another five used it occasionally. Some classes used the on-line news service for information on current events and the on-line encyclopedia as a resource. One highly-successful activity was an On-line conference call in which four classes were on the electronic network simultaneously. For the most part, however, there was little inter-classroom communication initiated by teachers and students.

Student Outcomes.   We were convinced that typical measures of mathematics performance would not be affected by students' experiences with the Jasper series. In fact, we were concerned that there might be a drop in performance on these standardized measures because students were spending time on activities not tested by traditional mathematics assessments (see for discussion Goldman, Pellegrino, and Bransford, in press). In essence, although the Jasper program might be facilitating the development of mathematics problem-solving skills of a complex nature, we had no assurance that such an effect would emerge on standardized tests or on traditional word problem tests.

We developed a set of assessment instruments for purposes of evaluating outcomes with respect to three goals of the Jasper program:

- Develop critical mathematical problem-solving and reasoning skills, assessed by the planning problems and word problems tests;
- Develop an appreciation of mathematics as a useful, interesting, and realistic part of the everyday world, assessed by a mathematics attitudes questionnaire;

• Develop an understanding of specific mathematics concepts and skills necessary to solve the adventures, including, for example, time, measurement, basic statistical sampling, assessed by a basic mathematics concepts test.

Jasper classrooms and a set of control classrooms received these tests at the beginning and end of the year. There was also a mid-year assessment in which planning problems and word problems were administered. In the present context, we focus only on data from the beginning and end of the year for planning, word problem, and attitude assessments. (Fuller reports of the student outcome data are available in CTGV 1992a, in press b and in Pellegrino et al. 1991).

The assessment sample represented a 739-student subset of those participating in the implementation project. These students represented 17 Jasper classrooms (one from each of 17 teachers at 9 sites), 10 of which (drawn from 5 sites) had "matched," non-Jasper-using control classes, selected by the school district administration on the basis of the demographic match to the Jasper classes. The spectrum of mathematics achievement levels was represented across the sample. Teachers provided us with the standardized mathematics and reading test scores from the previous spring for the control and for the Jasper classes; there were no differences between them at the beginning of the year on either measure. (For additional details see CTGV, in press b; Pellegrino et al. 1991).

Development of Complex Problem-Solving Skills.   A set of paper-and-pencil "planning" problems presented a scenario to students and asked them to generate the subproblems and subgoals involved in solving the problem. There were also questions for these problems that required students to determine to which subgoal of the problem a particular calculation belonged. A sample problem, and these two kinds of questions, are shown in figure 7.5. The problem shown in figure 7.6, the "Jack" problem, deals with trip planning, the theme of the first two Jasper episodes. The Jack problem was administered at the end of the year; a problem identical in underlying form, the Jill problem, was administered at the beginning of the year.

Table 7.1 presents the observed means and standard deviations for the control, matched-Jasper, and unmatched-Jasper students at the beginning and end of the school year. The control and Jasper groups performed about the same at the beginning of the year, while the planning and subgoal comprehension scores for both Jasper groups were greater than the control group at both the midyear and year-end tests. (Statistical tests on these data are reported in Pellegrino et al. 1991.)

Jack lives in Annaheim. He wants to drive his car from his house to a friend's house in Bakersville. As shown on the map, Jack can take the road from Annaheim to Donaldtown and Donaldtown to Bakersville. His car is filled with gasoline and ready to go. There is a gas station in Annaheim, Bakersville, and Cairo, but there is not one in Donaldtown. Jack plans to leave on his trip at 1:00 in the afternoon.

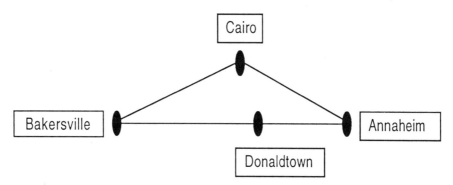

Top-Level Planning Challenge: What does Jack need to think about to figure out how long it will take him to make the trip?

Example Subgoal Comprehension Problems:

1.Jack divides the distance from Annaheim to Bakersville (350 miles) by the speed he will drive (50 miles per hour). Why does he do this?

2. Jack compares 240 miles (the distance his car can travel on one tank of gas) to 350 miles (the distance from Annaheim to Bakersville). Why does he do this?

Figure 7.5
Example of planning problem: The Jack problem

In addition to the planning problems, we assessed students' mathematics problem-solving skills with word problems of a more traditional sort. Jasper could easily have had no effect or a negative one on these problems because students in the Jasper groups spent *less* instructional time on these kinds of problems than they would have in their typical mathematics curricula. We examined single step, two-step, and multistep word problems. As the data in figure 7.6 show, Jasper students and their matched controls performed equally well on the beginning-of-the-year test; at the end of the year, Jasper students significantly outperformed their matched controls.

Developing Positive Attitudes toward Mathematics. Five scales assessed students' attitudes toward their mathematics ability and the utility of mathematics, as well as their mathematics self-confidence (the inverse

Table 7.1
Results for planning and subgoal comprehension

| | Beginning of year "Jill" problem | | | |
	n	Planning	Subgoal	Calculation
Control	257	18.5	32.8	73.9
		(24.0)	(27.5)	(25.5)
Matched Jasper	249	18.3	31.0	69.5
		(21.6)	(27.8)	(27.6)
Unmatched Jasper	189	21.9	33.2	72.6
		(21.3)	(27.7)	(27.8)
	End of year "Jack" problem			
	n	Planning	Subgoal	Calculation
Control	212	19.6	42.4	85.0
		(18.6)	(31.1)	(20.8)
Matched Jasper	231	34.2	48.5	85.3
		(24.5)	(33.0)	(22.0)
Unmatched Jasper	179	35.7	56.3	86.4
		(22.8)	(28.6)	(18.8)

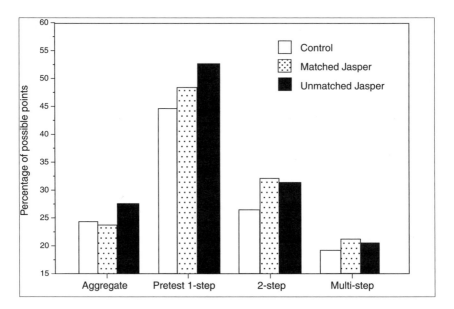

Figure 7.6
Performance on word problems

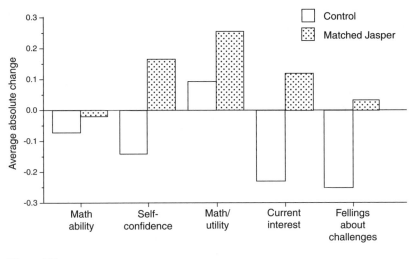

Figure 7.7
Changes in attitudes from beginning to end of year

of mathematics anxiety), their interest in mathematics, and their feelings about challenging mathematics problems. Each statement was responded to on a 5-point Likert scale from 1—Strongly Disagree to 5—Strongly Agree. As the data in figure 7.7 indicate, the Jasper groups showed more improved attitudes from pretest to year-end than did the control students on four of the five scales. (There was no difference on the mathematics ability scale.)

Teacher Reactions and Outcomes. Many of the Jasper teachers were able to attend a reunion held in June 1991. Teachers were quite excited about the Jasper series and glad to have had the opportunity to participate in the implementation. They were also all extremely grateful for the opportunity to talk with one another about their experiences. What was quite remarkable was the consistency of the teachers' stories in a number of areas (CTGV 1992b). First, the teachers all indicated that the characters in the episodes were extremely important. Second, they agreed that the Jasper series seemed to be especially beneficial for their lower-achieving students. Students who had previously not participated much in class were now much more actively involved during class discussions. Third, they reported that parents were generally quite pleased by the introduction of the Jasper series in the classroom. Several teachers received letters from parents commenting on the change in attitude that had occurred within their children. Parents were very curious and many of them participated in Jasper activities held for their benefit.

Teachers also shared feelings of inadequacy they experienced in trying to implement the Jasper series. Interestingly, discovering that others had also experienced these feelings made everyone feel better. Teachers indicated that their number one difficulty was with time constraints and conflicts between other curricular demands and the desire to teach the Jasper series. Many of the comments centered on what they would do "next time" they used a specific Jasper episode. Teachers indicated that they thought greater integration with their standing curriculum in mathematics would help in that regard. A number of the teachers reported lack of support from the principals as an issue. Some teachers wanted to know more about how to keep all children involved during small-group activity. Several teachers recommended group sizes no larger than four students.

Finally, teachers and students expressed universal dislike for the paper-and-pencil instruments we used for evaluation. They indicated these were totally inconsistent with the Jasper program. Students often groaned at the tests; it was an especially stark contrast to their motivation to work on the Jasper adventures. The teachers urged us to develop alternative means of assessing students. We explore some alternatives in the following section.

Another important outcome for teachers concerned the multimedia software and extensions of Jasper. They were looking forward to really working on these during their *second* year with Jasper. The feeling was that for a first time through, the episodes were more than enough to worry about. Now that they had those under their belts, so to speak, they were ready to extend their use of Jasper into other areas of the mathematics curriculum and into other content areas. Many of the teachers had also begun to train other teachers in their schools and districts and had become "media stars" in their own right, doing presentations and demonstrations for community and press groups.

Overall, our experiences with the school-based implementation research attuned us to the importance of breaking down the isolation of the classroom so that teachers, students, and research could more freely interact with one another. So we began to think beyond restructured classrooms by considering the design of systems that could support collaborative activity and community involvement in the schools. This led us to a concern with learning communities, a concern that is discussed next.

The Importance of Learning Communities

The third model of cognitive research that our experiences led us to adopt is a model that looks explicitly at ways to break the boundaries of isolated classrooms and schools in order to develop learning communities to engage people in continual processes of inquiry and knowledge building. We have come to believe that the cognitive sciences will fail to have a truly powerful impact on the quality of education unless the importance of learning communities is realized. And our research has helped us understand some of the components of learning communities that seem important for success.

Our discussion is divided into three major parts: our initial ideas about learning communities and how these ideas were expanded as we worked with our Jasper implementation sites in nine states; "The Peabody Perspective" for learning communities, which evolved from an extended seminar attended by Peabody faculty representing a broad spectrum of expertise (including curriculum, instruction, assessment, teaching, school leadership, family and community ties); and the evolution of our SMART Challenges, designed to build learning communities by breaking the isolation of the classroom and helping everyone—teachers, students, community leaders, researchers—continue to learn from one another.

Initial Ideas about Learning Communities

The decision to focus on learning communities arose from several different aspects of our research experiences, especially our experiences in implementing the Jasper program in nine different states. Some ideas about the importance of learning communities were available to us at the beginning of this project and guided our plans. For example, it seemed clear to us that teachers who were going to teach Jasper needed to feel part of a community larger than themselves. This was why we had attempted to have a minimum of two Jasper teachers per school, and why we had paired each Jasper site with someone from a local corporation who could offer technical and motivational support.

Based on the research literature on the development of skilled performance and expertise (e.g., Chase and Simon 1973a), it also seemed clear that even the two weeks of intensive professional development that we were able to offer the teachers and corporate representatives would need to be supplemented with ongoing opportunities for learning. We assumed that our corporate representatives would be particularly helpful in answering questions about the technology the teachers were using, but we also anticipated questions about pedagogy. This was why we provided all our teachers with an electronic account to America Online. Our thought was that teachers would use this to contact our center; we had people on staff whose job it was to monitor their messages and respond. As we discuss later, there were reasons why this resource was underutilized.

The Importance of Community Building.   As the first year of our Jasper implementation unfolded, we began to discover additional reasons for focusing on a model of learning communities. One involved the importance of support from within the school. Nearly all the teachers commented that their ability to implement the new ideas associated with the Jasper curriculum was affected strongly by the strength of support from their school principal. There is a research literature that emphasizes the importance of support from the principal (e.g., Murphy 1991; Murphy and Hallinger 1993), but we had been only dimly aware of it at that time. Therefore, we did not help teachers focus on plans for developing school-wide support.

Luckily, many of our teachers implemented their own plans for developing support, not only from within the school but also from the broader community. For example, we noted earlier that teachers invented ways to help parents and other community members understand the value of the Jasper series and the experiences related to it. Several of the teachers invited parents and other adults to solve a Jasper adventure, using students as "experts" to keep the adults from getting too far off track. This idea proved to be a very powerful approach to community building. We have used it many times in our own community—always with extremely favorable results (CTGV 1993a).

An additional positive outcome has been that community members often volunteer to help students learn more about topics featured in the Jasper adventures—topics such as boats, airplanes, principles of flight, eagles and other endangered species, recycling, and ideas for viable business plans. Furthermore, teachers often get community members to help when students create and implement their own projects, such as their own trips to interesting locations, funded by their own business plans.

Finding Time and Reasons to Communicate.   Several months into the year, we saw that only a few of the teachers were making regular use of America Online to communicate with us and with one another. A major reason (obvious in retrospect, but not in prospect) was that they had almost no free time during school hours for doing this, and since they did not have computers and modems at home, they could not communicate from there. In addition, there was usually no compelling reason for them to communicate with one another and with us. We began to think about the possibility of developing high-stakes events that would stimulate a greater exchange of ideas and information. We say more about this in our discussion of the Jasper challenge series, below.

Variability in Performance. At midyear of the Jasper implementation we began to receive data from the sites about performance on our assessment instruments. Some of these measured the degree to which students could independently solve the first two Jasper problems after working with them in class; others assessed students' abilities to transfer to new but similar problems. There were clear indications of effective learning and transfer in all sites (see especially CTGV 1992c; Pellegrino et al. 1991). Nevertheless, we also noted that many students were far from perfect on Jasper mastery and that there was often considerable variability in performance across different schools and classes within schools—even in cases where pretest scores on standardized mathematics achievement tests would suggest that students should perform similarly. This led to the conjecture that different teachers were probably teaching the Jasper adventures differently and that this affected the quality of their students' learning. Observations of classrooms within our local area reinforced the belief in the variability of how Jasper was being taught. So we began to think about ways to help our research team, as well as teachers, continually reassess the quality of teaching as well as the standards of achievement reasonable for students. In many classes, we felt that the standards were too low.

Competing Events. Our thoughts about the design of the learning communities were further influenced by observations of how busy our teachers were and how many local events took precedence over Jasper-related activities even though teachers and students wanted more time to work on Jasper. Events such as state-mandated testing represent cases in point. We began to see that attempts to change (and, we hope, improve) the nature of teaching and learning in classrooms will always compete with other priorities, and that a major factor for change might be to create new priorities viewed by the community as even more important than the competing ones. So we began to consider design principles for learning communities that involved high-stakes events. Our Jasper challenges (to be discussed below) represent cases in point.

Testing versus Mentoring. An additional aspect of our experiences with the nine-state implementation of Jasper had an especially profound effect on our thoughts about design principles for learning communities. As the year progressed, we discovered that teachers and students had grown to dislike the paper-and-pencil assessment instruments we had developed and administered (e.g., CTGV 1992b). This prompted us to think about ways to preserve the value of assessment (especially formative assessment) without making the students and teachers feel "tested." We wanted to give students a sense of being mentored by people who were on their side, helping them achieve remarkable levels of performance. So this became a very important goal for the learning communities we wanted to design.

The Need for Continual Learning.   A final reason for focusing on the importance of learning communities is the importance of mechanisms for creating a dynamic curriculum. For example, individual teachers frequently generated new ideas for teaching Jasper concepts and for linking them to other areas of knowledge; we wanted to be able to communicate these ideas to other teachers. At the same time, our observational and interview studies (e.g., CTGV 1993b; Goldman, Vye, Williams, Rewey, and Hmelo 1992) helped us find ways to improve students' learning. For example, using "what if" questions after solving particular Jasper adventures helped students deepen their understanding and make transfer more flexible (e.g., CTGV 1993a). Similarly, we discovered ways of constructing visual representations of situations that made especially difficult concepts easier to comprehend and communicate. And as we worked with local teachers to use these insights to improve the learning experiences of their students, we began to see that middle school students could reach higher levels of performance than we had anticipated initially. We wanted to find ways to communicate these possibilities to other members of our collaborative team.

"The Peabody Perspective"
During the fall semester of 1991 we had the opportunity to participate in a unique seminar at Peabody. Faculty members from each of the major areas at Peabody met for six two-hour sessions (distributed across the semester) to see if they could agree on principles for an ideal "school for the 21st Century." We wanted to hold the seminar because none of us knew what everyone else on campus was thinking, and we wanted to uncover areas of agreement and disagreement. A nagging concern was that we would agree only on a "lowest common denominator" that was not far removed from schools as they currently existed. Fortunately, we were pleasantly surprised.

The result of our extended discussions was a set of principles that reflected a shared vision of education and schooling for the twenty-first century. The cornerstone of these principles was the concept of learning communities. Going beyond traditional programs aimed solely at children, "The Peabody Perspective" on learning communities sought to make school a key community resource accessed by and contributed to by all members of the community.

"The Peabody Perspective" on learning communities is based on the assumption that students' capabilities and motivation to learn are shaped by many influences, including their families, peers, teachers, organizations to which they belong, national and community values and expectations, and opportunities for further education and employment. Serious attempts to significantly improve the quality of learning must focus on the entire community rather than changes in one or two instructional variables. In particular, it does little good to attempt to significantly change teaching strategies without also changing the curriculum, and both of these changes will do little good without changes in assessment. The potential of these changes will not be realized unless they are accompanied by changes in school organization and professional development. Furthermore, the latter must be integrated with changes in community values as a whole, including the assumption that children's progress in school must be coordinated with other aspects of their lives such as safety and health.

The learning communities concept as embodied in the Peabody principles includes five major areas: curriculum and instruction, assessment, professional development and school organization, community connections, and technology (see table 7.2). These design principles for learning communities embody new conceptions of teaching and learning and create new roles for teachers, students, parents, administrators, and community members. The principles allow flexible adaptation to local conditions, while providing a clear direction for the design of learning environments that emphasize excellence for all and adaptability to changing needs and conditions. Especially important is the emphasis on collaborative learning communities rather than on isolated classrooms and schools.

Building a Learning Community
Inspired by the importance of learning communities as reflected in our implementation of Jasper and extended discussions with Peabody faculty, we asked ourselves how we could at least begin to build these communities so we could assess what worked. Since our Jasper series was being used in a number of sites, we decided to use it as the basis of our efforts to enhance mathematics curricula, instruction, assessment, and professional development.

Our efforts to develop learning communities began as an attempt to use teleconferencing technology to create a Jasper challenge series. The challenge series linked classrooms together through live interactive

Table 7.2
The Peabody perspective on learning communities

---

1. Curriculum and instruction
- Emphasizes active, problem-focused teaching and learning.
- Integrates subject areas.
- Emphasizes varied instructional strategies depending on student needs.
- Relies on heterogeneous, collaborative student groups/teams.
- Focuses on project-based activities, while also giving attention to the development of key concepts and skills.

2. Assessment
- Focuses on thinking and communicating as well as on concepts and skills.
- Is authentic.
- Informs instruction.
- Gives schools the flexibility to respond to the uniqueness of the populations they serve, while still being held accountable to state and national goals and standards.

3. Professional development and school organization
- Provides meaningful opportunities for educators to learn and improve.
- Redefines "professionals as isolated experts" to "professionals as collaborators and facilitators of learning."
- Keeps decision making open and responsive to parent, student, and community input.

4. Community connections
- Keep parents involved in their children's education.
- Create shared responsibility for children and cooperative efforts to provide resources and support for learning.
- Ensure adequate and coordinated health and social services for children.
- Foster a concern for the common good.

5. Technology
- Supports all areas of the learning community—learning, assessment, management, professional development, and community connectedness.

---

shows that allowed students to "test their mettle" with respect to the Jasper adventures and their extensions. We have named our Jasper challenges SMART challenges, where SMART stands for "Special Multimedia Arenas for Refining Thinking." SMART challenges incorporate features of systemic and dynamic assessments tied to problem-based curricula (CTGV 1992c; Goldman Pellegrino, and Bransford, in press). In the context of the Jasper series, students and teachers work with an adventure as a starting point. They prepare much as one prepares for a speech, a business meeting, a musical performance, or an important football game. Students are then given the opportunity to compare their ideas, projects, and performances to those of peers from around the country, and to receive feedback and suggestions for improvement.

Sometime later, another challenge gives students an opportunity to try again. We have conducted four such challenges over the past 24 months; each contained the following features:

1. Solve one of the Jasper adventures
2. Solve relevant analog and extension problems
3. Participate as part of a larger community in a public performance arena created by technologies such as satellite uplinks or cable TV augmented by phone bridges that allow audio interaction.
4. Use the feedback present in the public performance arena to revise, refine, and improve one's own performance.

Some of our experiences with SMART challenges are discussed below.

Initial SMART Challenges.   The initial SMART challenges were cast in the form of game shows conducted on-line. Students played the "at home" audiences and called in their responses to the studio from which the program originated. The basic task for the students was to evaluate the performances of individuals featured on the game show. For example, our "Pick the Expert" game show was modeled after "What's My Line?" A panel of "experts" answered questions based on "Rescue at Boone's Meadow"; students decided which panelist was the "true" expert. To do so, they had to use knowledge they had acquired by completing the "Rescue at Boone's Meadow" adventure and a set of video-based analog and extension problems that engaged students in "what if" thinking (see "Cognitive Analyses," above). The information needed to distinguish among the experts should have been acquired through solving the adventure and the analog and extension problems.

A second game show format, "Rate That Plan," built on the mathematical and problem-solving skills associated with the business plan adventure "The Big Splash." In "The Big Splash," Jasper's young friend, Chris, wants to help his school raise money to buy a new camera for the school TV station. His idea is to have a dunking booth at the school fun fair, in which teachers could be dunked when students accurately hit a target. He must develop a business plan for the school principal in order to obtain a loan for his project. The overall problem centers around developing this business plan, including the use of a statistical survey to help him decide if his idea would be a money maker. The problem posed at the end of the video is to prepare the business plan Chris should present to the principal.

The problem in "The Big Splash" can be approached from multiple perspectives and requires the evaluation of multiple elements and options to construct an acceptable alternative that meets the constraints originally set by the principal. Analog and extension problems focus students' attention on the concepts of representative sampling, extrapolation to a population from a sample, acceptable levels of risk, systematic consideration of possible expenses, and the dangers of responding to sales pitches based on physical appearance rather than the content of the message. The "Rate That Plan" game show included presentations of three plans for raising money at a school fun fair. Students had to decide which plan they thought was best. They phoned in the class vote but also filled out individual response sheets with their explanations for their choice.

Reactions to the Initial Challenges. The reactions to each of our initial challenges were highly positive and in marked contrast to the reactions we had received to the written measures we had used in the implementation project, above. Teachers reported that the discussions following the uplinks were spirited and were motivated by the opportunity students had to compare their answers to those of peers across the country. A number of the teachers felt that the discussions were especially helpful to students who had originally missed flaws in various plans because it helped them improve their understanding of key concepts, such as random sampling, that were necessary in order to create effective business plans. Others indicated that students enjoyed the opportunity to learn something new rather than merely repeat already acquired skills.

SMART Challenges II. Although our initial challenges were highly popular with students, teachers, and community members, we noted considerable variability in data collected about students' individual performances. Our data indicated that some students appeared to have learned a tremendous amount from preparing for the Challenge while others had learned relatively little. We tried to understand why these differences existed. One possibility was that the concepts were simply too difficult for many of the students. Another, more plausible possibility was that some of the teachers had not adequately prepared their students for the challenges. This might be due to a lack of time, a lack of interest, or perhaps an inadequate understanding of some of the concepts required for the preparation. In order to explore these possibilities we decided that the next step in our research should be to keep a better eye on what happened in the classroom.

We worked intensively in a single classroom for eight weeks with an experienced Jasper teacher, who has become an invaluable colleague. We observed his classroom daily for the eight weeks of instruction it took to complete this unit, and we worked with him to introduce some new instructional tools we felt would facilitate student learning.[4] At the end of each day we were able to discuss ideas with the teacher through a computer-based two-way videoconferencing system that connected his classroom with our technology center.[5]

One of the tools we introduced was a simple mechanical device for promoting self-assessment on the part of the students. They assessed the functioning of their groups, their feelings about making presentations before the group, and their understanding of the parts of the problem focused on that day. We created a device for self-assessment that made the results immediately visible to the teacher and students. We intended these results to stimulate classroom discussions. For example, when students were asked to respond to how nervous they would feel about presenting in class, the results showed very clearly that a number of them were quite nervous.

We also observed the nature of classroom discussions about key mathematical concepts such as representative sampling, optimal sample sizes, and so forth. In addition, we collaborated with the teacher to give students multiple experiences for making presentations, and we videotaped the progress of the students as they made their presentations—first about the income portion of the solution to "The Big Splash," then about their thoughts on expenses, later about their thoughts on the entire plan (income, expenses, and degree of anticipated profit). Later presentations were about each group's own business plan and the data gathered to assess the feasibility of the plans.

Reactions to the Challenge.   Our teacher was extremely pleased by his students' progress. He had used Jasper for three years and felt that, without a doubt, his students had reached levels of understanding and skill (including presentation skill) he never before imagined possible for students of this age. At the end of the eight-week period the students presented their own business plan (complete with data about feasibility) to a panel of experts who interviewed the students. The experts were also extremely impressed by the high level of performance of the groups—including their ability to think on their feet while answering questions asked by panel members.

Lessons Learned.   Our classroom observations convinced us of the importance of helping teachers make the thoughts, feelings, and skills of their students visible. As discussed earlier, one way we had helped accomplish this was through our mechanical device that provided frequent opportunities for anonymous self-assessment by the students. The teacher felt that these assessments provided an excellent opportunity for him to understand better what the class was thinking or feeling, and then take appropriate action. For example, when self-assessment data indicated that some of the groups seemed to be functioning at a less-than-ideal level, the teacher was able to begin a discussion about how to help groups run more smoothly. Similarly, when data indicated that a number of students were extremely nervous about making public presentations, the teacher devised a plan to deal with this—a plan that meshed nicely with our goal of providing frequent opportunities for important performances such as presentations.

The use of frequent opportunities to practice important performances also allowed the teacher to implement a variety of strategies to accommodate individual differences. As an illustration, for each class presentation the teacher insisted that every group member had to participate in some way, but the manner of the presentation could vary. Thus, in presentations early in the semester, some members of each group played the role of a "pointer" who pointed to the relevant data on the group's flip chart as someone else discussed the data. For presentations later in the semester, everyone in each group had to have a speaking part.

Our classroom observations and discussions helped us discover a number of issues that pushed all of us—the teacher plus members of our research team—to the edges of our knowledge. For example, what was a way to clarify the reasoning underlying the mathematical procedure used to estimate the best ticket price in "The Big Splash"? What was a succinct way to help students understand why the procedure Chris used to draw a representative sample was adequate, and why he used a sample size of 60? At a more general level, what are the general principles for deciding on sample size? This became important for students developing their own business plans. If their school population size was twice as large as the one in the Jasper adventure (Chris's population size was 360), should the sample size be 120, remain at 60, or what? Many members of our research group were uncomfortable with these questions, and the same is true of teachers: most did not have the benefit of in-depth preparation in statistics when they attended school. In addition, most teachers with whom we have worked are not familiar with how visual diagrams can be used to help students understand complex concepts—diagrams that members of our research team found themselves using in order to communicate with one another.

These experiences helped us realize how much we as a research team rely on our own "learning community" as a source of information to help us make sense of new or complex situations. So we began to think about another important function for our SMART challenges—to provide access to new information for teachers as well as students and to provide opportunities for expanding the connection of teachers and students to the broader community and its resources, including business leaders and members of the university community.

SMART Challenge III: Toward More Frequent Opportunities for Mutual Learning

SMART Challenge III is just beginning to be implemented as we write this chapter. Based on lessons learned from the earlier SMART challenges, it is designed to assess the value-added of increasing the opportunities for mutual learning by teachers, students, and our research team. It culminates in a special live televized event called "The Big Challenge," which is a variant on SMART Challenge I's "Rate that Plan" game show. It involves a number of experimental and control classrooms, which differ in their preparation stages.

The control classrooms in SMART Challenge III receive experiences similar to those discussed in SMART Challenge I, above. Students prepare for "The Big Challenge" by solving "The Big Splash," solving analog and extension problems relevant to it, and then spending several days generating their own business plans and deciding how they would collect data to estimate the projected income for their plans.

Students and teachers in the experimental classrooms receive the same experiences as those in the control classrooms (preparing for the live TV show "The Big Challenge" by solving "The Big Splash," solving analog and extension problems relevant to it, and then spending several days generating their own business plans and deciding how they would collect data to estimate the projected income for their plans). In addition, students and teachers in the experimental classrooms are provided with more frequent opportunities for mutual learning. This occurs by way of four special video-based programs that occur prior to "The Big Challenge." The first program provides an introduction to the series; the purpose of the three remaining programs is to help students and teachers focus on specific subchallenges while also providing opportunities to (a) compare their answers to those of students in other experimental classrooms throughout the city, (b) receive feedback about various ideas for problem solution and extensions to other areas, and (c) see models of powerful ways to express ideas.

At the end of the preparation stages, both experimental and control classrooms participate in the live interactive "Big Challenge" show that allows them to test their mettle with respect to a number of issues relevant to business plans and "The Big Splash." Data we are collecting both during and after this challenge will help us assess the value-added of the video-based programs made available to classes in the experimental condition. We expect to find advantages for student understanding, for students' ability to give clear presentations (including their use of graphics to communicate effectively), and for teachers' understanding of statistics and how they can help students better understand statistical concepts.

Future Plans.   Our hope is that SMART Challenge III will provide us with information and experience that will allow us to refine our ideas during the summer of 1993 and prepare to implement key learning-community ideas in a larger number of schools in the Nashville Metropolitan School System during the 1993–94 academic year. Our next SMART challenge project will be extended to one year and will cover Jasper trip-planning adventures as well as statistics and business planning adventures. The school system's educational TV studio has given us permission to use their facilities to deliver SMART challenges throughout the school year.

An extremely important issue is one of ensuring that students will not be disadvantaged on state tests of accountability by spending so much time working on SMART challenges. Our current plan is to ask schools to agree to implement a year-long, daily "project hour" that provides time for problem-based and project-based activities such as Jasper without taking time away from ongoing instruction in mathematics, science, reading, or other key activities. We will then help teachers integrate the instruction in the mathematics classes by working backward from Jasper adventures to find relevant concepts and skills that students are covering in their mathematics classes. And we will use inexpensive, two-way desktop videoconferencing to link these classrooms to individuals in the university and business community who will help students prepare for the SMART challenges and generate extension ideas of their own to be shared on our broadcasts.[6]

Needless to say, our plans for next year are still only a small part of what is needed to develop an effective learning community. But the work should allow us to better understand the benefits of breaking the isolation of classrooms and creating systems that encourage continual learning by students, teachers, researchers, parents, and other community members. We will attempt to assess the value-added of the learning community concept for each of these constituent groups.

Summary and Conclusions

A great deal has happened throughout the five and a half years we have participated in the McDonnell CSEP program. Many of us have experienced greater changes in our thinking than in any other period in our professional lives. These changes include a much deeper appreciation of the range of issues that need to be considered in order to promote positive educational change. Our goal in this chapter has been to discuss these changes from the perspective of three models of how cognitive research can impact educational practice: (1) the curricular elaboration model (providing visual support for word problems); (2) the classroom restructuring model (designing materials and working with teachers to change the nature of classroom teaching and learning activities); and (3) the learning communities model (using technology to break the isolation of classrooms and provide a basis for continual learning). Our original proposal to the CSEP program was tacitly guided by the first model; we had very little idea that other possibilities existed. As our research progressed, the findings helped us see the need to continue to improve. Especially important was the opportunity to discuss research ideas and findings in the context of collaborative, multidisciplinary groups such as our local McDonnell group and the McDonnell CSEP group that met annually.

We believe that each of the models discussed above can guide research that has important implications for educational practice. Nevertheless, we believe that the learning communities model must be explicitly developed and elaborated in order for the cognitive sciences to have a truly powerful impact on the quality of education. The issue is not that the learning communities model provides researchers with a deeper appreciation of the difficulty of implementing ideas spawned in the laboratory, although it does help fulfill this function. The major value of the learning communities model is that it helps people identify and define a set of research issues that are unlikely to emerge in rarefied research settings. Several key issues include professional development in the context of extremely busy schedules; ongoing formative assessments that make thinking visible and, in the process, help students and teachers increase their abilities to think, reason, and communicate about important subject matters; and community events that help redefine the nature and purposes of schooling (e.g., use of the students as experts who help adults solve problems). Each of these issues requires a mechanism for ongoing, mutual learning by teachers, students, researchers, parents, and other community members. New technologies are making this more possible than ever before.

We close by considering the role of research in our five-and-a-half-year journey. For us, it played a fundamental role in driving conceptual change. It allowed us to move beyond a casual observation of what happened as we put ideas into practice. Almost anything new generates enthusiasm, especially when it involves volunteer teachers who get to use "gee whiz" technology such as computers and videodiscs. Given such enthusiasm, it is tempting to declare victory and move on rather than look beneath the surface. But whenever we did look more carefully, we found lots of room for improvement. Transfer was often not as flexible as it should have been (CTGV 1992c);

assessments were often less pleasant and informative for teachers and students than we would have wanted (CTGV 1992b); groups often functioned in a manner that was less than ideal (e.g., Barron 1991; Rewey and CTGV 1991); and our attempts to help teachers understand and implement new approaches to teaching and learning often failed because of a lack of support for change and because problem- and project-based curricula quickly push people to the edges of their knowledge (CTGV 1993b). In each of these cases, and others, we were able to find ways to improve the situation. Sometimes we improved our Jasper materials (e.g., by adding "what if" extensions to each adventure); sometimes we improved our procedures for professional development and formative assessment (e.g., by introducing our latest SMART challenges). But in all cases, the improvements stemmed from the identification of problems revealed by our research activities.

It is the commitment to research and theory that is the major strength of the cognitive science community. Without this commitment, theory does not develop systematically, and educational practice falls preys to fads. We are grateful for the opportunity to work on applications, theory, and research simultaneously through our participation in the McDonnell Foundation's CSEP program. Along with us, our CSEP colleagues have increasingly adopted models that focus on systems rather than isolated pieces of the curriculum. As this trend continues, we expect to see changes in education that improve practice and contribute to an increasingly well-defined, educationally relevant theory base.

Notes

The research reported in this chapter was supported in part by grants from the James S. McDonnell Foundation JSMF 91-6, NSF Jasper MDR-9252990, NSF SMART Assessment MDR-9252908, and U.S. Dept. of Education No. G008730072.

Members of the Cognition and Technology Group who contributed to this article are Brigid Barron, Linda Barron, John D. Bransford, Elizabeth S. Goldman, Susan R. Goldman, Ted Hasselbring, Daniel Hickey, Cindy Hmelo, Allison Moore, James W. Pellegrino, Anthony Petrosino, Bob Sherwood, Nancy J. Vye, Susan Williams, and Linda Zech.

1. The grant number was NSF MDR 9050191.

2. The grant number was NSF MDR-9252990.

3. The subset included seventeen teachers and one of each of their classes, randomly selected.

4. During the last several weeks of this unit, each group of students generated its own plan for a viable business, collected data to access its viability, and presented its plan to a panel of business experts.

5. We are grateful to Northern Telecom, South Central Bell, Vanderbilt Telecommunications, and the Tennessee Public Service Commission for making it possible to use this technology.

6. We used the VISIT Microcomputer-based technology developed by Northern Telecom and are grateful to them for the opportunity.

Chapter 8

The CSILE Project: Trying to Bring the Classroom into World 3

Marlene Scardamalia, Carl Bereiter, and Mary Lamon

As its name implies, the Computer Supported Intentional Learning Environments (CSILE) project was aimed at using computer technology in supporting intentional learning by students. *Intentional learning* was originally conceived as an individual phenomenon, involving students investing effort in learning, over and above the effort they invest in immediate school tasks (Bereiter and Scardamalia 1989). Other terms that refer to roughly the same phenomenon are *self-regulated learning* (Zimmerman 1989) and *autonomous learning* (Thomas and Rohwer 1986). The unifying idea is that students differ considerably in the extent to which they actively and strategically pursue learning as a goal, and this has significant consequences for their educational development. "Intentional learning" is not just a synonym for "motivation." There are students who are motivated to do well in school and who apply themselves seriously to school tasks, but who are not in fact pursuing cognitive goals. Instead, their goals are formed around doing well on the tasks themselves or on looking good in comparison to others (Ng and Bereiter 1991; Nicholls 1984).

Most work on fostering intentional learning has concentrated on the teaching of cognitive strategies. As indicated in the preceding paragraph, however, intentional learning is fundamentally a matter of goals rather than strategies. It is a matter of having knowledge as a goal. Accordingly, use of the computer medium can make a significant contribution to fostering intentional learning if it brings knowledge itself more to the forefront of students' attention. Schooling tends to focus on activities and on production—on schoolwork, in short (Doyle 1983). Learning—which in modern cognitive terms is conceived of as the construction of knowledge by students—is a by-product of schoolwork, rather than something actively attended to by students. To bring knowledge to the forefront, we wanted a medium in which knowledge would be objectified, represented in an overt form so that it could be evaluated, examined for gaps and inadequacies, added to, revised, and reformulated. Thus we were led to the idea of a student-generated database as the core of the computer-based system. Because we wanted to encourage the same intentional learning processes across the curriculum, we opted for a single communal database into which everything students generated could be put and made accessible to others. Such generalized access meant that commenting on one another's knowledge-building efforts could become a natural and important activity.

Thus was laid the groundwork for a system in which the construction of knowledge was a social and not just an individual activity. The subsequent history of the CSILE project has been a history of increasing emphasis on this social dimension of knowledge construction. We have preserved the original name, because intentional learning is still a central objective. But we have been increasingly concerned with intentionality as something that can exist at the group level. This represents a major break with traditional ways of thinking about educational processes. Cooperative learning is, of course, a popular notion; but typically, it refers to students either cooperating in a group task or else helping one another achieve individually realized cognitive objectives. Can a school class, as a collective, have the goal of understanding gravity or electricity? Can it sustain progress toward this goal even though individual members of the class may flag in their efforts or go off on tangents? Can one speak of the class—again, considered as a community, not as a mere collection of individuals—achieving an understanding that is not merely a tabulation of what the individual students understand? These questions have on the one hand led us into issues of educational epistemology, but on the other hand have led into what we believe are promising new avenues of educational design.

None of this is to deny the importance of the individual student's learning. The educational value of school experience depends on what students carry away from it, and this is inevitably carried in individual minds; the school culture, as such, is left behind. Consequently, to advocate an educational focus on social construction of knowledge is to imply that such a focus has advantages for the individual learner in comparison to the more typical focus on individual achievement and performance. This is an empirical claim, not easily established, but evidence to be summarized later in this chapter provides support for it.

Theoretical and Research Background

Although there has been a large amount of research on students' cognitive strategies, surprisingly little of it has attempted to delineate what students normally do in school situations and to explain why they do it. Instead, the tendency has been to identify the strategies used by the more expert-like students and then to characterize average or below-average students by the absence of such strategies. The expert-like strategies are ones that bespeak a high level of intentional learning. They involve noticing and formulating comprehension difficulties as problems, summarizing what has been understood so far, reconsidering previous conclusions, drawing nonobvious inferences, and explicitly connecting new information with prior knowledge (Bereiter and Bird 1985; Brown, Bransford, Ferrara, and Campione 1983; Pressley and Levin 1983). On the assumption that students who do not use such strategies do not know them, there have been various efforts to teach such strategies as school subject matter. While these efforts have been moderately successful, it is noteworthy that some cognitive researchers originally involved in cognitive strategy instruction have since moved to a more broadly social orientation, in which the emphasis is on building a classroom culture supportive of active knowledge construction rather than relying on strategy instruction aimed at the individual student.[1]

The reasons for this shift are various, but we can begin to see a justification if we look at the research on the cognitive strategies of ordinary students. John Holt (1964) was a pioneer in this kind of research, and his analysis of the highly adaptive strategies lying behind the seemingly stupid behavior of children in mathematics classes remains as a beacon illuminating a vital fact. Ordinary students, he found, do not lack cognitive strategies. They have effective cognitive strategies, but ones adapted to goals different from those of the curriculum, such as avoiding unproductive effort and minimizing damage to self-esteem—goals bound to have a high priority for any reasonable person.

Two lines of research have produced convergent findings on the strategies ordinary students use in dealing with informative texts. One line studied strategies used in summarizing such texts (Brown and Day 1983; Brown, Day, and Jones 1983); the other, strategies used in composing them (Scardamalia and Bereiter 1987). In the summarizing strategy, called "copy-delete," students evaluate propositions one by one as they encounter them, retaining those judged important and "deleting" those judged unimportant. In the composing strategy, called "knowledge telling," students evaluate items of information as they think of them, adding them to the text if they are judged appropriate to the topic and the genre, rejecting them if they are not. Thus the two strategies are quite parallel and might even be considered to be the same strategy applied to different tasks (Scardamalia and Bereiter 1984).

In the customary way of studying cognitive strategies, these students would be described in terms of what they do *not* do. In summarizing, they do not seek to identify the central point of the text. They do not consider text statements in relation to one another and thus do not pick up important points implicit but not explicitly contained within single text statements. In an unpublished study, we gave people texts of a dozen or so sentences and asked them to select the three that best summarized the text. In one condition, the sentences were given in scrambled order. Graduate students first rearranged the sentences to make a comprehensible text before attempting to judge what were the best summary statements. Elementary school students, true to the copy-delete strategy, went right to work evaluating the sentences one by one, without concerning themselves with order. It is as if "What's the point?" is not a question that occurs to young students to ask about a text. The same can be said of their approach to writing a text. Using thinking-aloud protocols, we again compared school children with graduate students as they composed opinion essays on the same topic (Bereiter, Burtis, and Scardamalia 1988). The more skillful of graduate students were found to engage in a variety of strategic moves aimed at working out the main point of what they were trying to write, whereas elementary school students did almost none of this.

If we look instead at what young students *do,* it turns out that their strategies are remarkably well adapted to the demands of school reading and writing tasks. Considering their simplicity, the copy-delete and knowledge-telling strategies produce good results. Evaluating statements one at a time, school children produce judgments of importance that agree fairly well with those of adults who base their judgments on more complex criteria (Brown and Smiley 1977). Writing down ideas as they come to mind, using simple criteria of relevance and appropriateness, children nevertheless manage to produce texts that are topically coherent and well formed (Bereiter and Scardamalia 1987, chap. 1). The strategies, moreover, are highly economical of time and effort. They are single-pass strategies. They avoid the necessity of going back over text, reconsidering decisions, or carrying out complex searches. The information processing load is small, compared to that of more sophisticated ways of processing text (Scardamalia 1981; Scardamalia and Bereiter 1984).

Why, then, would anyone want to replace these strategies? The short answer is that these strategies undermine educational purposes. Although they are efficient for accomplishing school tasks, they eliminate the very intellectual activities that the school tasks were intended for. Why are students asked to summarize a text in the first place? It is not primarily with a view to their mastering the art of summary writing.

It is so they will understand a text better, as a result of having thought it through at the level of main points. Similarly, students are not asked to write informative and opinion essays only in order to develop their writing skills. The writing is expected to help them develop and organize their knowledge and to reflect upon and consider the grounds for their beliefs. By using strategies that by-pass such intellectual effort, students render the school tasks largely pointless.

Yet these are not lazy or disaffected students. Most of the students we have worked with have been eagerly cooperative, and we can reasonably assume that the cognitive strategies they developed were not aimed at beating the system. Rather, we can assume that students were doing what adaptive organisms always do, behaving in ways that were locally optimal, given the environment (cf. Anderson 1990). The typical school environment, as noted, does not direclty confront students with needs for understanding, critical examination of beliefs, and the like. It confronts them with an essentially endless series of tasks to be done. Typically, the time constraints for completing a task are severe, whereas the task requirements are quite liberal. It is also fairly common in schools to reward early task completion with opportunities to do things that are more enjoyable, such as free reading or playing a computer game. Although school tasks may vary considerably, and are sometimes even selected by the students, they almost always center on a product—a completed workbook page, a piece of writing, a written problem solution, etc. Under these circumstances, any adaptive organism will develop strategies that minimize time to complete tasks, and the most likely way to do this is by trimming away activities that do not directly yield the deliverable product. In the case of research papers, this means minimizing research. In the case of producing a summary, this means minimizing rereading. In the case of writing a reflective essay, this means minimizing reflection.

At a symptomatic level, at least, all this is well known to educators. There have been two traditional ways of dealing with it. One is to try to design tasks that will, as the saying goes, "make students think." Give them thought-provoking questions to answer, challenging topics to write on. The trouble with this approach is that it depends on being able to outsmart the students, to find tasks for which their labor-saving strategies will not work. Alfred North Whitehead saw clearly the futility of such an effort. "You are up against too skillful an adversary, who will see to it that the pea is always under the other thimble." The other approach is to look for activities that will spontaneously engage students' intellectual efforts by arousing their curiosity or appealing to their existing interests. Often this means letting students plan their own activities, choose their own writing topics, set their own goals.

The strengths and weaknesses of this child-centered approach are too familiar to need repetition here. Worth noting, however, is the extent to which this approach relies on cognitive goals, questions, and interests already present in the individual child. Not surprisingly, some children's interests are much more compatible with traditional curriculum objectives than others, and so there is continual tension surrounding the issue of how far children's personal interests should be allowed to determine their educational future.

The common assumption underlying everything discussed thus far in this section has been that knowledge is an individual attainment—something acquired or, in the more modern view, constructed through the learner's own activity. It is very difficult for people brought up in the Western world to think of knowledge in any other way. The version of Vygotsky's sociocognitive theory that is gaining popularity among educators takes us halfway to another view of knowledge, with its proposal that cognitive structures are first formed socially and then reconstructed internally. However, as this idea has been taken up by North American educators, the emphasis is on the internal part, with social activity treated as a means of advancing the child's personal knowledge. That emphasis is problematic insofar as it has dictated a corresponding neglect of how cognitive structures are supported by social structures and hence fails to account for the internalization process itself.

This emphasis on individual learning (whether carried out through solitary or group activity) is understandable, given that the ultimate value of schooling is judged by what students individually carry away from it. The idea of knowledge having a *primarily* social existence thus does not enjoy a natural fit with educational thought. This idea has proved significant in the philosophy and sociology of science, however (Harré 1984; Latour 1987; Popper 1972). Karl Popper drew a sharp distinction between knowledge as it exists in individual minds ("World 2") and knowledge as an abstraction that (like the economy of a nation or the climate of a classroom) exists above the individual level ("World 3"). He saw the business of science as improving and advancing World 3.

There have been periodic attempts to model classroom learning upon the sciences and disciplines (e.g., Education Development Center 1969). The idea has been to bring into the classroom the excitement and dynamic quality of research enterprises, in place of the mere transmission of information that commonly goes on. In transferring the scientific model of knowledge building to the classroom, however, it has almost always been translated into a World 2 rather than a World 3 enterprise. That is, the emphasis has shifted from constructing a public, collective understanding of things to the individual pursuit of understanding, driven by individual students' curiousity and cognitive abilities. Even when the instructional medium is group discussions and investigations, the focus of analysis and evaluation has tended to remain the individual. The question is always to what extent do children think and act like scientists, not to what extent does a school class function like a scientific community.

The individualistic focus has tended to distort the knowledge-building process. It has given us, for instance, *Science: A Process Approach* (American Association for the Advancement of Science 1974), in which the scientific enterprise is reduced to the exercise of a variety of skills, such as observation, measurement, and experimentation. Although such skills are undeniably involved in science, focusuing on them results in a parody that misses the whole point of science. But so does an approach that focuses on individual efforts to construct meaning and satisfy curiosity. Neither one captures the essential character of science that Popper identified, the construction of a public understanding of things.

It may not be evident why, in the development of CSILE, we have been concerned with finding a way of objectifying knowledge and bringing it to the forefront of classroom activity. The goal is to get students involved in improving *the knowledge itself* rather than with improving their own minds. This is a radical turnabout for schooling, but it represents the normal arrangement of priorities in the "real" world of knowledge building. It is what all of us who consider ourselves active members of scholarly or scientific disciplines do. Our hope is to restructure school processes so that this becomes a normal and natural thing for students to do as well.

CSILE as a Medium for Working in World 3

Although computers have an important (we would say indispensable) function in CSILE, CSILE has never been primarily a software development project. Rather, as indicated earlier, we started with certain ideas about intentional learning and how to promote it, using computers as an adjunct to a more general effort to change educational processes in schools. As our ideas have changed, so has the computer software, but not to as great an extent as the uses to which the software has been put. It should also be acknowledged, however, that the software has played a role in changing our ideas. Children started to do things with the CSILE communal database that neither we nor their teachers had anticipated. In limited ways they were doing what could be described as creating World 3 for themselves.

Before proceeding with examples, some general description of CSILE is in order. The standard CSILE installation has eight networked computers per classroom, connected to a file server, which maintains the communal database. The database consists of text and graphical notes, all produced by the students and accessible through database search procedures. Anyone can add a comment to a note or attach a graphic note subordinate to another graphic note, but only authors can edit or delete notes. Authors are notified when a comment has been made on one of their notes. Various versions of CSILE have other features, such as a student-produced spell-checker dictionary. These are described elsewhere (Scardamalia, Bereiter, Brett, Burtis, Calhoun, and Smith Lea 1992). The features described here represent the basic functionality of the system, however, and are sufficient to discuss the knowledge-building activities.

Teachers work CSILE activities into the curriculum in any way they wish. They have been used in history, social studies, science, literature, geography, and to some extent mathematics. A limiting factor is computer time. Each student typically gets thirty minutes a day on a computer. This has generally meant that at any given time only one unit or subject is being worked on via CSILE. In some cases a unit will follow a definite sequence of activities. For instance, it might begin with a videotape, followed by whole-class discussion; then students will individually enter questions and study plans as CSILE notes; then they will do individual reading, entering what they learn as notes which others may comment on; whole-class discussions or readings will intervene; finally, selected text and graphic notes may be printed out and displayed on a bulletin board. In other cases, students will work in small groups and plan their own work, with only general guidance from the teacher. (Models of use are compared in Bereiter and Scardamalia, in press, and Lamon and Lee, in press). Information brought into CSILE notes may come from any sources: books, experimental observations, interviews, electronic media.

Obviously, CSILE can be used to support anything from very traditional schoolwork to student-initiated inquiry. Therefore it might seem that the software is entirely neutral and could not possibly have a significant role in shifting educational processes toward a World 3 focus. To be sure, it cannot do much by itself, but it has turned out that CSILE is not nearly so neutral a medium as one might suppose. It introduces certain biases and enables cetain kinds of information flow that are at least conducive to educational change. First, the physical conditions—especially the fact that not all children can be working on CSILE at the same time—militate against the traditional schoolwork model, where all the students are doing the same thing at the same time. Second, CSILE opens up a significant channel for communication in the classroom that is not mediated through the teacher. The following two examples give an idea of what this can mean.

We have cited several examples frequently because they influenced us to think about reshaping educational processes to focus on building public or World 3 knowledge. The first example arose within the context of a fairly traditional grade 6 biology unit. Each student was to select an animal, formulate questions about it, and then find and record information related to the questions. One student, wandering from the beaten track of elephants and polar bears, chose sponges. One of the questions he posed was how they reproduce, and this led to a note reporting that sponges have three ways of reproducing—sexual reproduction, budding, and regeneration. Even though reading one another's notes was not part of the assignment for this unit, CSILE students do on their own initiative spend time browsing the database. In particular, they do searches by author, checking up on classmates whom they know to produce interesting notes. Accordingly, the news about sponge reproduction spread. It resulted in a series of twelve notes, in which students offered speculations about why sponges should be favored with so many ways of reproducing. Reasons proposed included the defenselessness of sponges and the value of back-up systems in case one failed. One student went beyond this level of speculation and, in comments on other students' notes, kept raising the following question: If it is good to have three ways of reproducing, why do other creatures (such as humans) have only one? Eventually he was able to track down information that enabled him to answer his own question: It's structural simplicity that makes it possible for sponges to reproduce by budding and regeneration. "Lungs, a heart, and a brain, etc. could not grow on your finger if it was cut off."

Note the emergence here of a kind of evolutionary thinking that goes beyond the simplistic adaptationism found to characterize even university students (Ohlsson 1991). It recognizes the limitations that existing structures place on evolutionary possibilities. In the present instance, there is no reason to believe this sophisticated conception extended beyond the one student who expressed it, or even to suppose that it represented more than a glimmer of understanding in that one student's mind. Nevertheless, considering the whole episode, it seems fair to say that the focus of the students' activity was on *the nature of things in the world* rather than on some task that had been set by or for them or on their own states of mind. Thus it can be said that the students were working in World 3, trying to construct a piece of world knowledge. The construction did not get very far, but then it was quite extracurricular, something the students carried out not only without instructions but without the teacher's even being aware of it. (The whole episode, in fact, only came to light weeks later, when a researcher was scanning the database.)

The second example shows students not only pursuing questions that carried them beyond fact learning, but also devising a fairly sophisticated methodology for pursuing those questions. Students using CSILE for a project in medieval history were asked to write a series of questions about aspects of medieval life as CSILE notes. Some of the questions were simply factual ("What games did children play in medieval times?") but surprisingly many were concerned with how various castle defense systems worked ("How did drawbridges go up and down without motors?" "What chance did enemy archers have of getting through the portcullises?") Instead of simply using reference books for answering these questions, two students constructed a working model of a portcullis using Interactive Physics^{TM} and explained how their model worked in a CSILE note. Apparently, the note was read widely, for soon several other students' models began appearing in the database. Frequently, students' models of how a drawbridge worked relied on principles for how a catapult works. Earlier in the term students had worked on a researcher-conducted CSILE project concerning the relation between mass and distance on a balance beam. Since students had not been reminded of that project it is an interesting demonstration of students themselves spontaneously extending the project beyond the assigned task of acquiring declarative information to a goal of understanding how things worked by using knowledge from another domain.

The third example is highlighted by one key entry in the database. It occurred in the course of a series of notes and comments generated by a group of grade 5 and 6 students who were working on questions having to do with inheritance of characteristics—why a child will resemble one parent in some respects, the other in others, and some more distant relative in yet other respects. The students' efforts to arrive at a coherent explanation of this complicated phenomenon were quite impressive, but no more so than a number of other such episodes recorded in CSILE databases. What made this one memorable was a one-line note which stated simply, "Mendel worked on Karen's question."

The statement captured something that we had been vaguely aware of with CSILE students but have never seen so clearly before. It is the opposite of alienation. It is the sense of being part of a long tradition— a grand and endless dialogue—aimed at understanding the nature of things. It is not, as present-day exponents of cultural alienation like to say, studying the works of "dead white males." The fact of Mendel's being male, white, and dead was not what seemed to matter to this young thinker. What mattered was the realization that this problem was not just a classroom exercise or something that was a puzzle to them because they were young and naive, but that it was a problem that had a history, a problem that had mattered to other people, and that by working on it they became a part of something larger. Or so it seemed to us. We may be reading too much into a perhaps offhand remark (although for a student to have entered this one piece of information as a CSILE note suggests it could not have been all that offhand). All we really want to claim, however, is that the remark is suggestive of how working in World 3 might come to have a much deeper and richer significance for students than working in World 2, the world of their personal interests and puzzlements.

Evidence of Effects

Our objectives for CSILE have moved from promoting intentional learning in individual students to supporting the collective construction of public (World 3) knowledge. Note that World 3 and World 2 goals are not antagonistic. The claim is that the cognitive processes invoked to articulate ideas and beliefs in social interactions are then available to the child for self-reflection. Two sources of data then are relevant for testing the idea that construction of knowledge is a social and not just an individual activity: World 3 effects (e.g., improved knowledge quality and evidence of constructive activity in students' collective work) and World 2 effects (e.g., a shift toward mastery goals and away from performance goals, and evidence of deeper understanding). Although we are thinking about possibilities for assessment at a World 3 level (for instance, assessing the progress of a discourse), nothing of this sort is operational yet. Consequently, we focus on individual assessments, which may provide plausible suggestions of what is happening at the level of the classroom community.

Assessments that have been applied in evaluating CSILE range from standardized achievement tests to special-purpose instruments designed to get at students' conceptions of knowledge. Assessment data have been obtained from four classrooms, all in the same school, where CSILE is installed. They are all mixed-grade classrooms: one comprises grades 1 to 3, another grades 4 and 5[2], and two combined grade 5/6 classrooms. Comparison data for grades 1 to 4 come from other classrooms in the same school. Since the whole grade 5/6 population of the school is in CSILE classrooms, a comparison class from another school is used, comparable in grade mixture, socioeconomic level, and educational philosophy. The CSILE students are from a public school in midtown Toronto, serving a population characteristic of that area: extreme ethnic diversity, wide income range, and a large proportion of single-parent families.

Standardized Achievement Tests

Although standardized achievements cannot be expected to be sensitive to cognitive outcomes of the kind intended for CSILE, they serve as an important point of reference—so that it can be determined, for instance, whether sought-after gains are being obtained at the expense of losses on more traditional criteria. Five subtests from the Canadian Tests of Basic Skills (similar to the Iowa Tests of Basic Skills) are administered in the fall and spring of each year. Composite results for language and mathematics subtests are shown below.

Figures 8.1a and b show the grade equivalent scores for the language and math subtests for the three years of collection of this data. In order to compare these scores across the four grade levels, the grade is subtracted from the score, so that 0 represents one grade below grade level, 1 represents at grade level, and 2 represents one grade above grade level. A two-way analysis of covariance of posttest language scores (experience on CSILE by grade), using pretest as the covariate, revealed a significant effect of experience on CSILE, F (3,393) = 7.04, $p < .001$. A closer examination of this result, using post hoc comparisons, showed that the scores for the three CSILE groups together were higher than the control group, F (1,377) = 5.36, $p < .05$. Analyses also showed that the scores of the students in their second year in a CSILE class were significantly higher than those of the control students, F (1,377) = 10.69, $p = .001$. These second-year CSILE students also scored significantly higher than those in their first year of CSILE, F (1,377) = 3.85, $p = .05$. Students in their third year of CSILE, although higher at posttest than the control students, were not significantly so. This is an unexpected result, but it could be misleading due to the small sample size of CSILE students in their third year (control group, $n = 172$; CSILE year 1, $n = 122$; CSILE year 2, $n = 89$; CSILE year 3, $n = 21$). The analysis of covariance also showed a significant effect of grade, F (3,393) = 13.91, $p < .001$, but no interaction between grade and experience on CSILE. There were no significant results in a similar analysis of covariance on the mathematics subtests. Most use of the CSILE system to date has focused on language-based domains, and the difference between domains appears to reflect that focus. However, the results clearly indicate that CSILE students are not losing ground in either domain using traditional criteria.

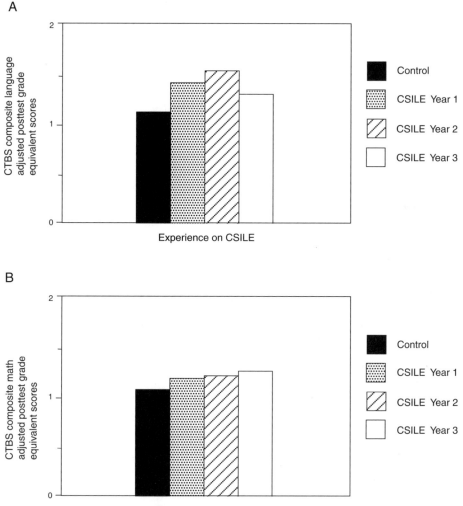

Figure 8.1
1990 to 1992 adjusted posttest scores (using pretest as a covariate) for students in grades
3 to 6 on the language subtests (vocabulary, reading comprehension, and spelling) and
the mathematics subtests (problem solving and computation) of the Canadian tests of
basic skills

Depth of Explanation

Students in the two grade 5/6 CSILE classes and the grade 5/6 comparison class were interviewed before and after a science unit. Because the topics and activities differed from class to class, the results cannot be interpreted with confidence. They do, however, show a significant advantage for the CSILE classes on indices relevant to knowledge-building. Students were asked to write on the topic, "What I have learned from doing this unit." Responses were scored on a holistic scale of depth of explanation. Responses scored at the low end were judged to consist of isolated bits of information, whereas those at the high end were judged to present an elaborated description of the topic area as a system. CSILE students scored significantly higher than the control students (M = 2.89 versus M = 1.20; t (35) = 7.09; p < .001). Their mean rating indicates that, on average, they were attempting to construct explanations or at least coherent accounts, rather than simply listing facts.

Graphical Knowledge Representation

An important but relatively unresearched aspect of using computer-based technology is the cognitive effects of increased availability and power of computer graphics. In past years, informal examination of student graphics created using CSILE suggested that students were not just using graphics for descriptive or illustrative purposes, but were also using them for a variety of explanatory and organizational ones. A study was conducted to test whether CSILE students did in fact create more conceptually advanced graphics than those of control students (Gobert Wickham, Coleman, Scardamalia, and Bereiter 1992).

In this study, all students were provided with a booklet containing a text about continental drift and two sets of questions requiring that they draw diagrams and give explanations. Three classes of grade 5/6 students participated in the study (n = 86). Two of the classes had prior experience constructing graphical and explanatory models using CSILE. Of these two, one class had prior knowledge of continental drift. A third group served as a control group (no prior content knowledge or CSILE experience).

All students produced diagrams using paper and pencil, so as not to give an advantage to those with computer graphics experience. Graphics were scored both for descriptive accuracy and for presence of dynamic/causal components—that is, components that served to show how the indicated process (e.g., formation of mountains) took place. Figure 8.2 shows an example of a student diagram that makes use of dynamic components such as arrows and sequential frames to serve explanatory purposes. Three written problems required students

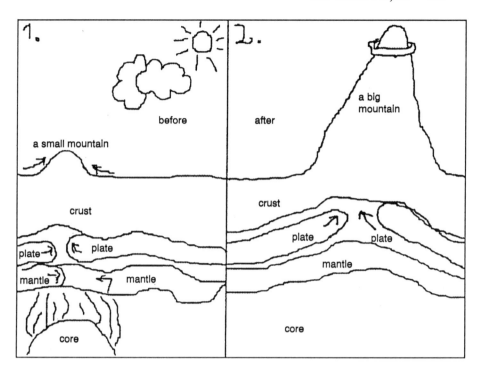

Figure 8.2
A student's dynamic explanation of continental drift

to apply information from the text to explain phenomena not dealt with in the text (e.g., "Using what you just learned about continental drift, explain how it is possible that kangaroo fossils were found in both South America and Australia"). Responses to these items were scored for degree of scientific adequacy.

A multivariate analysis of variance was conducted using five measures taken from the diagrammatic representations—3 descriptive and 2 dynamic/causal—and three conceptual measures of explanation. The analysis revealed an overall main effect for group (F (16,142) = 3.63, $p < .001$), indicating that the CSILE groups produced significantly more advanced explanations (F (2,77) = 6.88, $p < .002$) and diagrams which contained more causal/dynamic information (F (2,77) = 10.20, $p < .001$) (see figure 8.3).

Interestingly, no significant differences between groups were found in the students' depictions of descriptive components of continental drift. Furthermore, prior knowledge of continental drift did not have a significant effect on either the production of diagrams or of explanations.

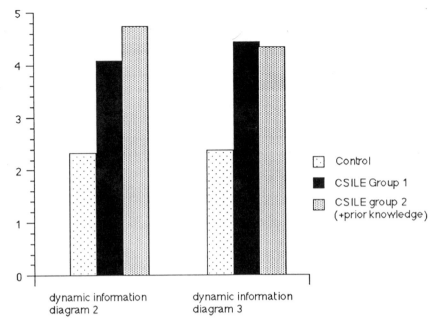

Figure 8.3
CSILE and control group differences in amount of dynamic information depicted in diagrams

Overall then, students in the CSILE classrooms constructed diagrams that contained more causal/dynamic information and also produced causal explanations that were much more advanced. These findings provide some evidence that CSILE experience leads to gains in graphical literacy and ability to work with scientific explanations.

Portfolio Ratings
In CSILE and comparison grade 5/6 classes, students maintain portfolios in which they place items of work that they are particularly pleased with or interested in. Separate portfolios are kept for writing, mathematics, and science. The actual contents of the portfolios are generally too heterogeneous to permit comparative assessment. Instead, comparisons are based on (a) students' comments on their own portfolio selections and (b) comments on the selections of another student in the same class. Rating scales for each question were based on children's depth of explanation. Generally, uninformative responses were given a score of 0, global descriptive responses a score of 1, detailed descriptions a score of 2, and explanatory responses a score of 3.

Tables 8.1a and b present the mean self- and peer commentary scores of CSILE and non-CSILE classes for each domain for the fall and spring data collections. Analyses of covariance of the self-commentary scores for writing, mathematics, and science showed that CSILE students, to a significantly greater extent than non-CSILE students, went progressively deeper in describing what their work was about, more often cited learning goals in their reasons for selecting a particular piece of work, and gave detailed descriptions of what they had learned from doing that work. And for all three domains, CSILE students made more reflective comments about others' work, about others' comments on that work, and gave more detailed responses to their editors' comments. Results replicate an earlier portfolio study (Lamon, Abeygunawardena, Cohen, Lee, and Wasson 1992) and, as such, support the hypothesis that CSILE students become more reflective about their own knowledge and learning than non-CSILE students.

Table 8.1a
Means and standard deviations of portfolio self-commentary, fall and spring scores for writing, mathematics and science as a function of CSILE

Domain		Control (*n* = 39)		CSILE (*n* = 74)	
		M	SD	M	SD
Writing	Fall	1.79	.52	1.81	.37
	Spring	1.89	.41	2.05	.49
Mathematics	Fall	1.72	.54	1.91	.52
	Spring	1.69	.44	1.79	.57
Science	Fall	1.76	.39	1.72	.51
	Spring	1.84	.57	1.97	.54*

Significance levels: * = < .05, ** = < .01, *** = < .001

Table 8.1b
Means and standard deviations of portfolio peer commentary, fall and spring scores for writing, mathematics, and science as a function of CSILE

Domain		Control (*n* = 39)		CSILE (*n* = 74)	
		M	SD	M	SD
Writing	Fall	1.49	.36	1.67	.45*
	Spring	1.40	.38	1.83	.60**
Mathematics	Fall	1.45	.48	1.65	.52
	Spring	1.21	.35	1.63	.54*
Science	Fall	1.37	.33	1.66	.40***
	Spring	1.41	.51	1.69	.57*

Significance levels: * = < .05, ** = < .01, *** = < .001

Constructive Processes in Reading
As was mentioned earlier in this chapter, a strategy that children commonly use in summarizing and composing texts (Brown and Day 1983; Brown, Day, and Jones 1983; Scardamalia and Bereiter 1987) is to look for single important points without evaluating the overall meaning of what is being read or written. Clearly, a strategy that leads students to focus on taking in or reporting new facts can lead to locally adequate understanding. However a surface approach to learning is unlikely to lead to new insights into a domain. In contrast, studies of what students *do* when trying to learn new information have shown that successful learners focus on cognitive goals, structural features of a problem and a transformational approach to learning.

If CSILE is effective in helping children to focus on understanding the nature of things (a World 3 orientation), the difference between active and passive approaches should become apparent when students are trying to learn something new, something for which they have inadequate prior knowledge. Lamon, Chan, Scardamalia, Burtis, and Brett (1992) asked students in CSILE and non-CSILE classrooms to read a text on either photosynthesis or evolution (texts were counterbalanced such that students who had read the evolution text in the fall were presented with the photosynthesis text in the spring) in order to solve an analogous problem. As an example, students who studied a text on evolution read about the change in the coloration of peppered moths in industrial England from primarily white to primarily black. The subsequent problem asked them to explain the emergence of long-legged deer in an area populated by cheetahs. These texts are difficult. In order to solve the problem, students need to extract underlying concepts. Dependent measures were quality of problem solution and recall of text information.

The data of primary interest are the changes in children's solutions and are presented in table 8.2. In the fall, no differences emerged

Table 8.2
Means and standard deviations of problem solving and recall, fall and spring scores as a function of CSILE

Task		Control (*n* = 40)		CSILE (*n* = 71)	
		M	SD	M	SD
Problem solving	Fall	4.05	1.23	4.11	1.32
	Spring	4.25	1.01	4.68	1.08*
Recall	Fall	4.25	1.97	4.66	2.22
	Spring	3.89	1.73	5.38	2.19***

Significance levels: * = < .05, ** = < .01, *** = < .001

between CSILE and non-CSILE students' solutions. CSILE students' solutions were now significantly more accurate, F (1,108) = 4.14, $p <$ .05. Moreover, CSILE students recalled significantly more of the text than non-CSILE students, F (1,108) = 13.95, $p < .001$.

Beliefs about Learning
Substantial evidence has accumulated showing that students' beliefs about learning are related to their academic achievement. A major contrast is that between a "shallow" conception of learning, which sees it as a matter of paying attention, doing assigned work, and memorizing, and a "deep" conception, which sees learning as dependent on thinking and understanding (Biggs 1984). It seemed reasonable to expect that, if CSILE was achieving some success in orienting students toward active construction of knowledge, this should be reflected in a deeper conception of learning being held by CSILE students. A nine-item three-alternative forced-choice instrument was assembled, based on statements that we had found in previous, more in-depth interview assessments to be significantly related to student beliefs about learning.

Results showed that 71 percent of choices made by children in CSILE classes were mastery-oriented but only 50 percent of choices made by children in the non-CSILE class were mastery-oriented. Specifically, 80 percent of children in CSILE classes said that they could tell they had learned if they came to understand something they didn't know before, but only 56 percent of students in non-CSILE classes said so. Conversely, 40 percent of children in non-CSILE classes said they could tell if they had learned something if they got a good mark on a test, but fewer than 15 percent of CSILE students assessed learning in terms of marks. Similarly, when asked about learning from text, 64 percent of students completing their first year in a CSILE class and 78 percent of students in CSILE classes for the second or third year said that thinking deeply about what the book said was most important for learning, but only 40 percent of students in non-CSILE classes selected that response. Conversely, 44 percent of students in non-CSILE classes thought that reading the book correctly was most important for learning but only 25 percent of first-year CSILE students and 13.5 percent of second- and third-year CSILE students selected that response. Differences in overall scores and specific responses showed a significant increment related to CSILE experience.

Comparison of CSILE-based with Face-to-Face Group Problem Solving
The preceding evaluations indicate some general effects favoring classrooms in which CSILE is used, but they do not of course indicate what

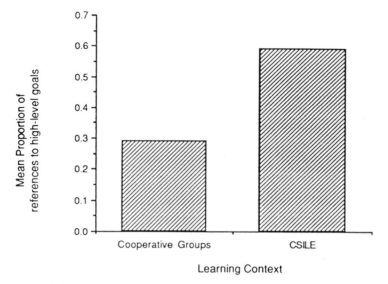

Figure 8.4
Differences between CSILE students and face-to-face cooperative groups in proportion of references to high-level goals

the causal factors may be. Of particular interest for further educational development is the question of how significant the computer support is. Might it not be possible, and perhaps even more effective, to have the children working on knowledge construction through face-to-face discussion rather than through the more impersonal medium of CSILE? This is not a simple question to investigate. CSILE students do often meet face-to-face, so it is not an either-or comparison. In order to make conditions comparable in other respects, it would be necessary to use learning activities that do not make optimal use of CSILE capabilities—by eliminating, for instance, activities that involved search and retrieval of other students' previous contributions. A recent study (Lamon 1992), however, provides an interesting comparison of students carrying out essentially the same activity with and without CSILE.

The study involved children working on one of the Jasper problems (see chapter 7). Students watched a videotape version of the problem drama and then worked either in small face-to-face groups or on CSILE to solve the problem. Solving a Jasper problem requires solving a large number of subproblems, which are hierarchically related so that solving the lower-level problems enables solution of the higher-level ones, there being one top-level problem that is the focus of the video drama. A difficulty that young students often exhibit is getting

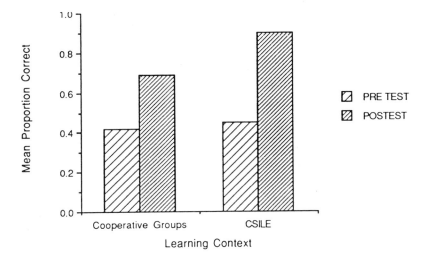

Figure 8.5
Pre- and posttest differences between CSILE students and face-to-face cooperative groups in solving problems

lost in lower-level problems and losing sight of the goal. Transcripts of the face-to-face discussions and the CSILE notes were scored by tallying the frequency of goal-related statements at different levels in the problem gaol hierarchy. As figure 8.4 indicates, students using CSILE showed a significantly higher proportion of references to high-level goals.

The other result of significance is the gain from pretest to posttest on sets of word problems mathematically similar to those encountered in the Jasper problem. Such gain may thus be taken as a measure of transferable knowledge gained from the experience. Here, too, as figure 8.5 indicates, students using CSILE outperformed classmates who worked in face-to-face groups.

Some suggestion of why CSILE may have advantages over face-to-face discussion is provided by a pilot study conducted by Andrew Cohen (1992). This study involved university students taking a physics course for nonscience majors. They were trying to understand standing waves, doing part of their work through CSILE and part of it in small group discussions. Cohen's data showed that in face-to-face discussions there were extreme variations in the extent to which group members contributed, with some contributing hardly at all. When working through CSILE, these same students showed virtually equal levels of participation.

This finding of equal participation is reinforced by tracking data from the elementary school CSILE classrooms. There are no significant differences between boys and girls and between high and low achievers in the number of notes they enter and in the amount of commenting they do. Studying similar students doing similar work in face-to-face groups, Elaine Coleman (1992) observed what she called the "social destruction of knowledge," where competitiveness or other social factors led to the rejection of good ideas (see also Eichinger, Anderson, Palincsar, and David 1991).

Another kind of advantage that CSILE offers over face-to-face collaborative problem solving is the record of past goal states and solution ideas. It was noted in the Lamon (1992) study that students using CSILE reviewed their previous work and moved on from there, whereas students in the control group were more likely to flounder or start over.

Discussion

Evaluations conducted to date show advantages for CSILE students that are consistent with the contemporary cognitive emphasis on understanding, metacognition, and active construction of knowledge. They also indicate that CSILE students are not handicapped in achievement according to conventional measures, and in fact show significant gains in the area of language skills. Although these favorable results indicate that something good is happening in CSILE classrooms, they cannot of course be claimed to validate the ideas behind CSILE. Neither do they provide evidence that what we intend to happen in CSILE classrooms is what actually takes place. On these matters, which are crucial in providing direction for further research and development, we currently rely to a great extent on informal classroom observations and examinations of notes in CSILE databases. Systematic assessments, of the kinds reported in the previous section, are mainly important in the development process as a protection against wishful thinking. We have had previous experience with an educational intervention where teachers were uniformly enthusiastic in reporting improvements in children's thinking, but where a three-year longitudinal assessment was unable to turn up the slightest evidence of gains (Bereiter 1984). Quantitative comparative assessments serve as an important kind of reality check and may on occasion signal problems, but one cannot expect much more from them.

Accordingly, in this discussion we shall deal in a more impressionistic way with what we see as progress to date and challenges to be met. We can point to instances where we feel CSILE is not being used to good advantage and to others where we feel it is. This is quite different, however, from having a definite program according to which different degrees of *implementation* can be judged. As we see it, a knowledge-building community is an idealization. The sciences are cited as prime examples of knowledge-building communities, but anyone actively involved in a science knows that it is stretching things to call it a community at all, let alone a community pristinely dedicated to the construction of knowledge. The concept of knowledge-building community captures an essence that only becomes visible from a broad and long-term perspective. What is going on at a particular time and place may have little evident fit to the concept. We should expect no more from a school. We should not expect to walk through the door and behold something recognizable as a knowledge-building community. What we have a right to expect from a science or scholarly discipline is progress in collective knowledge and understanding over some reasonable time span.

It remains, however, that judgments and diagnoses have to be based on what is locally observable. What we see in the four elementary school classrooms that we have been working with may be summarized as follows:

> In the primary grades, 1 to 3, we see the most marked development of a mutually supportive community, and we see the development of processes that are instrumental in the development of public knowledge—communicative representation of knowledge in graphical and text form, constructive commenting, and collaborative work. We do not want to declare that primary grade children are incapable of such a focus—who knows what clever instructional design might accomplish?—but we do feel there is no reason to rush it. Children at this age get very absorbed in their own work or work with a partner, and they can take an interest in what others are doing. CSILE facilitates this kind of activity, and it seems right for them. One teacher reports the beginnings of a World 3 focus in children's learning to recognize claims as claims rather than as immutable facts.
>
> In grades 4 to 6 there is a more evident focus on problems of understanding. Occasionally a topic takes off, as in the examples given earlier; several students become engaged with the same problem and there is an accumulation of information, an exchange of conjectures and criticisms, and occasionally progress toward a more powerful explanation. The extent of collaborative knowledge-building activity is considerably influenced by teacher encouragement (Bereiter and Scardamalia, in press; Lamon and Lee, in press). The kinds of knowledge problems

Table 8.3
Excerpt from a group-authored CSILE note

Jane: Problem: How does a balloon's surface change when it is rubbed on wool or hair?

MT: I think that the surface change is an electricity build-up on the balloon's surface. I also think that the surface change causes the balloon to be attracted to different surfaces. (Jane)

C: I like your theory but you should have explained how the balloon gets an electricity build-up. (Alan)

MT: I think that the surface change is an electricity build-up on the balloon's surface. I think that the electricity build-up is made by the travelling of electrons from your hair to the balloon. I also think that the surface change causes the balloon to be attracted to different surfaces. (Jane)

NI: The balloon's surface change is from no charge to a positive charge. I think it would be easier to understand this surface change if you understood how it happens. A balloon's surface change occurs by travelling electrons (from atoms). When you rub a balloon on your hair or on some wool the balloon will lose some of its electrons and your hair or wool will gain them. This makes them negatively charged. The balloon will instead gain protons, this makes the balloon positively charged. This is how a balloon's surface change happens. (Susan)

[discourse continues about how negative and positive changes shift]
INTU: Can a balloon's surface be changed by different temperatures?

---

children of this age will raise and pursue are on a par with those that nonspecialist adults will raise (Scardamalia and Bereiter 1991, 1992), but they tend to pursue them for a shorter time and to be satisfied with more limited explanations.

Much of our current effort is directed toward finding ways of supporting deeper and more extended discourse devoted to knowledge construction. We are looking for ways that allow the teacher's domain-specific knowledge and pedagogical knowledge to contribute, but that are not *restricted* by the teacher's knowledge. This seems to be essential for any approach that will work across a wide range of classrooms and knowledge domains.

A promising recent development is the "group note" (Hewitt and Webb 1992). This is a note focused on a particular problem. Students working on the problem keep appending their contributions, so that a linearly extended dialogue results. An example is provided in table 8.3 Each addition to the note is identified as to author and type of contribution—"My theory," "I need to understand," "New information," and "Comment." (The types are modifiable and extendable. For instance, one teacher has added the category "My feeling.") Group notes seem to result in deeper and more extended inquiry, with theories being modified in response to comments and new information. This has not been empirically tested yet. An interesting empirical result that bears on the issue, however, comes from a pilot study by James Hewitt (1992). When group notes are compared to separately created notes making use of the same contribution types, it is found that group notes contain a significantly higher proportion of epistemological terms—terms having to do with hypothesis, evidence, opinion change, and the like.

Although the group note seems to be effective for encouraging an extended exchange of ideas, it does not lend itself to synthesis—to pulling ideas together and establishing consensus. Thus it has serious limitations as a mechanism for constructing World 3 knowledge. To overcome this weakness, Jim Hewitt and Jim Webb have been experimenting with a "summary note," which sits on the screen beside the group note and which group members are supposed to update from time to time. The idea is that this should focus attention on World 3 knowledge, since the summary note is to reflect the group's progress rather than an individual's beliefs. In early trials, however, it seems that what the students put in the summary note are factual statements (usually from books) over which there is no dispute. Perhaps the summary note can be used as the basis for teaching students strategies for state-of-the-art assessment, such as identifying opposing theories, shifts in the weight of evidence, identification of impasses, and so on; and perhaps the summary note can be restructured in some way to support such assessment.

We mention the group note and the summary note as part of our own state-of-the-art assessment, as an illustration of the sorts of problems we are currently occupied with in the further development of CSILE.

Where's the Cognitive Science?

As the focus of our work has shifted from World 2 to World 3—from goings on within the individual mind to knowledge as a public construction—we of course have moved farther away from cognitive science as it has generally been conceived. But cognitive science itself is in a considerable state of flux, and many of its changes are in the same direction as our research and have had an important influence on how we think about what we are doing.

For educators to say that what they are doing is consistent with cognitive theory is a very weak claim. As J. B. Carroll (1976) showed, common sense or "naive learning theory," as he called it, is in close accord with cognitive theory—at any rate, the cognitive theory prevailing at the time Carroll wrote. Thus a more challenging question for the educational designer is, In what ways and to what extent is what you are doing different from what you would do if guided only by common sense?

Common sense or "folk psychology," as it is called, has received much attention from philosophically minded cognitive scientists (Stich 1983). It is the psychology we develop through ordinary social experience and that, regardless of our later scientific education, we tend to rely on in dealing with and making sense of the behavior of ourselves and others. It is a psychology in which the primary elements are beliefs and desires. The acquisition of this psychology has been charted by research on children's "theories of mind" (Astington, Harris, and Olson 1988). By age 6, but not at age 3, children can typically explain that Bozo the clown looked in the wrong box because Bozo *wanted* the candy, *believed* the candy was there, and did not *know* the candy had been removed. What has happened since the seventies, when Carroll wrote, is that increasing numbers of cognitive psychologists have come to believe that the cognitive psychology based on schemas, production systems, propositional networks, mental models and the like is not just *compatible* with folk psychology, it really *is* just folk psychology in a more refined and systematic form (Dennett 1987; Margolis 1987; Stich 1983). If this is true, then claims to be deriving educational innovations from mainstream cognitive theory are feeble indeed.

This is not the place to enter into the stormy controversy going on around this issue. We will simply state our own view, as a way of indicating how we are currently going about work we conceive of as applied cognitive science. It is a view very similar to that of Howard Margolis, and we recommend his *Patterns, Thinking, and Cognition* (1987) to readers interested in pursuing this line of thought. What happens when we or a six-year-old explain the behavior of Bozo the clown is that we *rationalize* it. That is, we reason abductively by creating premises that render the behavior rational (cf. Anderson 1990). These premises are then attributed to Bozo as beliefs, knowledge, goals, and the like. Hence, the psychological entities and processes that we attribute to the individual mind are actually a reflection back from an essentially public process of rational justification (Harré 1984). This view turns the relationship between World 2 and World 3 completely upside down from the way it is usually conceived. Instead of World 2 being primary and the source of a hypothetical World 3, World 3 is primary and is the basis for our hypothetical construction of a World 2 in the individual mind.

It remains that for many kinds of learning problems, cognitive analysis at the individual level is the best tool we have. If a student is having trouble grasping a certain mathematical or scientific idea, there is much to be gained by trying to construct and test a mental model of the student's knowledge and thinking in order to discover where the difficulties are and where possible points of entry might exist. Dangers arise only if the descriptive language is taken too literally (Bereiter 1991). One may, for instance, get caught up in trying to determine whether what is in the child's head is a theory or only a collection of notions, forgetting that what is actually in the child's head is a bunch of neurons and that the theories and beliefs are products of our descriptive language. Thus we should only be asking whether it is more *profitable* to describe the child as having a theory or as having something of a less organized sort at work.

But usually, in education, we are not dealing with problems of the individual learner. If we are teaching evolution, say, in a conventional lecture-and-recitation manner, we may remain quite unaware of the many distinctly non-Darwinian ideas afloat in the classroom. By giving students occasion to express their own understanding, we may become aware of a variety of misconceptions, which we will then be inclined to attribute to knowledge structures in the individual minds of students. Unable to argue things out with students individually, however, we will probably opt for addressing what we judge to be some common or underlying misconception. In this way, we are addressing evolutionary ideas at a World 3 level; the trouble is, however, that in a typical classroom there isn't any World 3 as far as evolution is concerned. That is, there is no collective understanding. Nothing has been done to achieve one. It should be little wonder, then, that all we are likely to produce is some minor disturbance or superficial alteration of beliefs. The world in which public knowledge of things like evolution is constructed exists elsewhere, and only fragmentary and confusing reflections of it enter the classroom. Hence the challenge of creating a community in the school that can construct and work with its own version of World 3.

The effective teacher or instructional designer, according to this conception, must be able to move flexibly between a World 3 view, in which the class's knowledge is regarded as a public, objective entity that the teacher must help develop optimally, and a World 2 view, in which the teacher works with hypothetical mental structures attributed to individual students. (Someone may ask, where is the actual flesh-and-blood child in this picture? Answer: Having a really good time, we hope.) When working at a World 2 level, the educator may be trying to get inside the child's head and to see evolution the way the child sees it. When working at a World 3 level, the teacher may ask whether the prevailing quasi-Lamarckian conception is impeding progress of the knowledge-building discourse or perhaps helping it to move ahead to a fuller understanding of adaptation.

Standard-brand cognitive science is helpful in working at the World 2 level, but it is essentially mute with respect to World 3. This makes cognitively oriented educators susceptible to a very serious confusion between (a) the way knowledge is organized in the mind of the child (World 2) and (b) the child's knowledge of the way knowledge is organized in a domain (World 3). It also prevents educators from considering misconceptions, simplified models, and the like as objective entities that can be evaluated, discussed (with the students), and investigated as to their effects on the course of knowledge building. We find that a cognitive science that makes a more radical break with folk psychology and commonsense epistemology offers a better basis for progress in educational design (Bereiter 1992).

Notes

The research reported in this chapter was supported by the James S. McDonnell Foundation. Development of the CSILE system has been supported by Apple Computer, Inc., External Research Division; IBM Corporation; the Ontario Ministry of Colleges and Universities; and the Ontario Ministry of Education. The authors wish to acknowledge the contributions of Clare Brett, Jud Burtis, and Nancy Smith Lea to the evaluation research and to preparing evaluation data for this chapter. We owe special thanks to the students we have worked with and their teachers: Kathy Frecker, Rosemary Kelly, Chuck Laver, and Jim Webb.

1. To name a few, besides ourselves, who have demonstrated this shift in emphasis, there are Ann Brown, John Bransford, Joe Campione, Jerry Duffy, Annemarie Palincsar, and Alan Schoenfeld.

2. Mechanical problems with the computers severely limited use of CSILE in the grade 4/5 classroom this year and so we report results for the grade 5/6 classes only.

Chapter 9

Guided Discovery in a Community of Learners

Ann L. Brown and Joseph C. Campione

The educational community in America is again facing a time of reform. Dissatisfied with the status quo, many are asking for widespread changes in public education. This is not new. Indeed, some have argued that education during the twentieth century has consisted of cycles of reform and retrenchment, with the actual business of schooling remaining largely unchanged (Cohen 1988; Cuban 1984, 1990).

Our current program is similar in many ways to earlier reform endeavors, most notably progressive education, discovery learning, and other movements influenced by the work of John Dewey (Cremin 1961; Dewey 1902; Graham 1967). Via a series of gradual steps leading from the laboratory to the classroom (Brown 1992), we find ourselves involved in a project that resembles the famous six-year experiment mounted by Dewey in the Chicago laboratory school at the turn of the century (Dewey 1894, 1897, 1936; Mayhew and Edwards 1936). We have, in effect, adopted a grade school.

As a result, when describing our work, we run up against some pervasive myths surrounding Dewey's laboratory school. We are often asked how the work differs from Dewey's, and why we think we can succeed where Dewey failed. Few, however, seem to know much about what Dewey actually did, or by what criteria his experiment can be viewed as a failure. Although it is undoubtedly true that our classroom research shares philosophical underpinnings with Dewey's approach, there are some subtle and not-so-subtle differences (Brown 1992). We will illustrate this point by considering two articles of Dewey's faith (1902) as received wisdom would have it: discovery learning and the nature of the curriculum.

The best-known tenet of Dewey's pedagogical creed (1897) is the concept of "discovery learning." It is argued that children learn best when discovering for themselves the "verities of life." This notion has been fully incorporated into constructivist theories of learning. Discovery learning, when successful, has much to recommend it. The motivational benefits of generating and testing one's own knowledge cannot be underestimated.

Discovery learning is often contrasted with didactic instruction. Both methods have their critics. On the one hand, there is considerable evidence that didactic teaching leads to passive learning. But, on the other hand, unguided discovery can be dangerous: children "discovering" in our classrooms are quite adept at inventing biological misconceptions (Brown 1992; Brown and Campione 1990; Brown and Palincsar 1989a). And, the exact role of the teacher in discovery learning classrooms is still largely uncharted.

We have argued in favor of a middle ground between didactic teaching and untrammeled discovery learning, that of "guided discovery" (Brown 1992; Brown and Palincsar 1989b), where the teacher acts as a facilitator, guiding the learning adventures of his or her charges. Guided discovery, however, is difficult to orchestrate. It takes sensitive clinical judgment to know when to intervene and when to leave well enough alone. To be successful, the guide must continually engage in on-line diagnosis of student understanding, and must be sensitive to the current "zone of proximal development" (Vygotsky 1978), the "region of sensitivity to instruction" (Wood and Middleton 1975), the "readiness arena," or "bandwidth of competence" (Brown 1979; Brown and Reeve 1987), where students are ripe for new learning. Guided discovery places a great deal of responsibility in the hands of the teacher, who must model, foster, and guide the "discovery" process into forms of disciplined inquiry that may not be reached without this expert guidance.

Dewey was also concerned about the curriculum of public education, again an enduring topic of debate (Kliebard 1987). What knowledge of enduring value should the child be guided to discover? And should this decision be colored by considerations of age, ability, ethnicity, etc? Most would agree with Bruner (1969) that knowledge in the form of "lithe and beautiful and immensely generative" ideas should form the basis of any curriculum. Immensely generative ideas may be few, and the idea behind education is to point students in the right direction so that they may discover and rediscover these ideas continuously, deepening their understanding in a cyclical fashion (Bruner 1969). It is surely unreasonable to expect students to reinvent such generative ideas for themselves, and it is the teacher who is called upon to orchestrate this discovery process. In this chapter we will focus primarily on ways of assisting discovery learning within rich content areas. We will also describe our attempts to relieve the demands on the official guide, the teacher, by introducing expertise into the system through drawing on a wider community of learners.

Brief History of the Project

The project that we currently refer to as the "Community of Learners" program, for want of a better name, has its historical roots not in the pedagogy of philosophers such as Dewey, nor in the cyclical reform movements of educational politics (Cuban 1990; Dow 1991), but in the changes that have occurred in psychological learning theory over the last thirty years. Under the auspices of the so-called cognitive revolution, major changes in psychological learning theory took place, changes that had important implications for educational practice.

The cognitive transformation of psychological learning theory led to renewed emphasis on several key ideas. First, although the concept of autodidactic learning (Bateson 1963; Binet 1909; Whitehead 1916) has a long history, it was not until recently that learners have become widely viewed as active constructors of knowledge, rather than passive recipients of others' expertise. Second, the contemporary ideal learner is imbued with powers of introspection, once verboten. We now recognize that one of the most interesting things about human learning is that the learner has knowledge and feelings about it (Tulving and Madigan 1970), sometimes even control of it—metacognition if you will (Brown 1975; Flavell and Wellman 1977). Third, we now recognize that humans, although excellent all-purpose learning machines, equipped to learn just about anything by brute force like all biologically evolved creatures, come predisposed to learn certain things more readily than others (Carey and Gelman 1991).

This concentration on active, strategic learning (Brown 1974), with the learner's understanding and control (Brown 1975, 1978), following domain-specific trajectories (Brown 1982, 1990; Carey and Gelman 1991; Gallistel, Brown, Carey, Gelman and Keil 1991) had a major influence on our research program in particular and on the gradual shift toward studying learning in educational settings in general.

Concomitant with the growing emphasis on active, self-conscious, self-directed learning were far-reaching modifications in what students were required to learn, together with the contexts in which they were asked to learn it. During the 1970s, psychologists began studying the acquisition of expertise within specific domains, gained over long periods of time via concentrated, and often self-motivated, learning (chess for example). More recently, learning theorists became concerned with the acquisition of disciplined bodies of knowledge, characteristic of academic subject areas (e.g., mathematics, science, computer programming, and even social studies). Learning theories had to change to reflect this shift in emphasis (Glaser and Bassok 1989). Furthermore, psychologists began to broaden their scope and consider input from other branches of cognitive science as well as from learning settings outside the laboratory, or even the classroom walls (Heath and McLaughlin, in press; Lave and Wenger 1991).

Reciprocal Teaching

Our original move outside the safe haven of the laboratory into classroom learning began with an extended series of studies of reading comprehension. We introduced a procedure, "reciprocal teaching," that was designed to improve reading in underachieving students (Brown and Palincsar 1982, 1989b; Palincsar and Brown 1984). In a typical reciprocal teaching session each participant in a reading group of approximately six members takes a turn leading a discussion. This "learning leader" begins by asking a question about the core content and ends by summarizing the gist of what has been read. Questioning provokes discussion, and summarizing helps students establish where they are in preparation for tackling a new segment of text. On chosen occasions the leader asks for predictions about future content and attempts to clarify any comprehension problems that might arise. These key activities of questioning, summarizing, clarifying, and predicting provide the repeatable structure necessary to get a discussion going, a structure that can be faded out when students are more experienced in leading and taking part in discussions.

Approximately a decade of research has seen significant changes in reciprocal teaching, as illustrated in table 9.1. We began working one-on-one with children who were reading unconnected passages in laboratory settings (Brown and Palincsar 1982), progressed to studying children "pulled out" in order to work in groups in resource rooms (Palincsar and Brown 1984), then to considering naturally occurring reading groups in the classroom (Brown and Palincsar 1989b), and finally to studying reading comprehension groups that were fully integrated into science classrooms (Brown and Campione 1990; Brown and Palincsar 1989a; Brown, Ash, Rutherford, Nakagawa, Gordon and Campione, in press). We began by concentrating on the few constrained strategies described above but quickly upped the ante by demanding that students describe the gist of entire texts and put their new knowledge to use via analogical extension and problem solving (Brown, Campione, Reeve, Ferrara, and Palincsar 1991). Next, we began modeling and supporting the development of complex explanation, argument, and discussion forms (Brown 1991). Most recently, we have fostered the development of complex reasoning and thought experiments as a method of building new knowledge (Brown et al., in press). Initially we looked at students reading unconnected passages, then proceeded to look at students reading coherent content (Brown

Table 9.1
Evolution of reciprocal teaching (RT)

Context	One-on-one in laboratory settings	Groups in resource rooms	Naturally occurring groups in classrooms	Work groups fully integrated into science classrooms
Activities	Summarizing, questioniong, clarifying, predicting	Gist and analogy	Complex argument structure	Thought experiments
Materials	Unconnected passages	Coherent content	Research-related resources	Student-prepared material
Pattern of use	Individual strategy training	Group discussion	Planned RT for learning content and jigsaw teaching	Opportunistic use of RT
Initiation of activity	Researcher-initiated	Researcher- and teacher-initiated	Teacher initiated with researcher guidance	Initiated by students

et al., 1991; Brown and Palincsar 1989a; Palincsar, Brown, and Campione, 1990). We are now observing reading comprehension as it takes place in social groups reading, discussing, and arguing about cohesive material they have prepared themselves. In our current classrooms students appropriate and adapt reciprocal teaching as a tool to enhance their comprehension. Faced with important material they have difficulty understanding, they call for a reciprocal teaching session to enhance and monitor their learning (Brown et al., in press).

Communities of Learners
In our current work, reciprocal teaching is only one component of a learning community designed to encourage distributed expertise (Brown 1992; Brown et al., in press). In order to foster such a community, we feature students as designers of their own learning: we encourage students to be partially responsible for designing their own curriculum. In addition to reciprocal teaching, we use a greatly modified version of the jigsaw method (Aronson 1978; Brown et al., in press) of cooperative learning. Students are assigned curriculum themes (e.g., changing populations), each divided into approximately five subtopics (e.g., extinct, endangered, artificial, assisted, and urbanized populations). Students form separate research groups, each assigned responsibility for one of the five or so subtopics. These research groups prepare teaching materials using commercially available, stable

computer technology (Campione, Brown and Jay 1992). Then, the students regroup into reciprocal teaching seminars in which each student is expert in one subtopic, holding one-fifth of the information. Each fifth needs to be combined with the remaining fifths to make a whole unit, hence "jigsaw." All children in a learning group are expert on one part of the material, teach it to others, and prepare questions for the test that all will take on the complete unit. It is important to note that all children are finally responsible for mastery of the entire theme, not just their fifth of the material. So the burden of teaching others from expertise is a real one, and a mainstay of these classrooms.

The Ideal Classroom

Working with a group of teachers, and with students at different grade levels[1], we have evolved a view of the essential features that characterize our ideal classroom environment. Because all new teachers are involved from the outset in the organic growth of their versions of the program, versions compatible with our underlying learning principles and their own practices, there is considerable variability in different classes. But there is also constancy at the level of underlying principles. Together with the teachers we have settled on several characteristics of successful classrooms that must be operating for the program to be judged in place. These essential characteristics are

Individual Responsibility Coupled with Communal Sharing.   Students and teachers each have "ownership" of certain forms of expertise, but no one has it all. Responsible members of the community share the expertise they have or take responsibility for finding out about needed knowledge. Through a variety of interactive formats, the groups uncover and delineate aspects of knowledge "possessed" by no one individual. Expertise is distributed deliberately through the jigsaw and reciprocal teaching collaborative learning activities that ensure students learn complementary material and can thus teach from strength.

Expertise is also distributed by happenstance; variability in expertise arises naturally within these classrooms (Brown et al., in press). We refer to this phenomenon as "majoring." Children are free to major in a variety of ways, free to learn and teach whatever they like within the confines of the selected topic. Children select topics of interest to be associated with: some become resident experts on DDT and pesticides; some specialize in disease and contagion; younger children often adopt a particular endangered species (pandas, otters, and whales being popular). Within the community of the classroom, these varieties of expertise are implicitly recognized, although not the subject of much talk.

Subcultures of expertise develop: varieties of expertise are recognized by the pattern of help seeking and the role students assume in small and whole class discussions. In these discussions, the class defers to expert children in both verbal and nonverbal ways. Status in discussions does not reside "in" the individual child, however, as in the case of established leaders and followers, but is a transient phenomenon that depends on a child's perceived expertise within the domain of discourse. As the domain of discourse changes, so, too, do the students receiving deferential treatment.

It is very much our intention to *increase diversity* in these classrooms. Traditional school practices have aimed at just the opposite, decreasing diversity, a traditional practice based on several assumptions: that there exist prototypical, normal students, that, at a certain age, they can do a certain amount of work or grasp a certain amount of material, and that they can do so in the same amount of time (Becker 1972). Now these are strong assumptions! They must serve a powerful administrative function (Cuban 1984), for there is little that we know about learning and development that would support them. So although we must aim at conformity on the basics, everyone must read eventually, we must also aim at increasing diversity of expertise and interests so that members of the community can benefit from the increasing richness of knowledge available. The essence of teamwork is pooling varieties of expertise. Teams composed of members with homogeneous ideas and skills are denied access to such diversity.

Ritual, Familiar Participant Structures.   Principal participation frameworks (Goodwin 1987) are few and are practiced repeatedly. One common classroom routine is for the students to be divided into three groups, one composing on the computers, one conducting research via a variety of media, and the last (the remaining children) interacting with the teacher in some way: editing manuscripts, discussing progress, or receiving some other form of teacher attention. A second repetitive frame is for the class to engage in reciprocal teaching research seminars or jigsaw teaching activities, with approximately five research/teaching groups in simultaneous sessions. Another activity, "crosstalk," was introduced by the students. In crosstalk, students from the various research groups periodically report in about their progress to date, and students from other working groups ask questions of clarification or extension. The various groups thereby talk "across groups" and provide comprehension checks to each other. And the final activity features the classroom teacher, or an outside expert, conducting a benchmark lesson, modeling thinking skills and self-reflection, introducing new information, stressing higher-order relationships or encouraging the class to pool their expertise in a novel conceptualization of the topic. The repetitive, indeed, ritualistic nature of these activities is an essential aspect of the classroom, for it enables children to make the transition from one participant structure (Erickson and Shultz 1977) to another quickly and effortlessly. As soon as students recognize a participant structure, they understand the role expected of them. Thus, although there is room for individual agendas and discovery in these classrooms, they are highly structured to permit students and teachers to navigate between repetitive activities as effortlessly as possible.

A Community of Discourse. It is essential that a community of discourse (Fish 1980) be established early in which constructive discussion, questioning, and criticism are the mode rather than the exception. Speech activities involving increasingly scientific modes of thinking, such as conjecture, speculation, evidence, and proof become part of the common voice of the community; conjecture and proofs are themselves open to negotiation in multiple ways (Bloor 1991) as the elements that compose them, such as terms and definitions, are renegotiated continuously. Successful enculturation into the community leads participants to recognize the difference between, and the appropriate place of, everyday versions of speech activities having to do with the physical and natural world and the discipline-embedded special versions of these activities (O'Connor 1991).

Multiple Zones of Proximal Development. Theoretically, we conceive of the classroom as comprised of multiple zones of proximal development (Vygotsky 1978) through which participants can navigate via different routes and at different rates (Brown and Reeve 1987). A zone of proximal development can include people, adults and children with varying expertise, but it can also include artifacts such as books, videos, wall displays, scientific equipment, and a computer environment intended to support intentional learning (Scardamalia and Bereiter 1991). The zone of proximal development defines the distance between current levels of comprehension and levels that can be accomplished in collaboration with other people or powerful artifacts. It embodies a concept of readiness to learn that emphasizes upper, rather than lower, levels of competence, boundaries that are not immutable, but rather constantly changing as the learner becomes increasingly independent at successively more advanced levels.

Seeding, Migration, and Appropriation of Ideas. In our classroom, teachers and students create zones of proximal development by *seeding* the environment with ideas and concepts they value and by harvesting those which "take" in the community. Ideas seeded by community members *migrate* to other participants and persist over time. Participants in the classroom are free to *appropriate* vocabulary, ideas, methods, etc., that appear initially as part of the shared discourse, and by appropriation, transform these ideas via personal interpretation. Ideas that are part of the common discourse are not necessarily appropriated by all, or in the same manner by everyone. Because the appropriation of ideas and activities is multidirectional, we use the term *mutual appropriation* (Moschkovich 1989; Newman, Griffin and Cole 1989; Schoenfeld, Smith and Arcavi, in press).

Mutual appropriation refers to the bidirectional nature of the appropriation process, one that should not be viewed as limited to the process by which the child (novice) learns from the adult (expert) via a static process of imitation, internalizing observed behaviors in an untransformed manner. Rather, learners of all ages and levels of expertise and interests seed the environment with ideas and knowledge that are appropriated by different learners at different rates, according to their needs and to the current state of the zones of proximal development in which they are engaged.

The Nature of the Curriculum

The Intended Curriculum

Although there is considerable room for discovery and individual majoring in these classrooms, we intentionally engineer the curriculum in certain ways. The teacher's role here is complex. Teachers must see that curriculum content is "discovered," understood, and transmitted efficiently and at the same time she must recognize and encourage students' independent majoring attempts. But what is the place of a set curriculum in discovery classrooms? True, it would be possible to allow the students to discover on their own, charting their own course of studies, exploring at will, but, in order to be responsive to the course requirements of normal schools, we believe it necessary to set bounds on the curriculum to be covered. In general, our approach is to select enduring themes for discussion and to revisit them often, each time at an increasingly mature level of understanding. For example, in biology we concentrate on interdependence and adaptation.

Changes in the curriculum occur over time because individual participating teachers help to design the actual expression of the main units, and the students themselves are allowed some freedom to nominate subunits for study, subunits constrained by a given theme. For example, the classroom teacher and the resident biologist select a unit theme, such as endangered species. The class meets for whole class sessions where they discuss what they already know and what they

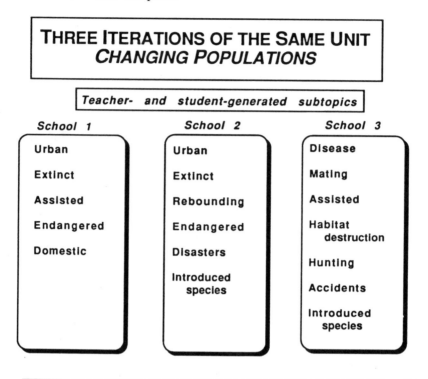

Figure 9.1
Changes in the curriculum of three sixth-grade classes (top) and two seventh-grade classes (bottom) as the result of teacher and student interests

want to find out. Questions thus generated are written on Post-its[TM], and placed on a bulletin board. Students then browse through a few highly selected books and generate more questions. Finally, the questions are grouped into subthemes and identified as the subunits. Thus, although there is a great deal of similarity across groups in the subunits, students feel ownership and volunteerism in what they select for study. The top half of figure 9.1 shows the variation in subthemes that three separate sixth grade classes helped generate under the unit, changing populations.

Similarly, teachers differed in how they orchestrated the study of units, partially in response to their own preferences and partially in response to student interest. The bottom half of figure 9.1 shows two different approaches to studying the food chain. In one case the focus was on mechanism; in the other on habitats and ecosystems. In the "Mechanism as Topic" class, students were led to consider different habitats as they concentrated on photosynthesis and energy exchange. Correspondingly, in the "Mechanism Folded In" class, those specializing in individual habitats were led to consider the basic mechanisms (photosynthesis, energy exchange, etc.) as they endeavored to understand their habitats (Ash and Brown 1993).

Under the general umbrella of the themes and subunits, students are introduced to some critical underlying notions. Grade school children become increasingly interested in cross-cutting themes that would form the basis of an understanding of such principles as metabolic rate, reproduction strategies, and hibernation as a survival strategy, although at a very elementary level. For example, a member of a group studying elephants became fixated on the amount of food consumed by his animal and subsequently by other animals studied in the classroom, notably the panda and the sea otter. Although relatively small, the sea otter consumes vast quantities of food because "it doesn't have blubber, and living in a cold sea, it needs food for energy to keep warm." When an adult observer mentioned the similar case of the hummingbird's need for a great deal of food, this student caught on to something akin to the notion of metabolic rate, a concept he introduced in all subsequent discussions. The notion of metabolic rate, seeded by one student, quickly migrated throughout the classroom, was appropriated by many, came to form part of the common discourse, and eventually made its way into the class book on endangered species.

As a further example, a group of girls studying whales became interested in fertility rates and the fate of low-birth-weight babies. They discovered that one reason that certain species of whales are endangered is that their reproduction rate has slowed dramatically.

The same was found to be true of sea otters. These students introduced the concept of declining fertility rates into the discussion, and it was taken up in the common discourse in two forms: simply, as the notion of the number of babies a species had, and more complexly, as the notion of reproductive strategies in general. The skilled teacher appropriates students' spontaneous interest in the common problems of endangered animals—amount of food eaten, amount of land required, number of young, and so on—and encourages them to consider the deeper general principles of metabolic rate, and survival and reproductive strategies.

The Unintended Curriculum

Because students are free to direct their research efforts broadly, each group of students develops an idiosyncratic set of concerns in which they choose to major. We will trace one set of issues that occupied a mixed fifth and sixth grade class (1992–93) for an entire semester: the spread of disease by mosquitoes.

The entry activity for a unit on endangered species, the anchoring events if you will (Bransford, Sherwood, Hasselbring, Kinzer, and Williams 1990), was a whole-class treatment of two pieces of literature: an expository text, "Saving the Peregrine Falcon" by Caroline Arnold, and a play, "The Day They Parachuted Cats into Borneo" by Charlotte Pomerantz. The students used reciprocal teaching to help them understand the endangered status of the peregrine falcon and the role of DDT in contributing to it. Simultaneously, we capitalized on the students' skills of dramatic play and art by having them enact and illustrate the play—which essentially describes the disruption in a food chain brought about by the introduction of DDT to eradicate mosquitoes. Through sociodramatic play (Heath 1991), the students were led to consider a biological theme that required deep understanding.

Shortly after these activities, an important idea was seeded by a student on "parents' night," a meeting where the students introduced their parents to the participant structures of the project. Students were, in effect, the teachers, while the adults were the students. The discussion centered around the use of DDT and other chemicals in combating malaria. One extremely confident student teacher informed the group that, like malaria, AIDS can be spread by mosquitoes. No one in the group argued with this statement. One of the authors (Brown), also in the group, then attempted to squash this spread of misinformation by arguing that this was not so. Challenged for her evidence by the student, she could manage only a feeble, "I saw it on television," the type of evidence justifiably impermissible in these classrooms. In the ensuing discussion, the child theorist clearly won the day by recourse to analogy and theory, "It's the same as with needles, infected blood gets into the needles and then spreads AIDS to another user—mosquitoes bite an infected host and then bite a healthy person—the blood commingles." Even his language was technical and impressive. This young theorist also made recourse to epidemiological data by arguing that the incidence of AIDS is higher in places where there are more mosquitoes, such as Florida and Africa. And to cap his argument, he introduced a little conspiracy theory, namely, that the CIA knows all about this but is repressing the evidence.

The next event followed immediately after parent night. The student theorist and the adult biologist called the San Francisco AIDS Hotline to find out whether, indeed, AIDS could be spread by mosquitoes. As it turns out, this is the third most frequently raised question for the hotline. The hotline operator answered from a crib sheet replete with deep biological terminology that neither the student/teacher interrogators, nor the hotline respondent, fully understood.

The information received from the hotline was as follows (from biologist Doris Ash's field notes):

> AIDS and Malaria are completely different in the way they are transmitted. The malaria *Plasmodium* parasite needs to live in the mosquito in order to complete its life cycle, and it has a very complex life cycle involving two hosts, a human and a mosquito. This is *not* true of AIDS.
>
> Where arthropod vectors (carriers, such as mosquitoes, ticks, fleas, etc.) are concerned, the parasite that causes the disease needs to both increase its numbers within the vector and also exit from it efficiently. This is true for malaria, but it is not true for the AIDS virus.
>
> With malaria, the parasites multiply, then concentrate in the salivary glands. When the mosquito injects the next victim, the parasites pass into the victim's blood. No such model exists for AIDS.
>
> During the decade that AIDS has been multiplying in the USA, researchers have been unable to locate multiplying HIV in mosquitoes and other anthropods, nor have they observed the virus in a place where they can exit the arthropod host.
>
> It should be noted that the mosquito does not inject blood into humans; it only sucks blood out of them. It does inject fluid from its salivary glands. Since the *Plasmodium* lives throughout the mosquito digestive system and migrates to the salivary glands, the *Plasmodium* parasite is injected into humans by carrier mosquitoes. To date, no animal intermediary has been identified with AIDS transmission.

Table 9.2
Seeding, migration, and appropriation of biological topics over a semester of student-directed inquiry

Student questions:	Bring up issue(s)
Do large amounts of DDT depress immune function?	Immunity and resistance.
If a human has malaria, can it be transmitted?—Can a baby get it inside the body?	Holoendemic areas vs. areas of new infection. Areas of endemic disease = high immunity. Immunity passed on to fetus. If first time infection, fetus at high risk.
What about babies outside the body?	After initial six month immunity, children 1–4 at high risk. Some children survive repeated bouts and develop immunity. The notion of vaccination.
In places in Africa with lots of malaria, is there more AIDS?	Epidemiological question: Answer is no.
Does plasmodium need mosquitoes to reproduce?	Transmission mechanism.
Does AIDS need mosquitoes?	Answer is no.
If they eat warm blood, why aren't they warm-blooded? This is a clarification question. How does plasmodium adapt to warm blood? Do mosquitoes have cold or warm blood?	Warm- vs. cold-bloodedness
Mosquito sucks blood out, spits saliva in?	Factors about blood clotting.
Does plasmodium go into the placenta?	Transmission mechanism.
If a child has it, and it grows, does the malaria get stronger and stronger?	Biological magnification.
If a mother breast feeds baby, can it get it?	Low possibility of AIDS spread through beast milk.
Do mosquitoes pass malaria on to young, or are they born with it? What started it?	Chicken/egg problem. Malaria around since recorded history.
Why didn't ice age kill it, like dinosaurs?	Mutation, drug-resistant strains.
In Kenya, people who have sickle-cell anemia don't get malaria as much?	Discussion of sickle-cell anemia as a protective factor.
Red blood cells are usually round. If you have sickling, your blood cells are like a sickle.	Sickle cell anemia. Red blood cells. Hemoglobin.
How do you get sickle cell?	Genetic transmission, recessive genes.

Table 9.2 (continued)

We heard that plasmodium eats what is called hemo . . . hemoglobin. What's hemoglobin?	Discussion of hemoglobin. Oxygen lack. Fever. Weakening. Shape of blood cells.
Ravaged blood cells clog the capillaries, deprive the brain of oxygen?	Brain/oxygen relation.
Why do babies die within a few hours of getting it?	Blood/oxygen/brain relations.
How do you get sickle cell? Is it in genes?	Genetic transmission. Genetic counseling. Genes, Nucleus, etc. Beginnings of DNA and gene altering.

Experiments with mosquitoes ingesting blood containing HIV indicate that they are not carriers, and epidemiological studies of AIDS-infected areas with mosquitoes do not indicate higher rates of AIDS than AIDS-infected areas without mosquitoes. If mosquitoes carried AIDS, for example, African children would have it in the same proportion as adults, but this is not the case. Since these children play outside and receive repeated bites, they would be expected to have AIDS if mosquitoes were carriers. However, this is not the case. In areas where there are both mosquitoes and AIDS, the incidence of AIDS is lower in children and adults over 60.

AIDS is transmitted most easily through direct transfer of blood or via vaginal and seminal body fluids. It is least likely to be spread via saliva. A human would need a large quantity of infected saliva in order to be in danger of transmission. To date, there are no proven cases of AIDS transmission via saliva.
[Distillation of AIDS Hotline information, from Ash and Brown 1993, and work in progress]

Complex ideas indeed, but this was the starting point that fueled a semester of sustained inquiry, highlights of which are featured in table 9.2.

We do not have space to detail the natural history of these ideas in the conventional way. Small-group and whole-group discussions, written documents, and so forth are too extensive for inclusive. Instead in table 9.2, we trace the student questions (in approximately verbatim form) and the biological issues that the questions led them to discuss. These are but a few of the questions raised by students in their search for deeper understanding of an issue of general concern, the spread of AIDS.

The discussion of sickle-cell anemia was introduced by a student knowledgeable about the topic, as she had sickle-cell anemia herself.

> S1: How do you get it?
>
> S2: Sometimes it's in the genes. My mother gave it to me.
>
> S3: Like if you kiss her?
>
> S4: No, it's like in your genes, like you great grandmother could have had it. Like you were in your mother's womb, you would have gotten it.
>
> S2: No, before that, in the genes.
>
> S4: What are genes?
>
> S6: Like what is in the blood. Like N.'s parents are really tall, so she is really tall. My mother has brown hair, so I have brown hair.
>
> S7: Genes are little things that are inside the nucleus which controls the cell. It depends—like what kind of cell it is and how it responds. Nucleus is like a little brain. Genes live inside the nucleus when the sperm and egg are forming one cell—then they reproduce the genes [pause] we better look this up again to get clear.

The discussion on the role of hemoglobin was motivated by both the sickle-cell anemia discussion and by a Newsweek article, "The Endless Plague" (January 11, 1993), brought in by a student. The biologist reported that in twenty years of teaching at all levels including college, this was the first time she had taught about hemoglobin to students who had a reason for wanting to know!

Success of the Program

Knowledge Building
We will concentrate first on the acquisition of biological knowledge. In short, did the students learn anything? And how would we know if they did? We use an extensive battery of static and dynamic pretest and posttest measures as well as on-line indices of conceptual change. We augment pretest and posttest scores by the use of portfolios and student products. The database is extremely rich, and we will concentrate in this chapter on the more traditional pretest/posttest tasks and extension activities of knowledge utilization.

All students receive short-answer quizzes on the entire theme before and after each unit. Half of the items are generated by the student

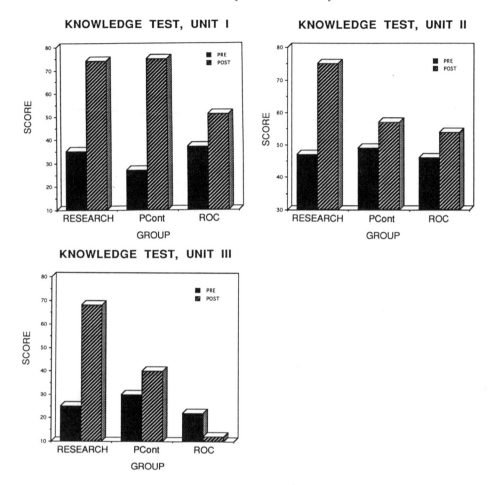

Figure 9.2
Results of unit content knowledge tests in a fifth and sixth grade full-year intervention.
PCont = partial control group, who were students in the first semester (unit 1), then
taught by their regular classroom teacher. ROC = a read-only control group that read
the key materials but did not research.

research teams and half by our staff. The results of short-answer
quizzes for one full-year intervention with fifth and sixth graders are
shown in figure 9.2. Students in the research classes were compared
with those in a partial control group (PCont) treated exactly the same
as the research classes for the first semester (unit 1), and then taught
environmental science by their regular science teacher. The partial
control group had exactly the same access to books, videos, computers,
and so forth, as the research classes. As figure 9.2 shows, the two

groups did not differ from each other on unit 1, where they were, in effect, both research groups, treated exactly the same; but the children in the research classrooms outperformed the partial control group on both units 2 and 3. A read-only control (ROC) group, who read the key materials but did no research performed poorly throughout. These "quick assessments" given to all students assure us that domain-specific content is retained better by students in the research classrooms.

Clinical Interview.   The next question is, can the students use the information flexibly? Students differ in their level of understanding and in the confidence with which they hold opinions. To test this we have developed a clinical interview (Ash and Brown 1993) consisting of a series of questions designed to be sensitive to the bandwidth of competence within which each individual student can navigate (Brown and Reeve 1987). To map the window of opportunity for learning, the interviewer raises a series of key questions, first eliciting basic expository information—for example, what does the student know about the food chain? If the student cannot answer, the interviewer provides hints and examples as necessary to test the student's readiness to learn that concept. If however, the student seems initially knowledgeable, the interviewer questions the stability of that understanding by introducing counterexamples to the student's beliefs ("Is a mushroom a plant?" "What about yeast?") and, if appropriate, asks the student to engage in thought experiments that demand novel uses of the information. For example, a student who has sorted pictures into herbivores and carnivores, and justified the choices, may be asked, "What would happen on the African plain if there were no gazelles or other meat for cheetahs to eat? Could they eat grain?" Some students are surprisingly uncertain about this, suggesting that cheetahs could eat grain under certain circumstances, although they would not live happily. Some even entertain a critical-period hypothesis—that the cheetah could change if it were forced to eat grain from infancy, but once it reached adolescence, it would be too set in its ways to change. Only a few invoked notions of form and function, such as properties of the digestive tract, to support the assertion that cheetahs could not change within their lifespan. In figure 9.3 we see one student's pre- and posttest attempts to negotiate such a thought experiment. These extension activities of thought experiments and counterexamples are far more revealing of the current state of students' knowledge than their first unchallenged answers.

Critical Thinking about Content.   We see the same benefit of being in the research classroom on novel application questions, such as "Design an animal to fit the following habitat" (desert, tundra, or rain forest)

THOUGHT EXPERIMENT

Question: Could a cheetah change from a meat diet to a vegetable diet and survive?

<u>First interview</u>

S: . . . well I mean if people can, like, are vegetarians, I mean I think a cheetah could change . . .

When asked how this might happen:

S: Well . . . just to switch off, but um, it would be easier for them to change on to plants than it would be for me; if I had been eating meat . . . because there would still be meat around for me to eat, but for them there wouldn't be . . . so if they wanted to survive, they're going to have to eat grass.

When asked if it would be easier for a baby cheetah to eat grass:

S: Well, if it was a baby, it would be easier because it could eat it . . . it would be right there, it would just have to walk a little bit to get it . . .

<u>Six months later</u>

S: No. No, their digestive systems isn't good enough . . . it's too uncomplicated to digest grasses and also their teeth wouldn't be able to chew, so then the grass would overpopulate . . . and the cheetah dies.

When asked if the baby cheetah could survive by eating grass, the student asserted that they would probably be the first to die.

Thrown a novel twist on the old question -- whether the gazelle might be able to eat meat if there were no longer grass, the newly confident student favored the interviewer with a broad smile and said:

S: Nice try . . . the digestive track of the deer is too complicated and also the teeth wouldn't be able to grind meat.

Figure 9.3
Thought experiment from a sixth grader showing changes in reasoning

or "Design an animal of the future." The sixth graders in the research classroom outperform control students in the number of biologically appropriate mechanisms they include in their designs (such as mechanisms of defense, reproductive strategies, etc.). Over time the research students introduce more novel variations of taught principles along with more truly novel ideas as can be seen in figure 9.4. For example, the class had discussed the notion of mimicry as a defense mechanism. In a response-scored taught/novel, one student said that the eggs of his animal were placed in a line and the markings made the eggs look like a "full grown cobra," a novel use of the mimicry principle. Another student incorporated the notion of behavioral mimicry that had

**Use of Biological Principles: Habitat Task
Design an Animal Version (6th Grade)**

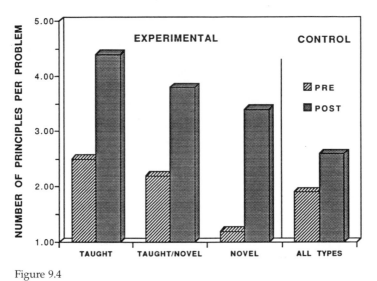

Figure 9.4
Pre- and posttest scores on a transfer test: Design an animal to fit a habitat

not been taught, still another introduced the concept of a predator's injecting a poison to which it was itself immune, so that the predator could safely devour the stunned prey.

Responses to clinical interviews, "what if" thought experiments, and analogy and transfer tests tell us a great deal about the status of the child's accumulating knowledge and ability to reason on the basis of incomplete knowledge. We regard them as fruitful avenues for promoting and evaluating students' ability to think critically about knowledge, an antidote to the stockpiling of passive, inert knowledge (White head 1916).

Reading
Although billed as a science curriculum, the program of research is very much an extension of the original reading comprehension work that began with reciprocal teaching (Palincsar and Brown 1984). Our main "transfer" data, therefore, take the form of: (1) improvement in students' reading comprehension scores on materials outside the domain of study and (2) gradual acquisition of increasingly complex

Comprehension Measures

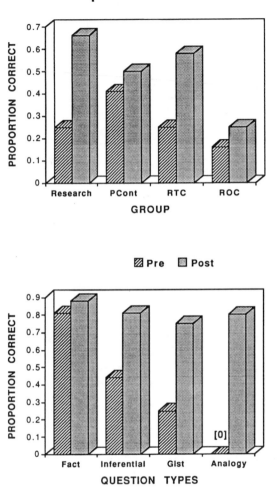

Figure 9.5
Reading comprehension measure in domain outside biology. PCont = partial control group as in figure 9.2. RTC = a reciprocal teaching control group. ROC = read-only control.

forms of argumentation and explanation strategies. We will limit ourselves here to a few representative samples.

We begin with an example of fifth and sixth graders' performance on criterion-referenced tests of reading comprehension. The data are from a full-year study, where we worked with approximately ninety students (Brown and Campione 1990). At the beginning and end of the year, students read age-appropriate expository passages unrelated to the curriculum and answered a set of questions from memory. These data are shown in the top half of figure 9.5. Students in the research classroom outperformed a comparison group reading the same passages via reciprocal teaching, even though the reciprocal teaching control group, (RTC) was given at least twice as much practice in the collaborative reading procedures and in taking tests of this nature. A read-only control (ROC) failed to show improvement. We also included a partial control group (Pcont) consisting of sixth graders who were treated the same as the experimental group for the first semester but taught by their regular classroom teacher after that. They also failed to achieve the same gains.

On each passage students were asked four fact and four inferential questions, together with a gist question requiring them to summarize the main theme of the entire passage, and an analogy question where they were asked to solve a problem analogous to the problem solved in the target passage. The bottom half of figure 9.5 shows the differential improvement according to question type for the research students (we include data from only those students tackling grade-appropriate texts). By design, students began scoring well on simple fact-based questions (to ensure that they achieved some success); as a result, there was no improvement on this measure. On inferential, gist, and analogy questions, however, there was significant improvement. In particular, regular practice greatly improved the students' ability to use analogous information to solve problems; that is, practice creates a mind-set to reason by analogy (Brown and Kane 1988).

Argumentation Skills.   Increasingly powerful comprehension-extending activities occurred in the student dialogues, such as those shown in table 9.3. The use of deep analogies and causal explanations increased over time. Explanations were more often supported by warrants and backings (Toulmin 1958). The nature of what constitutes evidence was discussed, including a consideration of negative evidence. A variety of plausible reasoning strategies (Collins and Stevens 1982) began to emerge. Argumentation formats developed, in which different points of view and defensible interpretations were compared. The nature and importance of prediction evolved, with students going beyond predictions of simple outcomes to considering possible worlds and engaging in thought experiments about them.

During the year, students progressed from using surface similarities (simple) to a reliance on deep analogies (advanced). For example, children initially make surface analogies, such as between human eyes

Table 9.3
Discourse activities

Analogy:

To note recurrent theme
To explain mechanism

Causal explanation:

Impasse driven
Resolving inconsistencies
For deeper understanding of mechanism

Explanation and evidence:

Claims and premises
Warrants and backings
Negative evidence

Argumentation:

Different points of view
Different interpretation

Predictions:

Of possible outcomes
Of possible worlds
Of perturbations in the system
Tought experiments—What if? Imagine that, etc.
Plausible reasoning

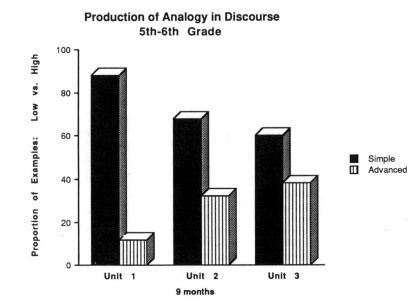

Figure 9.6
Production of analogy in the discourse

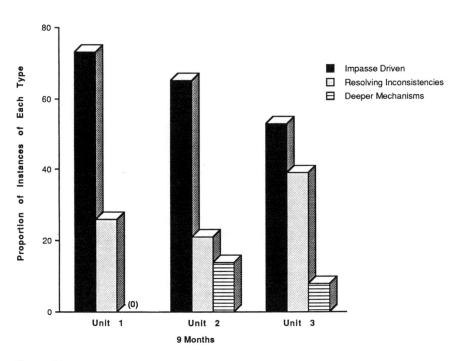

Explanations

Figure 9.7
Condition of production of explanations in the spontaneous discussion

and the headlights of a car (surface), while later they make the analogy between a car's engine and the human heart (deep). With increasing knowledge, children progress from accepting superficial analogy to using deep analogy to explain mechanisms. They question initially acceptable surface analogies (such as "plant stems are like straws"), then come to prefer analogies based on deeper understanding of the underlying biological mechanisms ("Plants are food factories"). This progression is shown in figure 9.6; over time, students make more effective use of analogy in their discussions. They use increasingly advanced analogies, both to help them learn new material and to communicate their new understanding to others.

There was a similar development in students' recourse to, and use of, causal explanations, where they go beyond specific facts and set out to understand relations among facts through attempting to explain the relevant mechanisms. As shown in figure 9.7, in the first unit of the year, students attempted to generate explanations when faced with an impasse or a breakdown in comprehension, that is, they sought an explanation in response to a comprehension failure. Later, students resorted to explanations in attempts to resolve inconsistencies. Finally, students used explanation spontaneously, in the absence of comprehension failure or obvious inconsistencies, as they continually revised and deepened their understanding of complex causal mechanisms (Brown 1991).

Extending the Learning Community

Inside the School

In order for the program to run optimally, adults are needed to lead jigsaw and reciprocal teaching seminars, but of course having a large number of adults available to serve this function is just not feasible. We try to conduct the intervention in such a way that dissemination across schools would be possible. As a rule of thumb, we have no more than two adults, the equivalent of a teacher and an aide, interacting with the children. Other adults in the classroom serve purely observational or data-collection roles.

For these reasons we rely heavily on the expertise of the children themselves. We use cross-age tutoring, both face-to-face and via electronic mail, and we also use older students as discussion leaders guiding the reciprocal teaching groups of younger students.

Cross-age Training.   Cross-age tutoring provides students invaluable opportunities to talk about learning. Cazden (1988) argues that there are four specific benefits of discourse among peers. First, peer discourse may act as a catalyst to other ideas. Talking with other students provides access to a variety of thoughts and perspectives. Second, peer discourse may allow students to adopt complementary roles so that when working together, they may draw on each other's strengths. Third, peer discourse gives practice in building a relationship with an audience. Students learn to question each other and make ideas clear to others through peer talk. Finally, peer discourse grants the opportunity for "exploratory talk," as opposed to producing "fully intact" thoughts. Bruner (1972) suggests that the higher goal of tutoring is the "building of community," where both the tutor and tutee get a "better sense of what it is to share." Peer and cross-age tutoring give students responsibility and purpose, and reinforce collaborative structures throughout the school.

Our cross-age tutoring program (Nakagawa and Brown, work in progress) involves fifth and sixth grade students working with second and third graders. The tutors receive a four-week training program.

The class discusses questioning, listening, relating personal experiences to text, and so on. In addition, the experienced fifth and sixth graders are reminded of: (a) reciprocal teaching procedures; (b) guided writing using computers; (c) pair editing; and (d) the content area of interest to both ages (note that both older and younger students focus on endangered species in their environmental science units). Finally, the older students are introduced to the rudiments of ethnographic methods—what to look for, field notes, interviewing tutees, and so forth (Heath and Mangiola 1991).

We intend to extend our work on cross-age collaboration by instituting a "one room schoolhouse" series in which students will be

Table 9.4
Cross-age tutoring (first session together; 31-page transcript)

Cast:

Fl	Fifth grade facilitator
Cr, Ke, Je, Da	Third grade returning students
Ri Ne, Tr	Third graders new to program

Tr Presents (p. 22 of transcript)

[Tells group of her urban wildlife: monkey flower and wild carrot Questioning begins]

Je: When the uhm, when the monkey flower dies, does it turn all brown and all the feathers come off? I mean, you know, the leaves. Whatever it is.

Tr: It limps. It goes like that [body movement of limp plant].

Ri: What does it eat?

Tr: Water. It eats water and, this is how you make its food. With air, sunlight and water.

Ri: What does the wild carrot eat?

Tr: It eats the same thing, and it can eat dirt too. That's what it eats—

Ke: Does you animal, I mean plant, need the ah, ah, the soil? Does it need soil?

Ne: Water.

Tr: [Calls on fifth grade facilitator, who has her hand up] Fl.

Fl: Plants don't eat soil. They don't eat soil at all. There was this experiment that was—

Je: Soil is dirt. That's where they growing.

Fl: They just grow in it, but they don't eat it. They make their own food. You know how, like how the carbon dioxide and everything, they mix that in, and that act is called photosynthesis. So they don't—

Tr: How do you spell that?

[Fl writes the word on paper, gives to Tr who copies it into her field notes]

Fl: For one thing, there was an experiment—a gallon, I think about five gallons of soil was put under a redwood tree that started growing, and as soon as it was real, real tall, the scientist took the barrel of soil away, and found out that only about two ounces were taken away. Only about two ounces were all.

Tr: It doesn't need the earth for food? It makes its own?

---

grouped together because of common research interests, rather than age, for several periods a week. All students interested in, say, urban wildlife, will meet as a club, all those working on rainforest destruction will be in another room, and so forth.

Students as Discussion Leaders.   We also train our older students to act as discussion leaders. Although we experience some of the same difficulties with students as with adult teachers, notably the tendency to be too directive, fifth and sixth graders are remarkably facile at leading discussions. They mimic activities modeled by their own adult teachers and enact them with their young charges. Again, children themselves introduced both examples of thinking activities and content area knowledge into the wider community. An example of this can be seen in table 9.4, where a fifth grader tries to dispel the common notion in her second graders that plants eat soil as food.

Guest Teachers.   As we work primarily with grade school teachers who are not subject-area specialists, we provide additional support in the form of outside subject-area experts who interact with the teachers and students, either in person or electronically. In table 9.5, an outside expert, a biologist, begins her second benchmark lesson by modeling thinking and research skills, and introducing biological ideas and terminology. In response to the student question, the teacher not only introduces the term *sexual dimorphism* but also points out that she has been thinking about the problem all week (2,5). The exact answer is not in the books she has, and she invites the students to join her in a thought experiment about how a biologist might reason this through (5,6). In utterance 6 she explicitly poses a thinking challenge and introduces the notion of advantages and disadvantages of a species adaptation. In utterance 16 she entertains a students' erroneous suggestion that the larger size of the female might allow her to have more eggs, a suggestion that is rejected by a student (17) by recourse to negative evidence.

Two weeks later they return to the topic; excerpts of the hour-long discussion are shown in table 9.6. Again, while accepting a student's correct solution (2), the teacher talks about her own thought process (3) and directs them to a crucial part of their readings (4) illustrating the notion of competitive advantage that the students understand.

A final example of teacher modeling that formed part of the third benchmark is what to do when there is disagreement:

> *Jo:* Do the peregrine falcons eat any other kind of prey besides birds?
>
> *Lav:* They eat prey, but I mean they eat, like meat.

Table 9.5
Discussion from second Benchmark lesson

(1)	*R:*	There's this one topic that I really want to find out about, is why female peregrine falcons are larger than males.
(2)	*T:*	I know that question has been on your mind; you've mentioned it three different times. It's been on my mind since Tuesday. Do you know the first thing I did when I got home? I got all my biology books out, and the topic I looked up is sexual dimorphism. I have my biology hat on. Right now I'm talking as a biologist. And I'm going to use some biological terms. Sexual has to do with male and female, right? "Di" means two. "Morph" has to do with how you look. It really means form.
(3)	*T:*	What's the question? The question was, R?
(4)	*R:*	Why are the female peregrine falcons larger than the males?
(5)	*T:*	I said OK, the male and female, having two looks, male and female. In my books do you know what they said? They said usually the male bird is more gorgeous and has better feathers and is red and blue. And the female is kind of drab. Drab means kind of dull looking. I said, "Huhh?" That's true right, but that's not the peregrine falcon. In your RT texts, it specifically said they look pretty much the same. Right? And the female is bigger. So we're not talking about pretty males and drab females are we? But the books said this: when you have pretty males and drab females, usually the male does not help take care of the babies. Hint. And I said that probably tells me that the male peregrine helps take care of the baby because he looks like the female. So then I said, "T, you're a biologist. How would a biologist think this problem through? Let's think like a biologist."

[Students make suggestions, mimic putting on biologist hats]

(6)	*T:*	Now here's a new thinking challenge for you. We need to think what is the advantage, the pros, of being bigger, and what are the disadvantages, the cons. The pros and cons. And in the biological world you add those pros and cons up, and usually you weigh them. Let's think about some advantages and disadvantages. And here is where we are all on the same ground I couldn't find it in a book, and I'm asking [student teachers] to help me because none of my books said anything about it. Really think, think, think. What might be an advantage of being bigger if you were a female peregrine falcon? Forget the male for now.
(7)	*El:*	She can scare people away because she's bigger.
(8)	*T:*	Scare away predators. Can I use that word? Is that OK, El?
(9)	*El:*	Yeah.
(10)	*N:*	She can keep the babies warmer?
(11)	*R:*	Protect her babies.
(12)	*T:*	What's a disadvantage? El?
(13)	*El:*	Oh, DDT has a better chance of hitting her because she is wider.
(14)	*Al:*	Well, if the female has DDT how is it going to have babies? La.
(15)	*La:*	This is an advantage because if she is bigger therefore she can produce more babies because she has enough womb to make a lot more babies than if she was smaller than the male.

Table 9.5 (continued)

(16)	*T:*	What La just said is what I came to, but I don't know if I'm right. In the car this morning I said well, if all things being equal it's OK for the female to be bigger and if she is bigger can't she lay more eggs? If she lays more eggs, can't she have more babies. If she has more babies, isn't she going to survive and be more successful?
(17)	*Ma:*	She's not going to have more babies because look, humans are bigger than peregrines, and they only have one baby, sometimes twins. And what about elephants? They only have one baby every three years. N?

Table 9.6
Two weeks later: Third Benchmark

(1)	*El:*	... like because all birds of prey are called raptors, and a lot of the raptors are bigger than the ... have females that are bigger than the males.
(2)	*Ta:*	Since the female is larger she's able to feed on a larger prey than the male is.
(3)	*T:*	All right now, we are talking about survival, having babies and not dying, and getting food, right? We talked about advantages and disadvantages. That's a big idea. Today, I have another big idea in mind. Our conversation two weeks ago had a lot to do with reproduction and babies and protecting and warm, right? But we all forgot something, including me. So I went home Tuesday night and I thought and thought and thought. Something's missing here.
		[Discussion by students]
(4)	*T:*	All right, let's direct our eyes back to our food chain. [Peregrine falcon food chain designed by students and displayed on board.] Now here's my thought process yesterday. Biologist's hat. I shared this with Ann [ALB] yesterday, and with Stella [classroom teacher] today. Now catch this. What if, because the female is a third larger, in their territory—the place that they live—what if she can take advantage of eating things like ducks and pigeons, which are relatively *large* birds, and the male, because he's a little smaller, maybe he can take advantage of eating relatively *small* birds, how might that give an advantage? Now think this through please. I want some thoughtful processes here. How might this help?
(5)	*Lee:*	Well, it would help them because they could, they could use a smaller place to live, like a territory. Because if the male, if it eats different food from the female, it would be less likely to run short on food. Uhm—
(6)	*Ned:*	It would make it better for them because they would like have, both of them go out and hunt at different times. It's like the female could bring back bigger prey, the male could bring back smaller prey. And they could put it together and have more food.

T: Uh-huh. They eat meat, which is prey—meat. Do they eat any other kinds of animals besides birds? Ned.

Ned: Yes, they eat like squirrels and stuff. And little rodents.

T: Not that I know of, actually. Can you prove that, Ned? That would be good if you could prove that. Because I thought I read that—in your, in the book—that they only eat birds. I thought I read that they *only* eat birds. This is the question. We better have a little question board here. Do they eat anything besides birds? That's important for us to consider, isn't it? Can somebody write that down in their journal please? Ned and I are disagreeing. And I'll try to get some proof, you try to get some proof. All right? Now where could we go to get the proof?

Lav: QuickMail

[Kids list examples of available sources, including outside experts]

Extending Community beyond the Classroom Walls

We turn next to the use of QuickMail to extend the research community beyond the classroom walls, thereby creating richer zones of proximal development for community members. For example, consider the following exchange between a biologist (MJ) and a group of students (Da 4 Girlz). The interaction was initiated by the students, who queried the status of hibernation for incarcerated bears.

> Our major questions are (WHAT HAPPENS TO THE BEARS THAT LIVE IN THE ZOO IF THEY CAN'T HIBERNATE?). DA [the science teacher] said that they don't need to hibernate because they are fed every day. But she said that was only a thought so I am asking you to please help us by giving us all you know and all you can find.

MJ responded with some information; admitting that he didn't really know the answer, he suggested an hypothesis and provided a phone number for the group to find out more information on their own. Throughout the interchange, MJ systematically seeded three pieces of information critical for an understanding of hibernation: the availability of resources, longevity, and warm- vs. cold-bloodedness.

> You probably think about hibernating in the same way as you think about sleeping, but they aren't the same. Bears hibernate in response to the weather conditions and the availability of food. If the conditions are reasonably fair (not too cold) and food is available the bear probably won't hibernate. I don't know, but I hypothesize that during the times when bears would usually

hibernate, bears in captivity are probably a bit slower, still showing signs of their tendency to hibernate at that time of the year.

How could you find out if my hypothesis is true? (Hint: Know-
land Park Zoo, 632-9523)

The topic is then dropped by the group but taken up by one group
member (AM), who is "majoring" in hibernation and wishes to know
about hibernation patterns in insects. She inquires to the network in
general.

I was wondering if you can find out an answer to this question.
The question is does insects hibernate? The reason why we ask
that is because MR [classroom teacher] read a book named Once
There was A Tree. And in it, it said something about the insects
slept in the bark of the tree when winter came. then when spring
came they got up and did what they usually do till winter comes
then they start all over again.

Receiving no response, the student then addresses MJ directly about
the topic. As a gesture of good faith, she begins by offering some facts
of her own before asking for information:

Bears hibernate because what ever they eat is gone during the
winter (like berries) and they can't eat so that's what hibernation
is for. It is for them to get away from starvation. So what does
truantula's eat? Can they always get their food? If they can't get
their food would they have to hibernate or die? Could we ask
somebody that knows about insects?

MJ responds with another prompt to encourage the student to take
the initiative and contact experts, this time at the San Francisco Zoo,
pointing out that the contact person there is ready and willing to help.
The persistent AM sends yet another request, and MJ reenters the fray.
Following a lengthy paragraph on the reproduction and survival
strategies of insects, he continues with a series of questions intended
to push the student to further and further depths of inquiry, a typical
strategy of guides in a zone of proximal development. In this communication, he introduces the notion of longevity, prompting AM to
consider the fact that if an insect lives only one season, hibernation
would not have much survival value for the species!

So you ask . . . what does this have to do with your questions
about hibernation? Consider the difference between the life style
of your typical mammal and that of the typical insect. Why is
hibernation important to some mammals? Why might hibernation not be a successful strategy for most insects? Some insect,

such as tarantula, live for 10 or more years. Do you think that they might hibernate? How might their life style be different from that of other insects.

Resisting this lead, AM again adopts the easier path of asking for direct information. "I'm not really sure if tarantula hibernates. What do you think?" to which MJ again responds with some critical information about warm-bloodedness.

I'm really not sure either. I do know that insects are cold blooded which means that they don't have a constant body temperature. This means that they depend on warmth from the sun or other objects in order to become active (move around and hunt). This happens pretty much every day. As the sun sets and it gets cold and cold blooded animals slow down. But hibernation is something that happens over a greater period of time (over a year rather than a day). Where do you think we could find out more about this question?

The interaction continued for several days. MJ gradually seeds the zone of proximal development with three critical pieces of information during this exchange. AM picks up on two of these features (availability of resources and longevity), although she never understand warm-bloodedness. QuickMail as a medium for sustaining and expanding zones of proximal development has exciting possibilities and is an essential feature of our learning environment, freeing teachers from the burden of sole knowledge guardian and allowing the community to extend beyond the classroom walls.

Strengths and Weaknesses of a Guided-Discovery Classroom

Strengths

Distributed Expertise.   Reliance on the two modes of cooperative learning, reciprocal teaching coupled with jigsaw, ensures that expertise is deliberately distributed across the members of the classroom (Brown et al., in press). In addition, variability in expertise arises opportunistically. The ploy of increasing rather than decreasing diversity and of allowing many "ways in" to full or legitimate peripheral participation (Lave and Wenger 1991) increases the richness of the knowledge base on which the community can draw. Everyone in the community is an expert responsible for sharing his or her expertise with others. Both inside and outside school, students and teachers have access to circles of ever-deepening domain expertise.

Teachers Capitalize on Student Expertise.   Teachers have at their disposal a variety of experts capable of peer and cross-age tutoring. Adult teachers are not the only source of knowledge. Many members of the community are knowledgeable. This knowledge can be harnessed to provide varieties of expertise, thus enriching the learning environment and at the same time providing opportunities for its members to take responsible leadership roles.

Multiple Roles are Modeled and Appropriated.   Because majoring is encouraged, even teachers are free to reveal ignorance of certain topics and to model ways of overcoming that ignorance by consulting outside sources and continuing to develop expertise over sustained periods of time. Children are free to be domain experts, be that in the subject area under study, in the use of technology, or the role of social facilitator.

Actors and Audience.   Everyone in the community is a teacher as well as a learner; everyone is at some stage an actor and an audience. The sense of audience for one's research efforts is an important aspect of the community. Audiences, be they adults or children, demand coherence; they push for higher levels of understanding; they require satisfactory explanations; they request clarification of obscure points. Students do not have to deal with a single audience, the teacher, as they usually do in school; the sense of audience is not imaginary, but palpable and real. Students are forced to teach what they know, and this is often the impetus for learners to recognize gaps in their knowledge that need attention before they take center stage again.

Sustained Complex Thinking.   Students in these learning communities are capable of deep, sustained, complex thinking, both in whole-class discussions and in their small groups. Consider the following example of a group of second graders dealing with the food chain involving a colleague's imaginary animal:

> S1: And, um, since it's the top of the food chain that I told you about, it has no predator, so. The baby ocrawhale has flat teeth when it's born, and two years later it gets sharper teeth so it can eat meat.
>
> S2: What do the little fish eat?
>
> S1: [Impasse] Well, the little fish are the bottom of the food chain, *so they don't have anything to eat.*
>
> S2: Oh! But how do they stay alive?
>
> S1: They probably just survive by their wits.
>
> [Five minutes later they are still puzzling about the sustenance of the fish at the bottom of the food chain]

S4: Yea, They can't live on, they can't live without food, just like we can't.

S1: Um, first the babies in those fish may be about this small.

S4: But, still, they have to eat.

S1: But then they get older and bigger.

S1: Well, first it eats seaweed and then . . .

S4: Well, that's what you should have said at first, because you said it would never eat nothing. [Bell rings]

[The children continue the discussion after class, telephone each other about it (parent report), and S1 agrees to "fix it" in his revision.]

Sloppy thinking is not tolerated by even our youngest community members.

Weaknesses

Limited Knowledge Capital.   Any learning community is limited by the combined knowledge of its members. Classrooms are constrained by four walls. Attempts to expand the knowledge capital of the community by recourse to libraries, field trips, and the like are as old as school itself. But even so, within traditional schools, members draw on a limited knowledge capital if the faculty and students are relatively static, or face jarring discontinuity if there is rapid turnover of personnel. Furthermore, both teachers' and students' expectations concerning excellence, or even what it means to learn and understand, may be limited if the or'y standards are local ones. Methods of extending the community beyond the classroom walls are needed to enrich and challenge the knowledge capital of a learning community.

Teacher Competence.   A major problem with guided discovery is the load placed on the guide, the official teacher. Invoking comfortable metaphors such as the teacher as coach does not tell us how and when the teacher should coach. How can the teacher foster discovery and at the same time furnish guidance?

The role of guide in the discovery process is difficult to maintain. Consider the position for a teacher who knows something that the students do not. Here the teacher is in the position of making a judgment call about whether to intervene or not. The teacher must decide whether the problem centers on an important principle or involves only a trivial error that she can let pass for now. Consider the case of the teacher who does not know the answer, or one who may share the students' puzzlement or misconception. In this case, the teacher is first required to recognize this fact (which the teacher might not be able to do), and, after admitting puzzlement or confusion, find ways to remedy it, for example by seeking help. This is not an easy role for many teachers; it requires them to admit that they do not know and seek help, thereby modeling this important learning strategy for their students.

Teacher as Critical-Thinking Model. In addition to guiding a course through the curriculum content, the teacher should also be a role model for certain forms of inquiry activities. If students are apprentice learners, then the teacher is the master craftsman of learning that they must emulate. In this role, the teacher models scientific inquiry through thought and real experiments. Ideally, children should witness teachers learning, discovering, doing research, reading, writing, and using computers as tools for learning, rather than exclusively lecturing, managing, assigning work, and controlling the classroom.

The teacher's job also includes efforts to model habits of mind by which children are encouraged to adopt, extrapolate, and refine the deep underlying themes to which they are exposed. As Bruner (1969, 126) argues, education

> should be an invitation to generalize, to extrapolate, to make a tentative intuitive leap, even to build a tentative theory. The leap from mere learning to using what one has learned in thinking is an essential step in the use of the mind. Indeed, plausible guessing, the use of the heuristic hunch, the best employment of necessarily insufficient evidence—these are the activities in which the child needs practice and guidance. They are among the great antidotes to passivity.

But again note this requires the expert guidance of a gifted teacher.

Misconceptions. Children "discovering" in our biology classrooms are quite adept at inventing scientific misconceptions. For example, they readily become Lamarckians, believing that acquired characteristics of individuals are passed on and that all things exist for a purpose. They overdetermine cause, the teleological stance, thus blinding themselves to essential notions of randomness and spontaneity (Mayr 1988). We encourage teachers to see these common problems as fruitful errors, way stations on the route to mature understanding that they can manipulate and direct in useful ways. Our teachers are also made aware of common misconceptions that students may harbor concerning, for example, the nature of plants or natural selection (Brumby 1979). Armed with this information, teachers are better able to recognize the occurrence of misconceptions and fallacious reasoning so that they may then introduce students to counterexamples or other challenges to their inchoate knowledge, for example, by having students who believe that plants suck up food through the soil conduct experiments on hydroponic gardening.

The Need for a New Theory of Learning

We argue that a major part of a research agenda such as the one described in this chapter is to contribute to a new theory of learning that would capture the richness of the environment and the flexible learning activities it engenders. This theoretical development is necessary for practical reasons as well. If one wants to disseminate the program on the basis of principles of learning rather than surface procedures, one must be able to specify what those principles are.

Dissemination is not simply a matter of picking up an innovative program and dumping it down in a new site unchanged. Even when we move from one class to another, the program undergoes significant change, depending on the interests of both students and teachers, the age of the children, the relative importance of literacy versus content knowledge, and so forth. Dissemination is a theoretical and practical problem of some complexity.

Any dissemination model consists of three overlapping parts: invention, diffusion, and consequences (Rogers and Shoemaker 1971). Change itself is of two main types: *immanent change* created within the social system and *contact change* created outside the social system in question. *Selective contact* occurs when people learn about a new idea and choose to implement it, and *directed contact* occurs when outsiders force the innovation to be adopted.

To date, our model of dissemination has been one of selective contact and immanent change, with teachers free to select new ideas and innovations based on their needs—*as long as they adhere to the first principles of learning on which the program is based.* As we expand our dissemination efforts to more distant sites, we will need to think deeply about this insistence that the first principles remain intact while allowing adaptation and modification as an organic part of the implementation process. This notion of "implementation as evolution (Majone and Wildavsky 1978) constrained by first principles" is our eventual goal.

First Principles of Learning. The development of a learning theory that can capture the essential features of our learning community is of paramount importance to this project. The development of theory has always been necessary as a guide to research, a lens through which one interprets data. But theory development is essential for practical implementation as well. Our dissemination attempts will rely heavily on our ability to specify first principles. In our past experience, procedures such as reciprocal teaching have enjoyed widespread dissemination: the term is used without the need to reference the originators. It has been picked up by researchers, teachers, and textbook publishers, and has become part of the discourse of the educational community.

If one looks closely at reciprocal teaching as practiced outside the control of the originators, however, the first principles of learning it was meant to foster are often lost, or at best relegated to a minor position. What is practiced are the surface rituals of questioning, summarizing, and so on, divorced from the goal of fostering understanding that the procedures were designed to serve. Teachers and students nationwide practice the "strategies," sometimes even out of the context of reading authentic texts. Rarely are the procedures modified and extended to enhance the learning principles upon which they were based.

It is the first principles, not the surface procedures, that we want to disseminate. And it is these that we wish to share with teachers, so that they are free to design or modify any surface activity in ways that are consistent with the principles. As we embark on more extensive dissemination efforts, it is necessary that we develop first principles of learning in such a way that they can guide dissemination and professional development, as well as inform our academic colleagues of our theoretical development.

The first principles of learning are by no means written in stone. Indeed, they are constantly evolving as the project itself evolves. Steps toward these inchoate principles are shown in table 9.7.

The first thing to note about the principles is that their development was influenced not just by psychology, and not just by a consideration of in-school learning. We have been strongly influenced by pertinent branches of linguistics, sociology, and anthropology, and by studies of out of school learning, such as after school, voluntary activities (Heath 1991; Heath and McLaughlin, in press; Laboratory of Comparative Human Cognition 1983), apprenticeships and on the job training (Becker 1972; Lave and Wenger 1991), and studies of communities of professional scientists (Latour 1987; Latour and Woolgar 1986); Medawar 1982; Starr 1983).

Strategies and Metacognition

The first two principles, however, not only show a clear influence of psychological theory, but they have guided our work since its inception. We have an enduring interest in the active, strategic nature of learning (Brown 1974, 1975) and metacognition (Brown 1975, 1978; Brown, Brandford, Ferrara, and Campione 1983; Campione and Brown

Table 9.7
Steps toward first principles of learning

- Active, strategic nature of learning
- Metacognition

  Awareness and understanding
  Intentional learning, self-selection, and direction
  Self-monitoring and other-monitoring for common good
  Reflective practice

- Multiple zones of proximal development

  Multiple expertise, multiple roles, multiple resources
  Mutual appropriation
  Guided practice, guided participation

- Dialogic base

  Shared discourse, common knowledge
  Negotiated meaning and defining
  Seeding, migration, and appropriation of ideas

- Legitimization of differences

  Diversity, identity, and respect
  Creation of community and individual identity
  Multiple access, multiple ways in
  Peripheral to full participation

- Community of practice

  Communities of practice with multiple overlapping roles
  Sense of community with shared values
  Volunteers establish curriculum
  Elements of ownership and choice
  Community beyond the classroom wall

- Contextualized and situated

  Purpose for activity, nothing without a purpose
  Theory and practice in action
  Repeatable participant structures
  Fantasy and sociodramatic play (being a researcher, being a teacher)
  Link between current practice and expert practice transparent

  Intellectually honest curriculum
  Responsive, transparent assessment

1978; Campione, Brown, and Ferrara 1982). We will not trace that history here.

Multiple Zones of Proximal Development
The third principle reflects our long-standing interest in American versions of Vygotsky's (1978) theorizing, notably the notion of a zone of proximal development. A zone of proximal development is the region of activity that learners can navigate with aid from a supporting

context, including but not limited to people. In our classroom, teachers and students create multiple zones of proximal development by seeding the environment with ideas and concepts. Participants in the classroom are free to appropriate vocabulary, ideas, methods, and so on that appear initially as part of the shared discourse, and by appropriation, transform these ideas into personal knowledge. Because expertise in the classroom is distributed by design and happenstance (Brown 1992; Brown et al., in press) the seeding and appropriation processes are essentially bidirectional. Everyone is expert in something: nobody, not even the classroom teacher, knows it all.

Dialogic Base
Our classrooms are intentionally designed to give place to multiple voices in Bakhtin's (Holquist and Emerson 1981) sense of *voice* as the speaking personality and the speaking consciousness. A major tenet of Bakhtin's (1986) creed was that "any true understanding is dialogic in nature."

In our classrooms there is the assumption of shared discourse and common knowledge (Edwards and Mercer 1987) as well as individual expertise. The core participant structures of our classrooms are essentially dialogic. Sometimes these activities are face-to-face in small- or large-group interactions; sometimes they are mediated via print or electronic mail; and at still other times they go underground and become part of the thought processes of the community members (Vygotsky 1978). Dialogues provide the format for novices to adopt the discourse structure, goals, values, and belief systems of scientific practice. Over time, the community of learners adopts a common voice and common knowledge base, a shared system of meaning, beliefs, and activity that is as often implicit as it is explicit.

Distributed Expertise.   Central to these learning activities is the display of distributed expertise. Ideas and concepts migrate throughout the community via mutual appropriation and negotiation. Some ideas and ways of knowing become part of common knowledge. Other forms of knowledge and knowing remain the special reserve of those who choose to major in a particular form of expertise. The classroom is designed to foster zones of proximal development that are continually the subject of negotiation and renegotiation among its citizens. Through their participation in increasingly more mature forums of scholarly research, students are encultured into the community practice of scholars. These classrooms encourage the development of a community of discourse pervaded by knowledge-seeking and inquiry processes. Expertise of one form or another is spread throughout and beyond the classroom, and this emergent expertise influences the discourse that provides the seeding ground for the mutual negotiation and appropriation activities of its members. The metaphor of a classroom supporting multiple, overlapping zones of proximal development that foster growth through mutual appropriation and negotiated meaning is the theoretical window through which we view the system of classroom activity and the community practices that arise within it.

Legitimization of Differences in a Community of Scholastic Practice
Differences are rarely tolerated in traditional schools. The common practice is for students to be arranged by age and subjected to "age-appropriate" segregated curricula. This common contemporary practice, not part of the one-room schoolhouse, is based on the assumption that students of the same age can do the same amount of work, or grasp a certain amount of material, at the same time.

Not surprisingly, given the tradition of twentieth-century schooling, the notion of legitimization of differences comes from out of school learning. Heath (1991) regards this principle as essential for understanding such activities as volunteer, after-school programs, notably little league baseball. Central features of Little League participation, for example, are that all participants are volunteers (coaches, kids, parents, back benchers, etc.); that they come in all shapes, sizes, and abilities; that the coach is many more things than a teacher; and that there is more than one coach. The role of the coach is central, but so is this distributed expertise:

> Central to the task of coaching many learners at the same time is acceptance of the value of differences among learners. A team cannot expect to have all members at the same level of ability in the same complex skills. Instead, the potential for division of labor depends on varying levels of performance in each niche; however, the general upgrading of performance for each individual rests in the social control potential of having knowledge about separate tasks shared and distributed among all members. Added to the general distributions of knowledge is the shared value of monitoring self and others . . . , which result in group improvement through individual achievement. (Heath 1991, 121)

Heath and McLaughlin (in press) describe several features of successful youth activities that inner-city youth volunteer to join. We try to mimic some aspects of these successful organizations in our restructuring of schools. In addition to the respect and legitimization of diversity, experience, and talent, we believe that the sense of imagined family, where older and more experienced participants guide new members is important. Seasonal cycles of planning, preparing, practicing, and performing to outside audiences, with real deadlines that provide points for self-reflection and taking stock, also provide the backbone of these organizations. An atmosphere of mutual monitoring and support, with assigned responsibility for group progress, makes these organizations safe havens for youth, havens they rarely experience in school.

To the extent we are able, we aim to mimic this philosophy within classrooms. We try to create a community of scholastic practice within which expertise is distributed (Brown et al., in press): everyone is a researcher, everyone is a teacher, everyone is a writer, everyone is an expert at something. Everyone is involved in a plan-prepare-practice-perform cycle with tangible results. Identities are created, and a sense of community with shared values emerges. Students say that they feel ownership, and although it can't be absolute, there is a sense of volunteerism and choice in these classrooms. There are multiple ways to full participation, and peripheral participation in some aspects of the work is legitimized (Campione, Rutherford, Gordon, Walker, and Brown, in press; Lave and Wenger 1991).

Respect.   Coupled with responsibility and the acceptance of legitimate differences comes respect, respect between students, between students and school staff, and between all members of the extended community, including experts available by electronic mail. Students' questions are taken seriously. Experts, be they children or adults, do not always know the answers: known-answer question-and-answering games (Heath 1983; Mehan 1979) have no home in this environment. Respect is earned by responsible participation in a genuine knowledge-building community (Scardamalia and Bereiter 1991).

One main goal of the project is to distill critical features of successful after-school activities and work (often subversively) to restructure school practices so that this type of learning environment can support academic work of some authenticity and integrity.

Contextualized and Situated
Wherever possible, we situate academic activities such that the goals of the enterprise are apparent to the participants. This is not an easy task, as academic "work" is notorious for its disassociated, inauthentic nature (see Scardamalia, Bereiter, and Lamon, chapter 8 of this volume). There is often a dramatic lack of continuity between school activities and the cultures of both childhood and legitimate adult occupations (Cole and Bruner 1971). We attempt to forge a link between school activity and outside activities. Even as young as seven,

students engage in sociodramatic play (Heath 1991) when they practice being a researcher, being a teacher, being a scientist, and so forth.

Because we are not running a Little League team, and are partially responsible for the education of a large number of students, we must be responsive to the agreed-upon guidelines of what it is that students should learn. We attempt to provide what Bruner referred to as an "intellectually honest curriculum," one that is tailored to a child's age and interests, but with fidelity to the content area in question. Similarly, we have attempted to provide transparent assessment and other self-assessment procedures (Frederiksen and Collins 1989) so that the name of the game is clear to all. Enlisting students as designers and evaluators of their own learning is one of the most important activities of the Community of Learners. The philosophy behind this emphasis is an outcome of our long-standing interest in metacognition. It is a fundamental tenet of our theory that students have a right to understand, evaluate, and orchestrate their own learning.

Notes

This research was supported by grants from the James S. McDonnell and Andrew W. Mellon Foundations, and from the Evelyn Lois Corey Research Fund to Ann L. Brown.

An inner-city grade school in Oakland, California, has for three years been the primary host to our program. Thanks are due to the teachers and students for their unfailing help and support. The authors thank Principal Sallyann Tomlin for her gracious encouragement. Special thanks are due to second grade teacher Jill Walker and sixth grade teacher Stella Kennedy, who have worked with us most intensively. Thanks are also due to the many colleagues who have worked on this project, most notably Doris Ash, Kathy Nakagawa, and Marty Rutherford. And of course we could not operate without the support of the children, whose patience, humor, and eagerness to learn are a constant delight.

1. The work of the project takes place in inner-city schools serving a diverse population of students at risk. The majority of students are African-Americans (approximately 65%), with the remaining students consisting of Asian (15%), Pacific Islanders (6%), Hispanic (2%), and Caucasian (12%). Many children are mainstreamed; the majority are from single-parent or grandparent homes, and approximately half are recipients of Aid to Families with Dependent Children.

CONCLUSION

Chapter 10

Classroom Problems, School Culture, and Cognitive Research

John T. Bruer

Classroom Problems: Obstacles to Learning

We send our children to school to learn things they might not learn without formal instruction so that they can function more intelligently outside school. If so, recommendations for school reform should explicitly appeal to and implement our best, current understanding of what learning and intelligence are. In the public debate on school reform, this is seldom the case. Common recommendations—raising standards, increasing accountability, testing more, creating markets in educational services—are psychologically atheoretical, based at best on common sense and at worst on naive or dated conceptions of learning.

Over the past three decades, cognitive research has helped advance our understanding of learning and intelligence. Cognitive science brings to education theories and methods that yield fine-grained analyses of the mental representations and processes that underlie learning and intelligent performance, analyses that provide fundamental insights for improving educational practice. This research gives us the theoretical basis we need "to teach a far broader range of students and take them farther than ever before as modern society demands" (Glaser 1988, 21).

Brown and Campione (chapter 9) distill the major themes of this theoretical basis into a single sentence: "This concentration on *active, strategic* learning, with the learner's *understanding* and *control*, following *domain-specific* trajectories has had a major influence . . . on the gradual shift toward studying learning and educational practice in general" (page 231, emphasis added). The preceding chapters show what can happen when researchers collaborate with experienced classroom professionals in applying these theory-based insights to identify classroom problems and to create more effective, productive learning environments. The chapters provide ample evidence that restructuring schools must begin with restructuring student-teacher, and student-student, interactions in the classroom.

William James (1890) described the world of the infant as one of "booming, buzzing confusion." The instructional problems addressed above suggest that, for many children, school can be a world of booming, buzzing confusion, a place where it can be hard to understand what is going on and why. The problems often arise because classroom practices and school culture are in conflict with how our minds work and how children best learn. Many school practices are insensitive to domain-specific learning trajectories, fail to impart understanding and control to the students, and ignore students' innate propensity to be active strategic learners. Thus, students fail to see the purpose of what goes on in the classroom and its relevance to intelligent behavior outside school. These problems are seldom articulated or acknowledged in our discussions of why children fail to learn or why they cannot function as intelligently as we would like in daily life, in higher education, or on the job. The proposed solutions collectively exploit each of themes mentioned by Brown and Campione. And, finally, applying our current understanding of learning and intelligence to classroom problems is in turn contributing to the development of new themes in the evolution of cognitive theory.

Domain-Specific Learning Trajectories

One of the first contributions of cognitive research to our understanding of intelligence was that intelligence and expert performance are highly domain-specific (Newell and Simon 1972). Detailed studies of experts, and novices struggling to become experts, yielded fine-grained descriptions of the efficient learning trajectories in various domains. One could think of these trajectories as paths through an (at least) two-dimensional space, where one dimension is declarative or factual knowledge and the other is procedural or skill knowledge. To become expert in a domain, a student must acquire the facts and concepts and know how to manipulate those facts and concepts. If we think of domain learning as a trajectory, certain points on that path, whose coordinates are concepts and skills, must be traversed successfully before others can be reached. Thus, what students can readily learn depends to a great extent on what they already know; prior knowledge enables or impedes future learning. Furthermore, we shouldn't assume that children start on these trajectories only with the onset of formal, school instruction. Based on informal learning and their everyday experience, students come to school on these developmental paths.

The chapters by Griffin, Case, and Siegler, Minstrell and Hunt, and Spoehr address instructional problems that arise when curricula and classroom practice ignore such domain-specific learning trajectories.

Griffin, Case, and Siegler (chapter 2) attempt to help children who are at risk of failing first grade arithmetic. Contrary to the pioneering work of Jean Piaget (Inhelder and Piaget 1958), from infancy children start to develop understanding of numbers, counting, and simple arithmetic without explicit instruction (Starkey et al. 1983; Gelman and Gallistel 1978). Most children have progressed a considerable distance on the trajectory toward mastery of numbers before reaching school. Their first, formal math instruction, if it is to be effective and intelligible, should build on this informally acquired knowledge.

As Case and Griffin found, however, not all children arrive at school with comparable understandings. Some children, disproportionately from low socioeconomic-status homes, arrive at school lacking an adequate understanding of the number line. Without this understanding of the number concept, it is exceedingly difficult for children to acquire the procedural knowledge—addition and subtraction skills—that operate on that conceptual structure and to use those procedures in turn to acquire a store of basic number facts. To these students, addition and subtraction no doubt appear unmotivated, mysterious, and largely meaningless procedures. For them, first, formal arithmetic is a booming, buzzing confusion. It has no connection to their prior understanding, and they can see little use for it beyond the classroom.

Somewhat surprisingly, many first grade curricula do not explicitly teach the number line concept and how it supports arithmetic operations. The Rightstart curriculum teaches the number line structure to students who have not acquired it prior to arriving at school. This relatively simple intervention has a profound impact on students' learning and allows them to progress on the early math learning trajectory.

Although involving older students in a different domain, Minstrell and Hunt's work (chapter 3) also illustrates problems that arise if school instruction is insensitive to where students are on domain-specific learning trajectories. High school students arrive in the classroom with a wealth of informal physics knowledge acquired from infancy through everyday interaction with objects and forces. This informally acquired, naive physics generally serves us well, but it can also lead us seriously astray. Traditional, school science instruction is ineffective for many students because it neither builds on this informal knowledge where it is correct, nor corrects it where it is in error.

Its ineffectiveness is dramatic and well documented. For example, Clement (1982) found that only 12 percent of students in a first-year college engineering course, students who were highly successful in school science, could correctly describe the forces that act on a coin when it is tossed into the air; yet, these students could write equations for Newton's Laws and could readily solve standard, quantitative textbook problems. Clement's students, like Minstrell's successful students, could manipulate equations to solve textbook problems, but did not understand what the equations meant, nor how to connect them with everyday experience. Students acquire a kind of procedural knowledge that allows them to succeed at school science, without understanding science.

Expertise in physics, as in other domains, requires that domain-specific conceptual knowledge be organized in such a way that domain-specific procedural knowledge (for physics, formal equations) can be applied to it. The difficulty is that our informally acquired physics knowledge is often not organized into a conceptual structure that can support formal physics reasoning and the intelligent use of formal equations. Minstrell and Hunt's "physics from a cognitive perspective" helps students recognize and modify their conceptual understanding of physics so that they can apply formal equations intelligently. Minstrell attempts to identify which pieces of students' informally acquired domain knowledge are correct and can serve as anchors for instruction and which are targets for conceptual change. Using students' everyday knowledge—starting from where they are on the physics learning trajectory—Minstrell slowly helps students reorganize their conceptual structures into ones that can support genuine physical reasoning. Imparting this level of qualitative, conceptual understanding helps students make sense of the instruction, lets them link classroom learning with everyday experiences, and enables them eventually to apply physics intelligently to the extracurricular world. They see that physics has a larger purpose and authentic use; it's not just a confusing, school-specific exercise in symbol manipulation.

In the ACCESS project, Kathy Spoehr (chapter 4) addresses a similar problem in high school social studies and humanities instruction; instruction that is almost as ineffective as physics instruction in helping students along the path to intelligent, expert performance in these domains. The National Assessments of Educational Progress suggests that students do acquire masses of factual knowledge, but are seriously inadequate in their understanding of history, literature, and civics (Ravitch and Finn 1987). Secretary of Education Richard Riley once described American students as having a "Trivial Pursuit" knowledge of these disciplines.

Failure to appreciate where children are on the domain-specific learning trajectories and failure to connect declarative and procedural knowledge are again at the heart of the problem. Even in middle school American history, textbooks and standard curricula fail to connect with children's prior, informally acquired knowledge (Beck et al. 1991; McKeown and Beck 1990). They assume more background knowledge than most children possess. Furthermore, standard materials and instruction are often not explicit about how historical or literary facts are interrelated temporally and causally. Thus, traditional instruction results in students accumulating isolated facts and knowledge fragments, which are never organized into appropriate domain-specific structures or schemas. If the declarative knowledge is not organized according to domain-specific principles, students are unable to apply appropriate domain-specific reasoning procedures to that knowledge.

The ACCESS project uses hypermedia to help students organize social studies and humanities knowledge according to the domain-specific principles that characterize these domains. Hypermedia allow students and teachers to build data structures where pieces of information are linked explicitly, making the previously abstract, covert structures visible for teachers and students, where they can be the focus of class discussion and reasoning. With the complex declarative knowledge structures now visible, students can see how expert-like, domain-specific reasoning procedures apply to them. When students acquire the organized knowledge and the appropriate procedural skills, they can reason with and about historical or literary knowledge in a way that makes it meaningful. With the knowledge structures and their related reasoning strategies at hand, students can raise questions, make inferences, and generate meaningful conclusions about the relevance of history or literature to their lives and situations outside school. Social studies becomes more than a trivial pursuit.

Active Strategic Learners

The discovery that where children are on domain-specific learning trajectories determines where they can readily go leads to a second fundamental insight about learning: Learning is an active, not a passive process. Students learn not by passively recording what teachers might tell them, but by interpreting and integrating new experiences, including classroom experiences, based on what they already know and understand. By doing so, they create their own knowledge structures.

Our propensity to be active learners and interpreters of our experience—our drive to understand—is a powerful one. Research in cognitive neuroscience even suggests that the human brain has a specialized module, the left-brain interpreter, the function of which is to try to make sense of our experience, no matter how bizarre that experience might be (Gazzaniga 1978). Our innate propensity to interpret, understand, and impose meaning can be the engine of learning, if it is directed to appropriate tasks and goals. Too often, though, school tasks and practices are inappropriate for the intended learning goals. In such situations, students, being clever, intelligent humans, will interpret their experience as best they can and develop suitable coping strategies that address the tasks and meet the goals as they understand them.

The Cognition and Technology Group at Vanderbilt (CTGV; see chapter 7) began their work on anchored instruction that led to "The Adventures of Jasper Woodbury" to address a problem of inappropriate tasks and practices in middle school math instruction. In the middle school math curriculum, word problems are supposed to teach students how mathematics applies to everyday situations. However, as the CTGV and others have found, word problems as used in school are highly artificial, decontextualized tasks that tend to subvert the intended learning goal. Standard word problems about cookies in jars or birds on wires state the goal and give the needed numbers, leaving the students only the task of picking a suitable computation to apply to the numbers. These are not the kind of quantitative problems students would have to solve outside school.

How do children interpret pages of these problems that seem to have no bearing on their extracurricular lives? Being clever, active learners who are trying to make sense of their experience, children develop strategies to solve these weird, school-specific problems. They develop strategies to help choose a suitable arithmetic operation. For example, they look for key words in the problem—"altogether" means add, "how many left" means subtract—and apply the cued operation to the given numbers. Although a useful, efficient, in-school strategy, it is useless when trying to apply math to formulate and solve problems like planning a trip or budgeting an allowance. The result is that children hate word problems, do not see their purpose, and fail to see any connection between school math and the outside world. The nature of the school task frustrates its purported educational purpose. Word problems are not unique in this regard. Other classroom practices surrounding science, reading, and writing are similarly counterproductive.

The Jasper series is an educational tool based on design principles derived from decades of research on memory and learning, that addresses this problem. The intent of Jasper is to promote a broader range of generative learning, learning that exploits the active, strategic nature of intelligence. In their research, the CTGV group found that students remembered and spontaneously used instructional information better when that information was presented in a learning context similar to the eventual problem-solving context where that information should be used. They discovered that such problem-oriented learning was superior to fact-oriented learning (Bransford et al. 1989). If students are active, strategic learners, then the problem-solving context should help students associate the new knowledge with conditions in which the knowledge should be used. If students learned and worked with knowledge in a variety of problem-solving contexts, they should be able to associate the knowledge with all those contexts and thus be able to use the knowledge more flexibly, even in novel situations.

The goal of CTGV researchers became the creation of shared problem-solving contexts that students and teachers could actively explore, where facts and skills were learned and used in context, rather than piecemeal, to solve holistic, authentic tasks. Their hope was that problem-solving environments would create an "anchor" for learning that would generate interest, allow students to formulate as well as define problems, and see the relevance of the material to their extracurricular lives. In the spirit of constructivist learning theory—the appreciation that students are active, strategic learners—they originally called their problem-solving contexts "invitations to thinking." These are instructional materials that appeal to children's natural propensity to understand. The Jasper series invites students to think by presenting interesting situations that afford children the opportunity to work collaboratively to construct knowledge.

The success of the Jasper series has stimulated an active educational research program that is attempting to develop better assessment tools to measure the active, strategic learning and to address the difficult but fundamental educational question of transfer of learning.

Understanding and Control: Metacognition

Around 1980, cognitive scientists began to focus on another element of human intelligence that is essential for efficient learning, metacognition. Metacognition is the ability to think about thinking, to be consciously aware of oneself as a thinker, and to monitor and control one's mental processing. It is our awareness of ourselves (and by extension, others) as intelligent thinking creatures (Flavell and Well-man 1977).

Just as there are basic, domain-specific knowledge and skills there are basic metacognitive knowledge and skills. Among them are the ability to predict the results of one's own problem-solving actions, to check the results of one's own cognitive processing, to monitor progress toward a problem solution, and to test one's actions and solutions against the realities of the larger world. These skills are "the basic characteristics of efficient thought" (Brown and DeLoache 1978, 15) and, as such, the basic skills of effective learning.

Some children develop metacognitive skills on their own without formal instruction and are naturally efficient learners. Others aren't so blessed and can have serious learning difficulties in school. Fortunately, research has shown that appropriate instruction can help children acquire metacognitive skills and the ability to use them. Successful programs to teach metacognitive skills and general learning skills share common features: "ideal cognitive skill training programs include practice in the specific task-appropriate strategies, direct instruction in the orchestrating, overseeing, and monitoring of these skills, and information concerning the significance of those activities" (Brown 1985a, 335). Children have to see the metacognitive strategies in use, be told explicitly what they are, practice them in contexts where they should be used, and be told explicitly when to use them. Most important the child must know *why* these strategies are useful. "Don't ask why, just do it" is not an effective learning principle for children who are actively trying to interpret their classroom experiences. The last four chapters above illustrate the importance of helping students develop their metacognitive skills, of helping them to understand and control their learning.

Reading is the fundamental learning skill. Students spend considerable time learning to read in the early primary grades, so that by fourth or fifth grade they will be able to read to learn in their other school subjects. Classroom teachers report one particularly striking reading problem some students manifest. Teachers are puzzled and amazed by students who can read well aloud, but have little understanding of what they have just read. (See Bruer 1993, chap. 6.) These children have adequate decoding, or word-recognition skills, but it as if they thought that the purpose of reading was to be able to say the written words aloud rather than to construct meaning from a text and store that meaning in memory for subsequent recall and use. When these students are placed in remedial reading classes that emphasize decoding skills, the instructor can make their problem worse rather than better. For these students who are trying to interpret their school experience, reading must appear to be a bizarre, pointless task indeed—sound out words from the page and say them aloud for the teacher. This is certainly not an understanding of reading as a fundamental, learning skill.

One of the first programs to teach metacognitive skills and general learning skills based on the features that Brown listed above was specifically designed to help these students. Annmarie Palincsar and Brown developed the method of reciprocal teaching that uses dialogues in reading groups to foster collaborative construction of meaning from texts (Palincsar and Brown 1984; Palincsar et al. 1988). Reciprocal teaching explicitly taught children to apply language comprehension strategies to reading and to monitor the comprehension process to assure the interpretations they were constructing made sense. After twenty days of reciprocal instruction, seventh grade remedial reading students, who had been reading at the third grade level, achieved reading comprehension levels comparable to that of their seventh grade peers. They were also able to apply their reading skills in classroom science and social studies reading assignments. They had learned to read and could now read to learn.

The work reported by Gaskins (chapter 6) builds on reciprocal teaching and other programs like it to teach metacognitive skills and strategies across the curriculum. Several years ago, the Benchmark faculty implemented a successful program to improve students' decoding skills, but they found that this did not necessarily result in improved reading comprehension in other school subjects. Gaskins and her faculty identified specific metacognitive strategies that would help their students improve their reading comprehension in their school subjects and to become more efficient learners. Gaskins relates how teachers in a school can implement Brown's formula for a successful strategy instruction program. They demonstrated, explained, and motivated the strategies, and created situations in which the students practiced the strategies and discussed when to use them, and why they work. Gaskins's Psych 101 class stressed the importance of metacognitive strategies, while making students aware of how their minds worked and how metacognitive skills they were learning in the context of domain-specific subject matter instruction built upon and extended their innate cognitive abilities.

Brown and Campione's "Communities of Learners" (chapter 9) extends reciprocal teaching, and supplements it with other pedagogical methods like the Jigsaw Classroom, to include reading, reasoning, and inquiry processes within scientific content domains. Their table 9.1 describes how reciprocal teaching with the learning principles it embodies has evolved from a method to help poor readers to a method students can use with teachers to help understand subject matter instruction in middle school biology.

"Communities of Learners" instantiates all facets of our current understanding of learning and intelligence. The focus is on developing domain-specific expertise, where students are active, strategic learners who are sufficiently aware and in control of their learning that they can pose their own questions, set their own learning goals, and borrow, for example, when a reciprocal session is needed to advance their learning goals. In the experimental classroom, this extension of reciprocal teaching increased student performance beyond that achieved by reciprocal teaching alone. Brown and Campione report elevated reading, writing, and problem-solving scores, along with impressive improvements in students' ability to understand and use content knowledge in novel situations. When students, guided by teachers, have such control over their learning, their motivation to learn increases. In such a context, school tasks have taken on a meaning and purpose that appeals to intelligent agents.

The work leading to CSILE, as reported by Scardamalia, Bereiter, and Lamon (chapter 8), grew out of research on how children develop writing skills and the role of metacognition in skilled writing. Research on the cognition of writing revealed that expertise derives from a writer's ability to retrieve and organize domain knowledge and then use rhetorical skills to present that information in a way that facilitates the audience understanding. Effective writers are reflective writers who are aware of their own topic knowledge, can envision the information and knowledge needs of an intended audience, and know how to apply their writing skills to foster comprehension in the audience. Skilled writers are aware of themselves and their envisioned audience as cognitive agents. Skilled writers are metacognitively adept.

Writing in school, one would hope, would help children acquire this metacognitive sophistication. But writing as it is done often impedes the development of metacognitive skills. Often school writing reduces to a form of recitation to the teacher, with no larger communicative purpose. Students can succeed at the task using strategies like "copy-delete" for writing summaries or "knowledge telling" for expository writing. These are unreflective, automatic strategies that work to solve writing problems as they are presented in school, but will work only for school-specific writing tasks—tasks where there is no real audience and the only point is to say what you know. Such tasks certainly do not engender metacognitive skills, and never metacognitive awareness. These, one might say, infracognitive strategies persist into college and are prevalent even among students at highly selective undergraduate institutions (Flower and Higgins 1990; Flower et al. 1992). In the culture of school, writing is another weird school task to be endured when it cannot be avoided.

In earlier work, Scardamalia and Bereiter contrast unreflective knowledge telling with the metacognitively demanding strategy of "knowledge transforming." Knowledge transforming requires that students take the knowledge they have and present it in such a way that it is relevant for and sensitive to the informational needs of others. Expert writing is one from of knowledge transforming, expert teaching is another (Bruer 1993, chap. 8), and being a member of a scholarly community is a third. In each instance, cognitive skills and intellectual effort are devoted to building intelligible links between what an individual knows and what a larger community knows.

Rather than teaching writing as knowledge transforming, CSILE is a piece of educational software that makes knowledge transforming the focus of classroom activity. CSILE redirects the flow of communication in the classroom so that students can interact, through text and graphics, in constructing a communal knowledge base. They write to and for each other to extend their common understanding of subject matter topics. This gives learning, not just writing, a larger, shared purpose. To participate in the community, students must be sensitive to the cognitive needs and demands of their fellow students as they actively collaborate in constructing domain-specific knowledge. Participation ensures metacognitive sophistication and an appreciation for the social dimensions of learning. Almost as a by-product, student writing improves as they participate in a culture that values constructing and communicating knowledge.

Intelligence in the Classroom

Chapter 5, by Gardner, Krechevsky, Sternberg, and Okagaki, addresses how contemporary theories of intelligence can be applied to improve schools. To the extent that a theory of intelligence is apparent in our schools, it is a highly parochial, stunted, and unproductive one. Standardized tests, already ubiquitous in American education and now being promoted as a means to enforce accountability to standards, suggest to students that intelligence is what the tests measure. Yet, anyone who has taken an intelligence, aptitude, or achievement test may well wonder how the test items and how we answer them are relevant to how we reason or solve problems in everyday life or in the workplace. Furthermore, although these tests, constructed on a well-established statistical theory, allow educators to compare students to a standard or norm group, the tests reveal next to nothing about what children know or understand (Bruer 1993, chap. 8). Test results tell teachers where students rank but are mute about where individual children are on domain-specific learning trajectories and what steps teachers, and the students themselves, might take to improve their performance and understanding. This deficit of prescriptive, therapeutic information creates an impression that the tests separate the academic sheep from the vocational goats based on a trait, intelligence, but that there is little students can do to improve their performance and raise their intelligence. This is not an appropriate message for young, strategic learners. School practices that support this "entity" theory of intelligence can seriously impair students' motivation and school goals (Henderson and Dweck 1990). In addition, school culture tends to define intelligence as success at school tasks; this is, after all, what achievement and aptitude tests assess. Yet we have seen repeatedly that many students perceive school tasks as meaningless and next to useless outside the culture of school. Worse, students can succeed at these tasks with little understanding of a subject domain's basic principles, often by employing strategies that are orthogonal to the tasks' purported educational goals. Should we be surprised, then, that many students adopt strategies to get by or to please the teacher and fail to see the purpose of school in terms of developing the knowledge, skills, and intelligence useful in the larger world?

Gardner, Krechevsky, Sternberg, and Okagaki suggest we can begin to address these problems if we apply a broader notion of intelligence in schools, one that embraces our understanding of domain-specific, active, metacognitively aware learning, that includes explicit emphasis on the purpose or goals of school activities, and that is sensitive to how intelligence functions within the culture of school.

Contemporary theories of intelligence, such as Sternberg's and Gardner's, help us see what underlies intelligent performance in school subject domains, rather than taking performance on school tasks and test items as definitive. Sternberg's triarchic theory, based in the information processing tradition, describes the component mental processes that contribute to intelligent behavior. Gardner's theory of multiple intelligence complements this computational approach with anthropological and neurological considerations. Domain specificity has an evolutionary history. Humans have innate sensitivities to certain classes of environmental stimuli, among them language, number, music, self-knowledge, and social knowledge. Successful formal instruction should build on and help students develop these innate intelligences. The PIFS curriculum is designed to serve these ends.

The PIFS curriculum also underscores the importance of active, metacognitively aware instruction: a practically intelligent student is aware of his or her own cognitive processes. Practically intelligent students appreciate their particular learning strengths, how to use them in the school environment, and the nature and demands of various school tasks. These sensitivities allow students to monitor, gauge, and control their learning, and to become effective and reflective learners. The curriculum attempts to make the purpose of school tasks and goals of schooling apparent and explicit for the students throughout. Understanding the demands and goals of the school environment can significantly reduce the booming, buzzing confusion.

The PIFS project also takes up a new theme in cognitive research, one that has also been mentioned by many of the other authors: sociocultural contexts matter. Gardner et al. are concerned with how intelligence unfolds within a specific sociocultural context, in the American middle school. To be practically intelligent, students must understand school as a social and cultural institution. We cannot ignore what intelligence is in school, how that context shapes the development of intelligence, and what the ramifications of the sociocultural contexts in particular schools are for the probability of successful school change. Their study of intelligence in the context of middle school, intended at first to help students function more effectively in that context, led to a more global recognition and recommendation. They, along with many others, recognized that authentic purposes may be lacking in school tasks. If so, the tasks, demands, and expectations of schooling must change to make them more attuned to how intelligence develops and to the demands of intelligent performance beyond the classroom. Helping children to function more effectively within the existing school culture may not be enough. We may also have to change the existing school culture.

Context, Communities, and Discourse

The significance of sociocultural context, communities, and discourse for cognition and learning has emerged in part because researchers have attempted to apply cognitive science to authentic classroom tasks rather than just artificial laboratory tasks. This foray into classrooms and work sites has had an impact on how researchers view cognition. The theory and research that originally motivated the interventions described above looked at how the individual problem solver performed in a circumscribed task environment (Newell and Simon 1972). When researchers brought ideas about domain-specific trajectories, active learning, and metacognition to the classroom and applied them with some success, they realized that other factors, factors not always emphasized in the cognitive research on problem solving, influence learning and support or inhibit intelligent behavior. Gardner et al. saw how the context of school shapes intelligence and saw the need to change school culture. The CTGV group evolved from attempting to change isolated aspects of the curriculum that would assist individual students to attempting to create dynamic learning communities that demonstrate how intelligence is distributed in the world. Most of Brown and Campione's learning principles go beyond those strictly motivated by research on individual problem solving and emphasize the impact of social and community values and speech practices in effective learning environments. Scardamalia and Bereiter emphasize the need to bring World 3, the world of public, collaborative knowledge building practiced by scholarly communities, into the classroom. All of the classroom interventions involve group and collaborative learning activities, where group dialogue and discussion are the vehicles of learning. Hence, the emphasis in the later chapters on discourse, the use of discourse in various kinds of learning communities, and a view of learning as enculturation into a discourse community.

How cognition is, or is not, determined, supported, or constrained by sociocultural factors is the central theoretical and methodological issue in the future development of cognitive science.

Originally, social interaction and dialogue solved a practical, pedagogical problem for those who wanted to provide informed, metacognitively aware instruction in the classroom. For example, in reciprocal teaching, the challenge was to teach children how to apply and monitor language comprehension skills when trying to construct meaning from written texts. Students did apply these skills in interpreting spoken language, so reciprocal teaching built on this prior understanding by using group discussions to make children aware of the skills, how they should be applied in reading, and how to monitor their successful application. By using language and language comprehension skills directed toward a specific learning goal, teachers could make thinking and problem solving within a domain public and shared and hence, the object of metacognitive reflection for their students.

The success of such classroom interventions makes clear that this approach works and improves classroom practice. The question for cognitive research then becomes *why* does it work? There are several possibilities. One is that social interaction and the dialogue surrounding it allow skilled thinkers to demonstrate expert strategies to the naive. Appropriately structured, guided dialogue could "make thinking visible" (Flower et al. 1992), making students aware of their own thought processes, those of others, and how to monitor their own thinking. In this view, social interaction through language makes hidden thought processes public and shared. Using Bereiter and Scardamalia's terminology, one might say working in World 3 makes World 2 public and shared.

Another possibility is that such communal interactions allow students to share and distribute the cognitive burdens of thinking. A group provides a more informationally rich context for learning because each participant's knowledge may be structured slightly different in long-term memory, so there are greater varieties of cues to trigger recall of information from individual memories. Also, the group has a larger collective working memory, so no one person's working memory is required to hold all the information needed to solve a problem.

A third possibility is that dialogue requires both language comprehension and language production. Production, either speech or writing, is cognitively more demanding than just listening or reading. Dialogue might then result in deeper processing of information. These three possibility all lay within the theoretical framework of problem solving and information processing psychology.

A fourth possibility is that social settings, particularly school, send the message that thinking and intelligence are socially valued. In such settings, students would become socialized as active, strategic, metacognitively aware beings. "Through participation in communities, students would come to expect thinking all the time, to view themselves as able, even obligated, to engage in critical analysis and problem solving" (Resnick and Klopfer 1989, 9). This explanation links individual cognitive psychology with social psychology. It suggests that social and cultural factors influence cognition and that any theory which overlooks this influence is seriously incomplete.

A fifth, more daring hypothesis, is that thought, learning, and knowledge are not just influenced by social factors and content, but are irreducibly social phenomena. Although knowledge is domain-specific, the activities that define a domain are framed by its culture: "Their meaning and purpose are socially constructed through negotiations among present and past members" (Brown, Collins, and Duguid 1989, 32). To learn is to become enculturated into a community of practice and to participate in the ongoing negotiations of knowledge or discourse building. This hypothesis is contributing to a reappraisal of the earlier theories of Vygotsky, Bakhtin, and Luria—for example, Vygotsky's claim that thought is the internalization of social behaviors and speech practices, Bakhtin's claim that all understanding is dialogue, and Luria's view that voluntary attention is social rather biological in nature. On this hypothesis, discourse doesn't make thought visible, rather thought is internalized discourse. As Scardamalia and Bereiter point out, this hypothesis reverses the relation between

Worlds 2 and 3. World 3 is primary and fundamental, giving rise to World 2. This hypothesis underscores the importance of anthropology, sociolinguistics, and even literary criticism for the further development of cognitive theory.

There probably is an element of truth in each of these hypotheses, and thus it would be a mistake to take any one of them as explaining why social interactions and discourse facilitate learning. Similarly, given what we presently know, it would be a mistake to choose definitely between the theories and methods of the information-processing and problem-solving tradition and the new sociohistorical, situated cognition approach.

The orthodox approach has been successful in extending our understanding of cognition and did, at least originally, provide the theoretical basis—domain specificity, active, metacognitively aware learners—for all the classroom interventions presented here. There is much to be gained by pursuing this line of research, while admitting its possible limitations. Situated theorists are making an important point when they argue for the inclusion of social and cultural variables in task analyses and descriptions of task environments and the content dependence of learning and intelligence. Also, the problem-solving tradition that has guided educational applications of cognitive research has proceeded on the assumption that mental function can and should be studied independently of brain structure, thus tending to see cognition apart from its biological and evolutionary basis. As Gardner points out, we have innate sensitivities to certain types of environmental stimuli, sensitivities hard-wired into the nervous system through a long evolutionary history.

Similarly, we should be reluctant to take the sociocultural view as the sole theoretical basis for the study of cognition, because it, too, may take insufficient account of cognition's biological basis and evolutionary history. Humans, despite our cultural attainments, share features for controlling behavior with other animals who negotiate the world without language and without socially and culturally defined goals and activities. "Animal cognition" is not necessarily an oxymoron.

Studies in child cognitive development have shown that infants have an awareness and understanding of domains such as number and physical object (Gelman and Gallistel 1978; Starkey et al. 1983; Baillargeon 1987). Among other things, this research has shown that children seem to process knowledge about numbers and objects without any behavioral signs of searching for or manipulating objects. This suggests that, contra Piaget, the origins of cognition cannot be traced to the internalization of motor behavior (Rothbart et al. 1990). A fortiori, it suggests, contra some extreme formulations of situated cognition, that the origins of cognition cannot be traced to the internalization of social interactions, either. Nonetheless, it leaves open the possibility that some forms of cognition might be just such internalizations, either of motor behaviors or social interactions.

A reasonable position, then, would be to admit that traditional cognitive science should be supplemented by cognitive neuroscience from below and by cognitive anthropology or cultural psychology from above. Biological theories, functional theories, and sociocultural theories proceed at different levels of analysis that for now cannot be seamlessly linked. Research at these levels should proceed in parallel, with each level looking to the other for possible constraints on its own theorizing. If this is to be scientific research, all that is required is that the disciplines at each level share a belief in an external reality that can be discerned through careful use of qualitative and quantitative research methods. All participants should share a conviction that their collaborative discourse is indeed about something.

Future Challenges

Our late twentieth-century expectations of what schooling should enable students to achieve pose an unprecedented societal challenge. To meet this challenge, we must create learning environments that will help all students meet our ever-rising expectations. To design better learning environments, we must start at the level of student-teacher and student-student interactions in the classroom. We must exploit what we already know about how children think, remember, and learn and we must strive to further our understanding of learning and how intelligence develops.

The work reported here provides examples of what can happen when cognitive research guides instructional design. To the extent current practices are based on common sense and outmoded theories, cognition research provides a needed corrective. The work also illustrates how our attempts to apply research to real-world problems of learning and teaching can serve to advance cognitive research. Ideally, there should be continuous feedback from theory to practice to theory, and an institutional structure to support this interaction. With each iteration of this feedback loop, we would then be able to improve educational outcomes for children and deepen our understanding of cognition and intelligence.

A start has been made, but many challenges remain for both educators and researchers. First, the research community will have to do a better job of making its methods and results comprehensible and accessible to teachers, educators, and parents. End users of the research need declarative and procedural knowledge about cognition and need to know when and why to use it, if they are to view the enterprise as meaningful. As Kathy Spoehr writes, "Broad educational reform based on a shared understanding of how thinking and learning occur from a cognitive point of view will require that all educators understand the basic insights cognitive science provides and that they practice applying them consistently."

There is a complementary challenge for educators, particularly those who control school systems, buildings, and working conditions. They must provide learning and working environments where teachers can appropriate the cognitive perspective. According to Irene Gaskins, "If the gap between research and practice is to be bridged, schools will need to cultivate environments where professional growth is valued, continuous high-quality staff development is provided, teacher input to the change process is encouraged, and adequate time is allowed for change to take place."

Constructive interaction between research and practice, as Brown and Campione emphasize, must take place around a set of first principles for learning: "As we embark on more extensive dissemination efforts, it is necessary that we develop first principles of learning in such a way that they can guide dissemination and professional development, as well as inform our academic colleagues of our theoretical development." Without explicit first principles, surface features of instructional innovations spread, but the innovations lose contact with the learning goals they were intended to serve. Without theory or first principles, instructional innovations can be divorced from their purpose and run the risk of becoming meaningless, superficial rituals.

Finally, the cognitive community itself must strive to assure that a coherent research program continues to evolve, a research program that incorporates the insights from cognitive neuroscience, builds on and refines the results and methods in the information-processing tradition, and pursues more recent insights about the importance of context, society, and culture for our understanding of cognitive intelligence. Given how little we currently know, research within each of the paradigms should be viewed as complementary rather than competing. Gardner et al. outline the challenge for cognitive research in the coming years: "A theory of intelligence sensitive to nuances of context is desirable, but it is also clear that, for scientific purposes, one does not want a theory for every content and for every context. Urgently needed is a research program that can tease out factors that remain constant from among those factors which vary with context . . . the search for generalizations will require both focused empirical investigations and powerful efforts at synthesis."

References

Adelson, B. 1981. Problem solving and the development of abstract categories in programming languages. *Memory and Cognition* 9:422–433.

Allington, R. L., and McGill-Franzen, A. 1989. School response to reading failure: Chapter 1 and special education students in grades 2, 4, and 8. *Elementary School Journal* 89:529–542.

American Association for the Advancement of Science, Commission on Science Education. 1974. *Science: A Process Approach.* New York: Ginn.

Ames, C. A. 1990. Motivation: What teachers need to know. *Teachers College Record* 91:409–421.

Anderson, J. R. 1974. Retrieval of propositional information from long-term memory. *Cognitive Psychology* 6:451–474.

Anderson, J. R. 1982. Acquisition of cognitive skill. *Psychological Review* 89:369–406.

Anderson, J. R. 1990. *The adaptive character of thought.* Hillsdale, NJ: Erlbaum.

Anderson, J. R., and Reder, L. M. 1979. An elaborative processing explanation of depth of processing. In L. S. Cermak and F. I. M. Craik, eds., *Levels of Processing in Human Memory.* Hillsdale, NJ: Erlbaum.

Anderson, M. 1992. *Intelligence and development.* London: Blackwells.

Anderson, M., and Diskin, S. 1987. Inspection time and the development of intelligence. Paper presented at the British Psychological Society Conference, Sussex University.

Arnold, C. 1985. *Saving the peregrine falcon.* Minneapolis: Carolrhoda Books.

Aronson, E. 1978. *The jigsaw classroom.* Beverly Hills, CA: Sage.

Ash, D., and Brown, A. L. 1993. After the jigsaw is over: Children's learning in socially and informationally rich environments. Paper presented at the annual meeting of the American Educational Research Association, Atlanta, GA.

Astington, J. W., Harris, P., and Olson, D. R., eds. 1988. *Developing theories of mind.* Cambridge: Cambridge University Press.

Atkinson, R. C., and Shiffrin, R. M. 1968. Human memory: A proposed system and its control processes. In K. W. Spence and J. T. Spence, eds., *The Psychology of Learning and Behavior: Advances in Research and Theory.* Vol. 2. New York: Academic Press.

Baddeley, A. D., and Hitch, G. 1974. Working memory. In G. H. Bower, ed., *The Psychology of Learning and Motivation.* Vol. 8. New York: Academic Press.

Baillargeon, R. 1987. Object permanence in 3 1/2- and 4 1/2-month-old infants. *Developmental Psychology* 23:655–664.

Bakhtin, M. M. 1986. *Speech genres and other late essays.* C. Emerson and M. Holquist, eds. V. W. McGee, trans. Austin: University of Texas Press.

Baron, J. 1985. *Rationality and intelligence.* New York: Cambridge University Press.

Barron, B. J. S. 1991. Collaborative problem solving: Is team performance greater than what is expected from the most competent member? Ph.D. diss., Vanderbilt University, Nashville.

Barron, B. J. S., Bransford, J. D., Kulewicz, S., and Hasselbring, T. S. 1989. Uses of macro-contexts to facilitate mathematical thinking. Paper presented at the annual meeting of the American Educational Research Association, San Francisco.

Bateson, G. 1972. *Steps to an ecology of mind*. New York: Ballantine Books.

Beck, I. L., and McKeown, M. G. 1987. Getting the most from basal reading selections. *Elementary School Journal* 87:343–356.

Beck, I. L., McKeown, M. G., Sinatra, G. M., and Loxterman, J. A. 1991. Revising social studies text from a text-processing perspective: Evidence of improved comprehensibility. *Reading Research Quarterly* 26:251–276.

Becker, H. 1972. A school is a lousy place to learn anything in. *American Behavioral Scientist* 16:85–105.

Beeman, W. O., Anderson, K. T., Bader, G., Larkin, J., McClard, A. P., McQuillan, P., and Shields, M. 1987. Hypertext and pluralism: From lineal to non-lineal thinking. In *Hypertext '87*, 67–85. New York: The Association for Computing Machinery.

Bereiter, C. 1984. How to keep thinking skills from going the way of all frills. *Educational Leadership* 42:75–77.

Bereiter, C. 1991. Commentary on "Special topic: Confronting the learning paradox." *Human Development* 34:294–298.

Bereiter, C. 1992. Referent-centered and problem-centered knowledge: Elements of an educational epistemology. *Interchange* 23:337–362.

Bereiter, C., and Bird, M. 1985. Use of thinking aloud in identification and teaching of reading comprehension strategies. *Cognition and Instruction* 2:131–156.

Bereiter, C., Burtis, P. J., and Scardamalia, M. 1988. Cognitive operations in constructing main points in written composition. *Journal of Memory and Language* 27:261–278.

Bereiter, C., and Scardamalia, M. 1985. Cognitive coping strategies and the problem of "inert knowledge." In S. F. Chipman, J. W. Segal, and R. Glaser, eds., *Thinking and learning skills*. Vol. 2, *Research and open questions*, 65–80. Hillsdale, NJ: Erlbaum.

Bereiter, C., and Scardamalia, M. 1987. *The psychology of written composition*. Hillsdale, NJ: Erlbaum.

Bereiter, C., and Scardamalia, M. 1989. Intentional learning as a goal of instruction. In L. B. Resnick, ed., *Knowing, learning, and instruction: Essays in honor of Robert Glaser*, 361–392. Hillsdale, NJ: Erlbaum.

Bereiter, C., and Scardamalia, M. In press. Two models of classroom learning using a communal database. In S. Dijkstra, ed., *Instruction Models in Computer-based Learning Environments* NATO-ASI Series F: Computer and Systems Sciences. Berlin: Springer-Verlag.

Biggs, J. B. 1984. Learning strategies, student motivation patterns and subjectively perceived success. In J. R. Kirby, ed., *Cognitive strategies and educational performance*, 111–134. Orlando FL: Academic Press.

Binet, A. 1909. *Les idées modernes sur les enfants*. Paris: Flammarion.

Binet, A., and Simon, T. 1905. Méthodes nouvelles pour le diagnostic du niveau intellectuel des anormaux. *L'année Psychologique* 11:191–244.

Block, N., and Dworkin, G. 1976. *The IQ controversy: Critical readings*. New York: Pantheon.

Bloor, D. 1991. *Knowledge and social imagery*. Chicago: University of Chicago Press.

Blumenthal, A. L. 1970. *Language and psychology*. New York: Wiley.

Boring, E. G. 1923. Intelligence as the tests test it. *New Republic* June 6:35–37.

Bransford, J. D., Franks, J. J., Vye, N. J., and Sherwood, R. D. 1989. New approaches to instruction: Because wisdom can't be told. In S. Vosniadou and A. Ortony, eds., *Similarity and analogical reasoning*. Cambridge: Cambridge University Press.

Bransford, J. D., Goin, L. I., Hasselbring, T. S., Kinzer, C. K., Sherwood, R. D., and Williams, S. M. 1988. Learning with technology: Theoretical and empirical perspectives. *Peabody Journal of Education* 64 (1): 5–26.

Bransford, J. D., Hasselbring, T. S., Barron, B. J., Kulewicz, S., Littlefield, J., and Goin, L. I. 1988. Uses of macrocontexts to facilitate mathematical thinking. In R. I. Charles and E. A. Silver, eds., *The teaching and assessing of mathematical problem solving*, 125–147. Hillsdale, NJ: Erlbaum and National Council of Teachers of Mathematics.

Bransford, J. D., and Nitsch, K. E. 1978. Coming to understand things we could not previously understand. In J. F. Kavanaugh and W. Strange, eds., *Speech and language in the laboratory, school, and clinic*, 267–307. Cambridge: MIT Press, Reprinted in H. Singer and R. Ruddell, eds., *Theoretical models and processes of reading*. Newark, DE: International Reading Association.

Bransford, J. D., Sherwood, R. D., Hasselbring, T. S., Kinzer, C. K., and Williams, S. M. 1990. Anchored instruction: Why we need it and how technology can help. In D. Nix and R. Spiro, eds., *Cognition, education, and multimedia: Exploring ideas in high technology*, 115–141. Hillsdale, NJ: Erlbaum.

Bransford, J. D., Sherwood, R. D., Vye, N. J. and Rieser, J. 1986. Teaching thinking and problem solving: Research foundations. *American Psychologist* 41:1078–1089.

Bransford, J. D., and Stein, B. S. 1984. *The IDEAL problem solver*. New York: Freeman.

Brown, A. L. 1974. The role of strategic behavior in retardate memory. In N. R. Ellis, ed., *International review of research in mental retardation* 7:55–111. New York: Academic Press.

Brown, A. L. 1975. The development of memory: Knowing, knowing about knowing, and knowing how to know. In H. W. Reese, ed., *Advances in child development and behavior* 10:103–152. New York: Academic Press.

Brown, A. L. 1978. Knowing when, where, and how to remember: A problem of metacognition. In R. Glaser, ed., *Advances in Instructional Psychology* 10:77–165. Hillsdale, NJ: Erlbaum.

Brown, A. L. 1979. Theories of memory and the problem of development: Activity, growth, and knowledge. In L. S. Cermak and F. I. M. Craik, eds., *Levels of Processing in Human Memory*, 225–258. Hillsdale, NJ: Erlbaum.

Brown, A. L. 1982. Learning and development: The problem of compatibility, access, and induction. *Human Development* 25:89–115.

Brown, A. L. 1985a. Mental orthopedics, the training of cognitive skills: An interview with Alfred Binet. In S. F. Chipman, J. W. Segal, and R. Glaser, eds., *Thinking and learning skills*. Vol. 2, *Research and open questions*. Hillsdale, NJ: Erlbaum.

Brown, A. L. 1985b. Teaching students to think as they read: Implications for curriculum reform. Reading Ed. Rep. No. 58. Urbana-Champaign: University of Illinois, Center for the Study of Reading.

Brown, A. L. 1987. Metacognition and other mechanisms. In F. E. Weinart and R. H. Kluwe, eds., *Metacognition, motivation, and understanding*. Hillsdale, NJ: Erlbaum.

Brown, A. L. 1990. Domain-specific principles affect learning and transfer in children. *Cognitive Science* 14:107–133.

Brown, A. L. 1991. Explanation, analogy, and theory in children's spontaneous learning. The Kenneth Craik Memorial Lecture Series. St. John's College, Cambridge, October.

Brown, A. L. 1992. Design experiments: Theoretical and methodological challenges in creating complex interventions in classroom settings. *Journal of the Learning Sciences* 2:141–178.

Brown, A. L., Ash. D., Rutherford, M., Nakagawa, K., Gordon, A., and Campione, J. C. In press. Distributed expertise in the classroom. In G. Salomon, ed., *Distributed cognitions*. New York: Cambridge University Press.

Brown, A. L., Bransford, J. D., Ferrara, R. A., and Campione, J. C. 1983. Learning, remembering, and understanding. In J. H. Flavell and E. M. Markman, eds., *Handbook of child psychology*. Vol. 3, *Cognitive development*, 77–166. New York: Wiley.

Brown, A. L., and Campione, J. C. 1990. Communities of learning and thinking, or a context by any other name. *Human Development* 21:108–125.

Brown, A. L., Campione, J. C., Reeve, R. A., Ferrara, R. A., and Palincsar, A. S. 1991. Interactive learning, individual understanding: The case of reading and mathematics. In L. T. Landsmann, ed., *Culture, schooling and psychological development*. Hillsdale, NJ: Erlbaum.

Brown, A. L., and Day, J. D. 1983. Macrorules for summarizing texts: The development of expertise. *Journal of Verbal Learning and Verbal Behavior* 22:1–14.

Brown, A. L., Day, J. D., and Jones, R. S. 1983. The development of plans for summarizing texts. *Child Development* 54:968–979.

Brown, A. L., and DeLoache, J. S. 1978. Skills, plans, and self-regulation. In R. S. Siegler, ed., *Children's thinking: What develops?* Hillsdale, NJ: Erlbaum.

Brown, A. L., and Kane, M. J. 1988. Preschool children can learn to transfer: Learning to learn and learning from examples. *Cognitive Psychology* 20:493–523.

Brown, A. L., and Palincsar, A. S. 1982. Inducing strategic learning from texts by means of informed, self-control training. *Topics in Learning and Learning Disabilities* 2:1–17.

Brown, A. L., and Palincsar, A. S. 1989a. Coherence and causality in science reading. Paper presented at the annual meeting of the American Educational Research Association, San Francisco, CA.

Brown, A. L., and Palincsar, A. S. 1989b. Guided, cooperative learning and individual knowledge acquisition. In L. B. Resnick, ed., *Knowing, learning, and instruction: Essays in honor of Robert Glaser*, 393–451. Hillsdale, NJ: Erlbaum.

Brown, A. L., and Reeve, R. A. 1987. Bandwidths of competence: The role of supportive contexts in learning and development. In L. S. Liben, ed., *Development and learning: Conflict or congruence?*, 173–223. Hillsdale, NJ: Erlbaum.

Brown, A. L., and Smiley, S. 1977. Rating the importance of structural units of prose passages: A problem of metacognitive development. *Child Development* 48:1–8.

Brown, J. S., Collins, A., and Duguid, P. 1989. Situated cognition and the culture of learning. *Educational Researcher* 18:32–42.

Brown, R., and Herrnstein, R. 1975. *Psychology*. Boston: Little, Brown.

Brown, W. F., and Holtzman, W. H. 1967. *Survey of study habits and attitudes, form H.* (SSHA). New York: The Psychological Association.

Bruer, J. T. 1993. *Schools for thought: A science of learning in the classroom*. Cambridge: MIT Press.

Brumby, M. 1979. Problems in learning the concept of natural selection. *Journal of Biological Education* 13:119–122.

Bruner, J. S. 1985. Vygotsky: A historical and conceptual perspective. In J. V. Wertsch, ed., *Culture, communication, and cognition*, 21–34. New York: Cambridge University Press.

Bruner, J. S. 1972. Toward a sense of community. Review of Gartner et al. 1971, Children Teach Children, *Saturday Review* 55(15 January): 62–63.

Bruner, J. S. 1969. *On knowing: Essays for the left hand*. Cambridge: Harvard University Press.

Campione, J. C., and Brown, A. L. 1978. Toward a theory of intelligence: Contributions from research with retarded children. *Intelligence* 2:279–304.

Campione, J. C., Brown, A. L., and Ferrara, A. 1992. Mental retardation and intelligence. In R. J. Sternberg, ed., *Handbook of human intelligence.* New York: Cambridge University Press.

Campione, J. C., Brown, A. L., and Jay, M. 1992. Computers in a community of learners. In E. DeCorte, M. Linn, H. Mandl, and L. Verschaffel, eds., *Computer-based learning environments and problem solving.* NATO ASI series F: Computer and Systems Science 84:163–192. Berlin, Springer-Verlag.

Campione, J. C., Rutherford, M., Gordon, A., Walker, J., and Brown, A. L. In press. Now I'm a REAL boy: Zones of proximal development for those at risk. In N. C. Jordan and J. Goldsmith-Phillips, eds., *Learning disabilities: New directions for assessment and intervention.* Needham Heights, MA: Allyn & Bacon.

Carey, S., and Gelman, R., eds. 1991. *Epigenesis of mind: Essays on biology and cognition.* Hillsdale, NJ: Erlbaum.

Carr, E., and Ogle, D. 1987. K-W-L Plus: A strategy for comprehension and summarization. *Journal of Reading* 30:626–631.

Carroll, J. B. 1976. Promoting language skills: The role of instruction. In D. Klahr, ed., *Cognition and instruction,* 3–22. Hillsdale, NJ: Erlbaum.

Case, R. 1975. Social class differences in intellectual development: A neo-Piagetian investigation. *Canadian Journal of Behavioral Sciences* 7:78–95.

Case, R. 1985. *Intellectual development: Birth to adulthood.* New York: Academic.

Case, R. 1992. Defining the notion of a central conceptual structure, and placing it in an educational context. Paper presented at the annual meeting of the American Educational Research Association, San Francisco, April.

Case, R., and Garrett, N. B. 1992. New approaches to the teaching of mathematics and the role of the Rightstart program in laying an appropriate foundation for them. In S. Griffin and R. Case, Number Sense, Interim Report submitted to the James S. McDonnell Foundation, St. Louis.

Case, R., and Griffin, S. 1990. Child cognitive development: The role of central conceptual structures in the development of scientific and social thought. In C-A. Hauert, ed., *Developmental psychology: Cognitive, perceptuo-motor and psychological perspectives.* North-Holland: Elsevier.

Case, R., and Sandieson, R. 1987. General developmental constraints on the acquisition of special procedures (and vice versa). Paper presented at the annual meeting of the American Educational Research Association, Baltimore, April.

Cazden, C. 1988. *Classroom discourse: The language of teaching and learning.* Portsmouth, NH: Heinemann.

Ceci, S. 1990. *On intelligence . . . more or less.* Englewood Cliffs, NJ: Prentice Hall.

Chan, L. K. S., and Cole, P. G. 1986. The effects of comprehension monitoring training on the reading competence of learning disabled and regular class students. *Remedial and Special Education* 7:33–40.

Chase, W. G., and Simon, H. A. 1973a. Perception in chess. *Cognitive Psychology* 1:33–81.

Chase, W. G., and Simon, H. A. 1973b. The mind's eye in chess. In W. G. Chase, ed., *Visual information processing.* New York: Academic Press.

Chi, M. T. H., Feltovich, P. J., and Glaser, R. 1981. Categorization and representation of physics problems by experts and novices. *Cognitive Science* 5:121–152.

Chi, M. T. H., Hutchinson, J. E., and Robin, A. F. 1989. How inferences about novel domain-related concepts can be constrained by structured knowledge. *Merril-Palmer Quarterly* 35:27–62.

Chi, M. T. H., and Koeske, R. D. 1983. Network representation of a child's dinosaur knowledge. *Developmental Psychology* 19:29–39.

Chiesi, H. L., Spilich, G. L., and Voss, J. F. 1979. Acquisition of domain-related information in relation to high- and low-domain knowledge. *Journal of Verbal Learning and Verbal Behavior* 18:257–273.

Clement, J. 1982. Students' preconceptions in introductory mechanics. *American Journal of Physics* 50:66–71.

Cobb, P., and Merkel, G. 1989. Thinking strategies: Teaching arithmetic through problem solving. In P. Trafton, ed., *1989 Yearbook of the National Council of Teachers of Mathematics,* 70–81 Reston, VA: National Council of Teachers of Mathematics.

Cobb, P., Wood, T., Yackel, E., Nicholls, J., Wheatley, G., Trigatti, B., and Perlwitz, M. 1991. Assessment of a problem-centered second grade mathematics project. *Journal for Research in Mathematics Education* 22(1): 3–29.

Cohen, D. 1988. Teaching practice—plus ça change. In P. Jackson, ed., *Contributions to educational change: Perspectives on research and practice, National Society for the Study of Education.* Berkeley, CA: McCutchan.

Cohen, A. 1992. Using CSILE in a progressive discourse in physics. Paper presented at the annual meeting of the American Educational Research Association, San Francisco.

Cognition and Technology Group at Vanderbilt. 1990. Anchored instruction and its relationship to situated cognition. *Educational Researcher* 19(6): 2–10.

Cognition and Technology Group at Vanderbilt. 1991. Technology and the design of generative learning environments. *Educational Technology* 31:34–40.

Cognition and Technology Group at Vanderbilt. 1992a. The Jasper experiment: An exploration of issues in learning and instructional design. *Educational Technology Research and Development* 40:65–80.

Cognition and Technology Group at Vanderbilt. 1992b. The Jasper series: A generative approach to mathematical thinking. In K. Sheingold, L. G. Roberts, and S. M. Malcolm, eds., *This year in science series 1991: Technology for teaching and learning,* 108–140. Washington, DC: American Association for the Advancement of Science.

Cognition and Technology Group at Vanderbilt. 1992c. The Jasper series as an example of anchored instruction: Theory, program description and assessment data. *Educational Psychologist* 27:291–315.

Cognition and Technology Group at Vanderbilt. 1993a. Anchored instruction and situated cognition revisited. *Educational Technology* 33:52–70.

Cognition and Technology Group at Vanderbilt. 1993b. Toward integrated curricula: Possibilities from anchored instruction. In M. Rabinowitz, ed., *Cognitive science foundations of instruction,* 33–55. Hillsdale, NJ: Erlbaum.

Cognition and Technology Group at Vanderbilt. In press a. The Jasper series: Theoretical foundations and data on problem solving and transfer. In L. A. Penner, G. M. Barsche, H. M. Knoff, D. L. Nelson, and C. D. Spielberger, eds., *Contributions of psychology to mathematics and science education.* Washington, DC: American Psychological Association.

Cognition and Technology Group at Vanderbilt. In press b. The Jasper series: A design experiment in complex, mathematical problem solving. In J. Hawkins and A. Collins, eds., *Design experiments: Integrating technologies into schools.* New York: Cambridge University Press.

Cole, M., and Bruner, J. S. 1971. Cultural differences and inferences about psychological processes. *American Psychologist* 26:867–876.

Coleman, E. B. 1992. *Facilitating conceptual understanding in science: A collaborative explanation-based approach.* Ph.D. diss., University of Toronto, Toronto.

Collins, A., and Stevens, A. 1982. Goals and strategies of inquiry teachers. In R. Glaser, ed., *Advances in instructional psychology* 2:65–119. Hillsdale, NJ: Erlbaum.

Crabtree, C., Nash, G., Gagnon, P., and Waugh, S. In press. *Lessons from history: Essential understanding and historical perspectives students should acquire.* Berkeley: Regents of the University of California.

Cremin, L. A. 1961. *The transformation of the school: Progressivism in American education, 1876–1957.* New York: Alfred A. Knopf.

Crews, T., and Biswas, G. In press. A tutor for trip planning: Combining planning and mathematics problem solving. In *1993 World Congress on AI in education in August, 1993.* Edinburgh, Scotland.

Cuban, L. 1984. *How teachers taught: Constancy and change in American classrooms, 1890–1980.* New York: Longman.

Cuban, L. 1990. Reforming again, again, and again. *Educational Researcher* 13:3–13.

Dansereau, D. F. 1987. Transfer from cooperative to individual studying. *Journal of Reading* 31:614–619.

Dawson, V. L., Zeitz, C. M., and Wright, J. C. 1989. Expert-novice differences in person perception: Evidence of experts' sensitivities to the organization of behavior. *Social Cognition* 4:1–30.

Dee-Lucas, D., and Larkin, J. H. 1986. Novice strategies for processing scientific texts. *Discourse Processes* 9:329–354.

Dennett, D. C. 1987. *The intentional stance.* Cambridge: MIT press.

Derry, S. J., and Murphy, D. A. 1986. Designing systems that train learning ability: From theory to practice. *Review of Educational Research* 56:1–39.

Dewey, J. 1894. Plan of organization of the University Primary School, In J. A. Boydston, ed., *The early works of John Dewey, 1882–1898.* Vol. 5, *1895–1898: Early essays,* 223–243. Carbondale: Southern Illinois University Press, 1972.

Dewey, J. 1897. The University Elementary School: History and Character. *University* [of Chicago] *Record* 2:72–75.

Dewey, J. 1902. *The child and the curriculum.* Chicago: University of Chicago Press.

Dewey, J. 1936. The theory of the Chicago Experiment. In K. C. Mayhew and A. C. Edwards, eds., *The Dewey School: The Laboratory School of the University of Chicago, 1896–1903* (pp. 463–466). New York: Appleton-Century.

diSessa, A. 1983. Phenomenology and the evolution of intuition. In D. Gentner and A. L. Stevens, eds., *Mental models.* Hillsdale, NJ: Erlbaum.

diSessa, A. 1988. Knowledge in pieces. In G. Forman and P. Pufall, *Constructivism in the computer age.* Hillsdale, NJ: Erlbaum.

Dole, J. A., Duffy, G. G., Roehler, L. R., and Pearson, P. D. 1991. Moving from the old to the new: Research on reading comprehension instruction. *Review of Educational Research* 61:239–264.

Dow, P. 1991. *Schoolhouse politics.* Cambridge: Harvard University Press.

Doyle, W. 1983. Academic work. *Review of Educational Research* 53:159–199.

Duffy, G. G., and Roehler, L. R. 1987a. Improving reading instruction through the use of responsive elaboration. *Reading Teacher* 40:514–520.

Duffy, G. G., and Roehler, L. R. 1987b. Teaching reading skills as strategies. *Reading Teacher* 41:414–418.

Duffy, G. G., Roehler, L. R., Sivan, E., Rackliffe, G., Book, C., Meloth, M. S., Vavrus, R., Putnam, J., and Bassiri, D. 1987. Effects of explaining the reasoning associated with using reading strategies. *Reading Research Quarterly* 21:347–368.

Education Development Center. 1969. *Goals for the correlation of elementary science and mathematics: Report of the Cambridge Conference on the Correlation of Science and Mathematics in the Schools.* Boston: Houghton Mifflin.

Edwards, P., and Mercer, N. 1987. *Common knowledge.* London: Open University Press.

Eichinger, D. C., Anderson, C. W., Palincsar, A. S., and David, Y. M. 1991. An illustration of the roles of content knowledge, scientific argument, and social norms in collaborative problem solving. Paper presented at the annual meeting of the American Educational Research Association, Chicago, April.

Erickson, F., and Shultz, J. 1977. When is a context? Some issues and methods on the analysis of social competence. *Quarterly Newsletter of the Institute for Comparative Human Development* 1:5–10.

Fennema, E., and Carpenter, T. P. 1989. *Cognitively guided instruction readings.* Madison: University of Wisconsin, Wisconsin Center for Education Research.

Fischer, K. W. 1980. A theory of cognitive development: The control and construction of hierarchies of skill. *Psychological Review* 87:477–531.

Fish, S. 1980. *Is there a text in this class: The authority of interpretive communities.* Cambridge: Harvard University Press.

Flavell, J. H., and Wellman, H. M. 1977. Metamemory. In R. V. Kail, Jr., and J. W. Hagen, eds., *Perspectives on the development of memory and cognition,* 3–33. Hillsdale, NJ: Erlbaum.

Flower, L., and Higgins, L. 1990. Collaboration and the construction of meaning. Unpublished manuscript.

Flower, L., Schriver, K. A., Carey, L., Haas, C., and Hayes, J. R. 1992. Planning in writing: The cognition of a constructive process. In S. Witte, N. Nakadate, and R. Cherry, eds., *A rhetoric of doing.* Carbondale: Southern Illinois University Press.

Frederiksen, J., and Collins, A. 1989. A systems approach to educational testing. *Educational Researcher* 18(9):27–32.

Fulwiler, T. 1980. Journals across the curriculum. *English Journal* 69:14–19.

Furman, L., Barron, B., Montavon, E., Vye, N. J., Bransford, J. D., and Shah, P. 1989. The effects of problem formulation training and type of feedback on math handicapped students' problem-solving abilities. Paper presented at the annual meeting of the American Educational Research Association, San Francisco, April.

Fuson, K. C. 1982. Analysis of the counting-on solution procedure in addition. In T. P. Carpenter, J. M. Moser, and T. A. Romberg, eds., *Addition and subtraction: A cognitive perspective.* Hillsdale, NJ: Erlbaum.

Gallistel, C. R., Brown, A. L., Carey, S., Gelman, R., and Keil, F. C. 1991. Lessons from the study of animal learning. In S. Carey and R. Gelman, eds., *Epigenesis of mind: Essays on biology and cognition.* Hillsdale, NJ: Erlbaum.

Galton, F. 1892. *Hereditary genius.* London: Macmillan.

Gambrell, L. B., Kapinus, B. A., and Wilson, R. M. 1987. Using mental imagery and summarization to achieve independence in comprehension. *Journal of Reading* 30:638–642.

Gardner, H. 1982. *Art, mind, and brain.* New York: Basic Books.

Gardner, H. 1983. *Frames of mind.* New York: Basic Books.

Gardner, H. 1985. *The mind's new science.* New York: Basic Books.

Gardner, H. 1988. Creative lives, creative works. In R. J. Sternberg, ed., *The nature of creativity.* New York: Cambridge University Press.

Gardner, H. 1989. *To open minds.* New York: Basic Books.

Gardner, H. 1991. *The unschooled mind: How children think and how schools should teach.* New York: Basic Books.

Gardner, H. 1993a. *Creating minds: On the breakthroughs that shaped our era.* New York: Basic Books.

Gardner, H. 1993b. Intelligence in seven phases. In H. Gardner ed., *Multiple intelligences: The theory in practice.* New York: Basic Books.

Gardner, H. 1993c. *Multiple intelligences: The theory in practice.* New York: Basic Books.

Garner, R. 1987. *Metacognition and reading comprehension.* Norwood, NJ: Ablex.

Gaskins, I. W. 1984. There's more to a reading problem than poor reading. *Journal of Learning Disabilities* 17:467–471.

Gaskins, I. W. 1988. Teachers as thinking coaches: Creating strategic learning and problem solvers. *Reading, Writing, and Learning Disabilities* 4:35–48.

Gaskins, R. W. 1992. When good instruction is not enough: A mentor program. *Reading Teacher* 45:568–572.

Gaskins, I. W., Anderson, R. C., Pressley, M., Cunicelli, E. A., and Satlow, E. 1993. Six teachers' dialogue during cognitive process instruction. *Elementary School Journal* 93:277–304.

Gaskins, I. W., and Baron, J. 1985. Teaching poor readers to cope with maladaptive cognitive styles: A training program. *Journal of Learning Disabilities* 18:390–394.

Gaskins, I. W., Cunicelli, E. A., and Satlow, E. 1992. Implementing an across-the-curriculum strategies program: Teachers reactions to change. In M. Pressley, K. Harris, and J. T. Guthrie, eds., *Promoting academic competence and literacy in schools,* 407–425. San Diego, CA: Academic Press.

Gaskins, I. W., Downer, M. A., Anderson, R. C., Cunningham, P. M., Gaskins, R. W., Schommer, M., and the Teachers of Benchmark School. 1988. A metacognitive approach to phonics: Using what you know to decode what you don't know. *Remedial and Special Education* 9:36–41, 66.

Gaskins, I. W., and Elliot, T. T. 1991. *Implementing cognitive strategy instruction across the school: The Benchmark manual for teachers.* Cambridge, MA: Brookline Books.

Gaskins, R. W., Gaskins, J. C., and Gaskins, I. W. 1991. A decoding program for poor readers—and the rest of the class too! *Language Arts* 68:213–225.

Gaskins, I. W., Guthrie, J. T., Anderson, R. C., Satlow, E., Boehnlein, F., Cunicelli, E. A., and Benedict, J. In preparation. Patterns of growth among poor readers during three years of strategy instruction.

Gazzaniga, M. S. 1978. *The integrated mind.* New York: Plenum.

Gelman, R., and Gallistel, C. R. 1978. *The young child's understanding of number.* New York: Harvard University Press.

Gibson, J. J. 1977. The theory of affordance. In R. Shaw and J. Bransford, eds., *Perceiving, acting, and knowing,* 67–82. Hillsdale, NJ: Erlbaum.

Ginsburg, H. P., and Russel, R. L. 1981. Social class and racial factors on early mathematical thinking. *Monographs of the Society for Research in Child Development,* vol. 46, serial no. 913.

Glaser, R. 1988. Cognitive science and education. *International Social Science Journal* 40(1): 21–44.

Glaser, R. 1989. To plan for a century. *Educational Researcher* 18:5.

Glaser, R., and Bassok, M. 1989. Learning theory and the study of instruction. *Annual Review of Psychology* 40:631–666.

Gobbo, C., and Chi, M. T. H. 1986. How knowledge is structured and used by expert and novice children. *Cognitive Development* 1:221–237.

Gobert Wickham, J., Coleman, E. B., Scardamalia, M., and Bereiter, C. 1992. Fostering the development of children's graphical representation and causal/dynamic models through CSILE. Paper presented at the annual meeting of the American Educational Research Association, Atlanta. April.

Goddard, H. H. 1910. A measuring scale for intelligence. *Training School* 6:146–154.

Goldman, J., Krechevsky, M., Meyaard, J., and Gardner, H. 1988. *A developmental study of children's practical intelligence for school.* Harvard Project Zero Technical Report.

Goldman, S. R., Pellegrino, J. W., and Bransford, J. D. In press. Assessing programs that invite thinking. In H. O'Neill and E. Baker, eds., *Technology assessment: Estimating the future.* Hillsdale, NJ: Erlbaum.

Goldman, W. R., Vye, N. J., Williams, S. W., Rewey, K., and Hmelo, C. E. 1992. Planning net representations and analyses of complex problem solving. Paper presented at the annual meeting of the American Educational Research Association, San Francisco. April.

Goldman, S. R., Vye, N. J., Williams, S. W., Rewey, K., Pellegrino, J. W. 1991. Problem space analyses of the Jasper problems and students' attempts to solve them. Paper presented at the annual meeting of the American Educational Research Association, Chicago. April.

Goldman, S. R., Vye, N. J., Williams, S. W., Rewey, K., Pellegrino, J. W., and the Cognition and Technology Group at Vanderbilt. 1991. Solution space analyses of the Jasper problems and students' attempts to solve them. Paper presented at the annual meeting of the American Educational Research Association, Chicago. April.

Goodwin, C. 1987. Participation frameworks in children's argument. Paper presented at International Interdisciplinary Conference on Child Research. University of Trondheim, Norway.

Gould, S. J. 1981. *The mismeasure of man.* New York: Norton.

Greeno, J. G., Smith, D. R., and Moore, J. L. 1993. Transfer of situated learning. In D. K. Detterman and R. J. Sternberg, eds., *Transfer on trial: Intelligence, cognition, and instruction,* 99–167. Norwood, NJ: Ablex.

Graham, P. S. 1967. *Progressive education, from arcady to academe: A history of the Progressive Education Association, 1919–1955.* New York: Columbia University Teachers College.

Griffin, S. A., Case, R. and Capodilupo, S. In press. Teaching for understanding: The importance of central conceptual structures in the elementary school mathematics curriculum. In A. Strauss, ed., *Educational environments.* Norwood, NJ: Ablex.

Griffin, S., Case, R., and Sandieson, R. 1992. Synchrony and asynchrony in the acquisition of everyday mathematical knowledge: Towards a representational theory of children's intellectual growth. In R. Case, ed., *The mind's staircase: Exploring the central conceptual underpinnings of children's theory and knowledge.* Hillsdale, NJ: Erlbaum.

Groen, G. J., and Parkman, J. M. 1972. A chronometric analysis of simple addition. *Psychological Review* 79:329–343.

Guttman, L. 1992. The irrelevance of factor analysis for the study of group differences. *Multivariate Behavioral Research* 27:175–204.

Halford, G. S. 1982. *The development of thought.* Hillsdale, NJ: Erlbaum.

Hammond, N. V. 1989. Hypermedia and learning: Who guides whom? In H. Maurer, ed., *Computer-assisted learning,* 167–181. Berlin: Springer-Verlag.

Hammond, N. V., and Allinson, L. J. 1989. Extending hypertext for learning: An investigation of access and guidance tools. In A. Sutcliffe and L. Macaulay, eds., *People and computers V,* 293–304. Cambridge: Cambridge University Press.

Harré, R. 1984. *Personal being: A theory for individual psychology.* Cambridge: Harvard University Press.

Hatano, G., and Osawa, K. 1983. Digit memory of grand experts in abacus-derived mental calculation. *Cognition* 15:95–110.

Heath, S. B. 1991. "It's about winning!": The language of knowledge in baseball. In L. B. Resnick, J. M. Levine, and S. D. Teasley, eds., *Perspectives on socially shared cognition,* 101–126. Washington, DC: American Psychological Association.

Heath, S. B. 1983. *Ways with Words.* Cambridge: Cambridge University Press.

Heath, S. B., and Mangiola, L. 1991. *Children of promise: Literate activity in linguistically and culturally diverse classrooms.* Washington, DC: National Education Association.

Heath, S. B., and McLaughlin, M. W. In press. Learning for anything every day. *Journal of Curriculum Studies.*

Henderson, V. L., and Dweck, C. S. 1990. Motivation and achievement. In S. Feldman and G. Elliot, eds., *At the threshold: Adolescent development.* Cambridge: Harvard University Press.

Hewitt, J. 1992. A comparison of hypertext and discourse environments with regard to knowledge-building and collaboration. Poster presented at the annual meeting of the American Educational Research Association, Atlanta. April.

Hewitt, J., and Webb, J. 1992. Designs to encourage discourse in the OISE CSILE system. Poster presentation at the Computer and Human Interaction Conference, Monterey, CA. May.

Hiebert, E. H., and Hutchison, T. H. 1991. Research directions: The current state of alternative assessments for policy and instructional uses. *Language Arts* 68:662–668.

Hiebert, J. 1986. *Conceptual and procedural knowledge: The case of mathematics.* Hillsdale, NJ: Erlbaum.

Hmelo, C. E., Williams, S. M., Vye, N. J., Goldman, S. R., Bransford, J. D., and the Cognition and Technology Group at Vanderbilt. 1993. A longitudinal study of the effects of anchored instruction in mathematical problem-solving transfer. Paper presented at the annual meeting of the American Educational Research Association, Atlanta, April.

Holquist, M., and Emerson, C. 1981. *Glossary for the dialogic imagination: Four essays by M. M. Bakhtin.* M. Holquist, ed. M. Holquist and C. Emerson, trans. Austin: University of Texas Press.

Holt, J. 1964. *How children fail.* New York: Pitman.

Inhelder, B., and Piaget, J. 1958. *The growth of logical thinking from childhood to adolescence.* New York: Basic Books.

James, W. 1890. *The Principles of Psychology.* New York: Henry Holt.

Jenkins, J. J. 1979. Four points to remember: A tetrahedral model and memory experiments. In L. S. Cermak and F. I. M. Craik, eds., *Levels and processing in human memory,* 429–446. Hillsdale, NJ: Erlbaum.

Johnston, P. 1985. Teaching students to apply strategies that improve reading comprehension. *Elementary School Journal* 85:635–645.

Joyce, B. 1985. Models for teaching thinking. *Educational Leadership* 42:4–7.

Kamii, C. K. 1985. *Young children reinvent arithmetic: Implications of Piaget's theory.* New York: Teachers College Press.

Kerkman, D. D., and Siegler, R. S. In press. Individual differences and adaptive flexibility in lower-income children's strategy choices. *Learning and Individual Differences.*

Kirst, M. 1991. Research news and comment: Interview on assessment issues with Lorrie Shepard. *Educational Researcher* 20:21–23, 27.

Kletzien, S. B. 1991. Strategy use by good and poor comprehenders reading expository text of differing levels. *Reading Research Quarterly* 26:67–86.

Kliebard, H. M. 1987. *The struggle for the American curriculum, 1893–1958.* New York: Rutledge.

Laboratory of Comparative Human Cognition. 1982. Culture and intelligence. In R. J. Sternberg, ed., *Handbook of human intelligence,* 642–719. New York: Cambridge University Press.

Laboratory of Comparative Human Cognition. 1983. Culture and Cognitive Development. In P. H. Mussen, ed., *Handbook of child psychology.* Vol. 1, *History, theory, and methods,* 295–356. New York: Wiley.

Lamon, M. 1992. Learning environments and macro-contexts: Using multimedia for understanding mathematics. Paper presented at the annual meeting of the American Educational Research Association, San Francisco, April.

Lamon, M., Abeygunawardena, H., Cohen, A., Lee, E., and Wasson, B. 1992. Students' reflections on learning: A portfolio study. Paper presented at the annual meeting of the American Educational Research Association, San Francisco, April.

Lamon, M., Chan, C., Scardamalia, M., Burtis, P. J., and Brett, C. 1992. Beliefs about learning and constructive processes in reading: Effects of a computer-supported intentional learning environment (CSILE). Paper presented at the annual meeting of the American Educational Research Association, Atlanta, April.

Lamon, M., and Lee, E. In press. Cognitive technologies and peer collaboration: The growth of reflection. In J. Hawkins and A. Collins, eds. *Design, experiments: School restructuring through technology.* New York: Cambridge University Press.

Landow, G. P. 1989. Hypertext in literary education, criticism, and scholarship. *Computers and the Humanities* 23:173–198.

Latour, B. 1987. *Science in action: How to follow scientists and engineers through society.* Cambridge: Harvard University Press.

Latour, B., and Woolgar, S. 1986. *Laboratory life: The construction of scientific facts.* Princeton, NJ: Princeton University Press.

Lave, J., and Wenger, E. 1991. *Situated learning: Legitimate peripheral participation.* New York: Cambridge University Press.

Levidow, B., Hunt, E., and McKee, C. 1991. The DIAGNOSER: A Hypercard tool for building theoretically based tutorials. *Behavior Research Methods, Instruments, and Computers* 23:249–252.

Lipsitz, J. 1984. *Successful schools for young adolescents.* New Brunswick, NJ: Transaction Books.

Liu, P. 1981. An investigation of the relationship between qualitative and quantitative advances in the cognitive development of preschool children. Ph.D. diss., University of Toronto, Toronto.

Lodge, D. 1989. *Nice work.* London: Penguin.

Majone, G., & Wildavsky, A. 1978. Implementation as evolution. In H. E. Freeman, ed., *Policy studies review annual* 2:103–117. Beverly Hills, CA: Sage.

Marchionini, G., ed. 1988. Special issue on hypermedia. *Educational Technology* 29, no. 11.

Margolis, H. 1987. *Patterns, thinking, and cognition: A theory of judgment.* Chicago: University of Chicago Press.

Marini, Z. A. 1992. Synchrony and asynchrony in the development of children's scientific reasoning: Re-analyzing the problem of decalages from a neo-Piagetian perspective. In R. Case, ed., *The mind's staircase: Exploring the conceptual underpinnings of children's thought and knowledge.* Hillsdale, NJ: Erlbaum.

Marzano, R. J., and Arredando, D. E. 1986. Restructuring schools through the use of teaching of thinking skills. *Educational Leadership* 43:20–26.

Mayhew, K. C., and Edwards, A. C. 1936. *The Dewey school: The laboratory school of the University of Chicago, 1896–1903.* New York: Appleton-Century.

Mayr, E. 1988. *Toward a new philosophy of biology.* Cambridge: Belknap Press.

McKeown, M. G., and Beck, I. L. 1990. The assessment and characterization of young learners' knowledge of a topic in history. *American Educational Research Journal* 27:688–726.

McLarty, K., Goodman, J., Risko, V., Kinzer, C. K., Vye, N., Rowe, D., and Carson, J. 1990. Implementing anchored instruction: Guiding principles for curriculum development. In J. Zutell and S. McCormick, eds., *Literacy theory and research: Analyses from multiple paradigms,* 109–120. Chicago: National Reading Conference.

Medawar, P. 1982. *Pluto's republic.* Oxford: Oxford University Press.

Mehan, H. 1979. *Learning lessons: Social organization in the classroom.* Cambridge: Harvard University Press.

Meichenbaum, P. M. 1977. *Cognitive behavior modification: An integrated approach.* New York: Plenum.

Meltzer, L. 1991. Problem-solving strategies and academic performance in learning-disabled students: Do subtypes exist? In L. V. Feagans, E. J. Short, and L. J. Meltzer, eds., *Subtypes of learning disabilities: Theoretical perspectives on research,* 163–188. Hillsdale, NJ: Erlbaum.

Minsky, M. 1985. *The society of mind.* New York: Simon & Schuster.

Minstrell, J. 1982. Explaining the "at rest" condition of an object. *The Physics Teacher* 20:10–14.

Minstrell, J., and diSessa, A. In press. Explaining falling bodies. Submitted to *The Physics Teacher.*

Montavon, E., Furman, L., Barron, B., Bransford, J. D., and Hasselbring, T. S. 1989. The effects of varied context training and irrelevant information training on the transfer of math problem-solving skills. Paper presented at the annual meeting of the American Educational Research Association, San Francisco, April.

Moschkovich, J. 1989. Constructing a problem space through appropriation: A case study of tutoring during computer exploration. Paper presented at the annual meeting of the American Educational Research Association, San Francisco, CA.

Murphy, J. 1991. *Restructuring schools: Capturing and assessing the phenomena.* New York: Teachers College Press.

Murphy, J., and Hallinger, P. 1993. *Restructuring schools successfully: Learning from ongoing efforts.* Beverly Hills, CA: Corwin/Sage.

National Assessment of Education Progress. 1983. *The third national mathematics assessment: Results, trends, and issues.* Denver: Educational Commission of the States.

National Assessment of Education Progress. 1988. National Center for Educational Statistics, U.S. Department of Education, Office of Educational Research and Improvement.

National Commission on Excellence in Education. 1983. *A nation at risk: The imperative for educational reform.* Washington, DC.

National Council of Teachers of Mathematics. 1989a. *Curriculum and evaluation standards for school mathematics.* Reston, VA.

National Council of Teachers of Mathematics. 1989b. *Professional standards for teaching mathematics.* Reston, VA.

Neves, D. M., and Anderson, J. R. 1981. Knowledge compilation: Mechanisms for the automatization of cognitive skills. In J. R. Anderson, ed., *Cognitive skills and their acquisition,* 5–84. Hillsdale, NJ: Erlbaum.

Newell, A., and Simon, H. A. 1972. *Human problem solving.* Englewood Cliffs, NJ: Prentice-Hall.

Newman, D., Griffin, P., and Cole, M. 1989. *The construction zone.* Cambridge: Cambridge University Press.

Ng, E., and Bereiter, C. 1991. Three levels of goal orientation in learning. *Journal of the Learning Sciences* 1(3–4):243–271.

Nicholls, J. G. 1984. Achievement motivation: Conception of ability, subjective experience, task choice, and performance. *Psychological Review* 91:328–346.

Nickerson, R. S. 1988. On improving thinking through instruction. In E. Z. Rothkopf, ed., *Review of Educational Research* 15:3–57.

Nist, S. L., and Simpson, M. L. 1987. Facilitating transfer in college reading programs. *Journal of Reading* 30:620–625.

Novak, J. D., and Gowin, D. B. 1984. *Learning how to learn.* Cambridge: Cambridge University Press.

O'Connor, M. C. 1991. Negotiated defining: Speech activities and mathematical literacies. Unpublished manuscript, Boston University.

Ohlsson, S. 1991. *Young adults' understanding of evolutionary explanations: Preliminary observations*. Technical report to OERI. Pittsburgh: University of Pittsburgh, Learning Research and Development Center.

Okamoto, Y. 1992. Implications of the notion of central conceptual structures for assessment. Paper presented at the annual meeting of the American Educational Research Association, San Francisco, April.

Olson, D. R., ed. 1974. *Media and symbols*. Chicago: University of Chicago Press.

Palincsar, A. S., and Brown, A. L. 1984. Reciprocal teaching of comprehension-fostering and comprehension-monitoring activities. *Cognition and Instruction* 1:117–175.

Palincsar, A. S., Brown, A. L., and Campione, J. C. 1990. First grade dialogues for knowledge acquisition and use. In N. Minick and E. Forman, eds., *The institutional and social context of mind: New directions in Vygotskian theory and research*. Oxford: Oxford University Press.

Palincsar, A. S., Ransom, K., and Derber, S. 1988. Collaborative research and the development of reciprocal teaching. *Educational Leadership* 46: 37–40.

Paris, S. G., Lipson, M., and Wixson, K. 1983. Becoming a strategic reader. *Contemporary Educational Psychology* 8:293–316.

Paris, S. G., and Oka, E. R. 1986. Children's reading strategies, metacognition, and motivation. *Developmental Review* 6:25–56.

Paris, S. G., Wasik, B. A., and Turner, J. C. 1991. The development of strategic readers. In R. Barr, M. L. Kamil, P. Mosenthal, and P. D. Pearson, eds., *Handbook of reading research* 2:815–860. New York: Longman.

Peabody Group at Vanderbilt. 1990. The Peabody perspective. Unpublished manuscript, Vanderbilt University, Nashville.

Pearson, P. D. 1985. Changing the face of reading comprehension instruction. *Reading Teacher* 38:724–738.

Pellegrino, J. W., Hickey, D., Heath, A., Rewey, K., Vye, N. J., and the Cognition and Technology Group at Vanderbilt. 1991. *Assessing the outcomes of an innovative instructional program: The 1990–1991 implementation of the "Adventures of Jasper Woodbury."* Technical Report no. 91-1. Nashville: Vanderbilt University, Learning Technology Center.

Perkins, D. 1992. *Smart schools: From training memories to educating minds*. New York: Macmillan.

Perkins, D., Lochhead, J., and Bishop, J. C. 1987. *Thinking: The Second International Conference*. Hillsdale, NJ: Erlbaum.

Polya, G. 1957. *How to solve it*. Princeton, NJ: Princeton University Press.

Pomerantz, C. 1971. *The day they parachuted cats into Borneo*. Reading, MA: Young Scott Books.

Popper, K. R. 1972. *Objective knowledge: An evolutionary approach*. Oxford: Clarendon Press.

Porter, A. 1989. A curriculum out of balance: The case of elementary school mathematics. *Educational Researcher* 18:9–15.

Premack, D. 1976. *Intelligence in ape and man*. Hillsdale, NJ: Erlbaum.

Prescott, G. A., Balow, I. H., Hogan, T. P., and Farr, R. C. 1978. *The Metropolitan Achievement Test*. New York: Harcourt, Brace, & Janovich.

Pressley, M., Gaskins, I. W., Cunicelli, E. A., Burdick, N. J., Schaub-Matt, M., Lee, D. S., and Powell, N. 1991. Strategy instruction at Benchmark School: A faculty interview study. *Learning Disability Quarterly* 14:19–48.

Pressley, M., Gaskins, I. W., Wile, D., Cunicelli, E. A., and Sheridan, J. 1991. Teaching literacy strategies across the curriculum: A case study of Benchmark School. *National Reading Conference Handbook*. Chicago: National Reading Conference.

Pressley, M., Goodchild, F., Fleet, J., Zajchowski, R., and Evans, E. D. 1989. The challenges of classroom strategy instruction. *Elementary School Journal* 89:301–342.

Pressley, M., and Levin, J. R., eds. 1983. *Cognitive strategy research: Educational applications.* New York: Springer-Verlag.

Ravitch, D., and Finn, C. E., Jr. 1987. *What do you 17-year-olds know? A report on the first national assessment of history and literature.* New York: Harper & Row.

Reitman, J. S. 1976. Skilled perception in Go: Deducing memory structures from inter-response times. *Cognitive Psychology* 10:438–464

Resnick, D. 1991. Historical perspective on literacy and schooling. In S. Grabard, ed., *Literacy: An overview,* 15–32. New York: Hill & Wang.

Resnick, L. B. 1989. Developing mathematical knowledge. *American Psychologist* 44(2): 162–169.

Resnick, L. B. 1983. A developmental theory of number understanding. In H. P. Ginsburg, ed., *The development of mathematical understanding.* New York: Academic Press.

Resnick, L. B. 1976. Task analysis in instructional design: Some cases from mathematics. In D. Klahr, ed., *Cognition and instruction.* Hillsdale, NJ: Erlbaum.

Resnick, L. B., Bill, V., and Lesgold, S. In press. Developing thinking abilities in arithmetic class. In A. Demetriou, M. Shayer, A. Efklides, eds., *The modern theories of cognitive development go to school.* London: Routledge.

Resnick, L. B., and Klopfer, L. E. 1989 Toward the thinking curriculum: An overview. In L. B. Resnick and L. E. Klopfer, eds., *Toward the thinking curriculum: Current cognitive research,* 1018. Alexandria, VA: Association for Supervision and Curriculum Development.

Resnick, L. B. and Klopfer, L. E., eds. 1989. *Toward the thinking curriculum: Current cognitive research.* Alexandria, VA: Association for Supervision and Curriculum Development.

Resnick, L. B., Levine, J. M., and Teasley, S. D. 1991. *Perspectives on socially shared cognition.* Washington, DC: American Psychological Association.

Resnick, L. B., Wang, M. C., and Kaplan, J. 1973. Task analysis in curriculum design: A hierarchically sequenced introductory mathematics curriculum. *Journal of Applied Behavioral Analysis* 6:679–710

Rewey, K. L., and the Cognition and Technology Group at Vanderbilt. 1991. Scripted cooperation and anchored instruction: Interactive tools for improving mathematics problem solving. Paper presented at the Annual Meeting of the James S. McDonnell Foundation Program in Cognitive Studies for Educational Practice.

Riley, M. S., and Greeno, J. G. 1988. Developmental analysis of understanding language about quantities and of solving problems. *Cognition and Instruction* 5(1): 49–101.

Rogers, E. M., and Shoemaker, F. F. 1971. *Communication of innovations: A cross-cultural approach.* 2d ed. New York: Free Press.

Rogoff, B. 1990. *Apprenticeship in thinking.* New York: Oxford University Press.

Rothbart, M. K., Posner, M. I., and Boylan, A. 1990. Regulatory mechanisms in infant development. In J. Enns, ed., *The development of attention: Research and theory.* North-Holland: Elsevier.

Salomon, G. In press. *Distributed cognition.* New York: Cambridge University Press.

Saxe, G. B., Guberman, S. R., and Gearhart, M. 1989. Social processes in early number development. *Monographs of the Society for Research in Child Development* 52, serial no. 216.

Scardamalia, M. 1981. How children cope with the cognitive demands of writing. In C. H. Frederiksen and J. F. Dominic, eds., *Writing: The nature, development, and teaching of written communication* 2:81–103. Hillsdale, NJ: Erlbaum.

Scardamalia, M., and Bereiter, C. 1984. Development of strategies in text processing. In H. Mandl, N. L. Stein, and T. Trabasso eds., *Learning and comprehension of text*, 379–406. Hillsdale, NJ: Erlbaum.

Scardamalia, M., and Bereiter, C. 1985. Fostering the development of self-regulation in children's knowledge processing. In S. F. Chipman, J. W. Segal, and R Glaser, eds., *Thinking and learning Skills.* Vol. 2, *Research and open questions*, 563–577. Hillsdale, NJ: Erlbaum.

Scardamalia, M., and Bereiter, C. 1987. Knowledge telling and knowledge transforming in written composition. In S. Rosenberg, ed., *Advances in applied psycholinguistics.* Vol. 2, *Reading, writing, and language learning*, 142–175. Cambridge: Cambridge University Press.

Scardamalia, M., and Bereiter, C. 1991. Higher levels of agency for children in knowledge building: A challenge for the design of new knowledge media. *Journal of the Learning Sciences* 1:37–68.

Scardamalia, M., and Bereiter, C. 1992. Text-based and knowledge-based questioning by children. *Cognition and Instruction* 9:177–199.

Scardamalia, M., Bereiter, C., Brett, C., Burtis, P. J., Calhoun, C., and Smith Lea, N. 1992. Educational application of a networked communal database. *Interactive Learning Environments* 2:45–71.

Scarr, S., and Carter-Saltzman, L. 1982. Genetics and intelligence. In R. J. Sternberg, ed., *Handbook of human intelligence.* New York: Cambridge University Press.

Schoenfeld, A., Smith, J., and Arcavi, A. In press. Learning: The microgenetic analysis of one student's evolving understanding of a complex subject matter domain. In R. Glaser, ed., *Advances in instructional psychology.* Vol. 4. Hillsdale, NJ: Erlbaum.

Shaw, R., Turvey, M. T., and Mace, W. 1982. Ecological psychology: The consequence of a commitment to realism. In W. B. Weimer and D. S. Palermo, eds., *Cognition and the symbolic processes* 2:159–226. Hillsdale, NJ: Erlbaum.

Shulman, L. S. 1986. Paradigms and research programs in the study of teaching: A contemporary perspective. In M. C. Wittrock, ed., *Handbook of research on teaching*, 3d ed., 3–36. New York: Macmillan.

Siegler, R. S. 1976. Three aspects of cognitive development. *Cognitive Psychology* 8:481–520.

Siegler, R. S. 1987. The perils of averaging data over strategies: An example from children's addition. *Journal of Experimental Psychology, General* 116:250–264.

Siegler, R. S. 1988. Individual differences in strategy choices: Good students, not-so-good students, and perfectionists. *Child Development* 59:833–851.

Siegler, R. S. In press. Adaptive and non-adaptive characteristics of low income children's strategy use. To appear in L. A. Penner, ed., *Contributions of psychology to science and math education.* Washington, DC: American Psychological Association.

Siegler, R. S., and Jenkins, E. 1989. *How children discover new strategies.* Hillsdale, NJ: Erlbaum.

Siegler, R. S., and Robinson, M. 1982. The development of numerical understandings. In H. W. Reese and L. P. Lipsitt, eds., *Advances in child development and behavior* 16:241–312. New York; Academic Press.

Siegler, R. S., and Shrager, J. 1984. Strategy choices in addition and subtraction: How do children know what to do? In C. Sophian, ed., *Origins of cognitive skills.* Hillsdale, NJ: Erlbaum.

Smith, E. E., Adams, N., and Schorr, D. 1978. Fact retrieval and the paradox of interference. *Cognitive Psychology* 10:438–464.

Snow, R. E., and Yalow, E. 1982. Education and intelligence. In R. J. Sternberg, ed., *Handbook of human intelligence*, 493–585. Cambridge: Cambridge University Press.

Spearman, C. 1923. *The nature of intelligence and the principles of cognition.* London: Macmillan.

Spielberg, S. (director) 1981. *Raiders of the Lost Ark* (film). Hollywood: LucasFilm Ltd. Productions.

Spiro, R. J., and Jehng, J.-C. 1990. Cognitive flexibility and hypertext: Theory and technology for the nonlinear and multidimensional traversal of complex subject matter. In D. Nix and R. J. Spiro, eds., *Cognition, education, and Multimedia: Exploring ideas in high technology,* 143–162. Hillsdale, NJ: Erlbaum.

Spiro, R. J., Vispoel, W., Schmitz, J., Samarapungavan, A., and Boerger, A. 1987. Knowledge acquisition for application: Cognitive flexibility and transfer in complex content domains. In B. C. Britton and S. Glynn, eds., *Executive control processes in reading,* 177–199. Hillsdale, NJ: Erlbaum.

Spoehr, K. T., and Katz, D. B. 1989. *Conceptual structure and the growth of expertise in American history.* Technical Report 89-3, Department of Cognitive and Linguistic Sciences. September.

Staff. 1993. The endless plague. *Newsweek,* January 11, p. 56.

Stanovich, K. 1986. Matthew effects in reading: Some consequences of individual differences in the acquisition of literacy. *Reading Research Quarterly* 21:360–406.

Starkey, P., Spelke, E. S., and Gelman, R. 1983. Detection of intermodal numerical correspondences by human infants. *Science* 222:179–181.

Starr, S. L. 1983. Simplification in scientific work: An example from neuroscientific research. *Social Studies of Science* 13: 205–228.

Steinberg, A. 1992. The seventh grade slump and how to avoid it. *Harvard Education Letter* 8(1): 1–5.

Stern, W. 1912. *Psychologische Methoden der Intelligence-Prufung.* Leipzig: Barth.

Sternberg, R. J. 1977. *Intelligence, information-processing, and analogical reasoning: The componential analysis of human abilities.* Hillsdale, NJ: Erlbaum.

Sternberg, R. J., ed. 1982. *Handbook of human intelligence.* New York: Cambridge University Press.

Sternberg, R. J. 1984. Toward a triarchic theory of human intelligence. *Behavioral and Brain Sciences* 8:269–315.

Sternberg, R. J. 1985. *Beyond IQ: A triarchic theory of human intelligence.* New York: Cambridge University Press.

Sternberg, R. J., ed. 1988. *The nature of creativity.* New York: Cambridge University Press.

Sternberg, R. J. 1990a. *Metaphors of mind.* New York: Cambridge University Press.

Sternberg, R. J. 1990b. Thinking styles: Keys to understanding student performance. *Phi Delta Kappan* 71:366–371.

Sternberg, R. J., ed. In press. *Encyclopedia of intelligence.* New York: MacMillan.

Sternberg, R. J., and Detterman, D., eds., 1986. *What is intelligence?* Norwood, NJ: Ablex.

Sternberg, R. J., and Lubart, T. 1991. An investment theory of creativity and its development. *Human Development* 34:1–31.

Sternberg, R. J., Okagaki, L., and Jackson, A. 1990. Practical intelligence for success in school. *Educational Leadership* 48:35–39.

Sternberg, R. J., and Wagner, R. 1986. *Practical intelligence.* New York: Cambridge University Press.

Stevenson, H., Lee, S., and Stigler, J. 1986. Mathematics achievement of Chinese, Japanese, and American children. *Science* 231:693–699.

Stich, S. P. 1983. *From folk psychology to cognitive science: The case against belief.* Cambridge: MIT Press.

Stigler, J., Lee, S. Y., and Stevenson, H. W. 1990. *Mathematics knowledge of Japanese, Chinese & American children.* National Council of Teaching of Mathematics Monographs.

Stigler, J., and Perry, M. 1988. Mathematics learning in Japanese, Chinese, and American classrooms. In G. Saxe and M. Gearhart, eds., *Children's mathematics: New directions for child development*, no. 41. San Francisco: Jossey-Bass.

Stigler, J., Shweder, R., and Herdt, G. 1990. *Cultural psychology.* New York: Cambridge University Press.

Swanson, H. L. 1989. Strategy instruction: Overview of principles and procedures for effective use. *Learning Disability Quarterly* 12:3–14.

Swanson, H. L. 1990. Influence of metacognitive knowledge and aptitude on problem solving. *Journal of Educational Psychology* 82:306–314.

Swing, S. R., Stoiber, K. C., and Peterson, P. L. 1988. Thinking skills versus learning time: Effects of alternative classroom-based interventions on students' mathematics problem solving. *Cognition and Instruction* 5:103–121.

Terman, L. 1916. *The measurement of intelligence.* Boston: Houghton Mifflin.

Thomas, J. W., and Rowher, W. D., Jr. 1986. Academic study: The role of learning strategies. *Educational Psychologist* 21:19–41.

Thomson, G. 1948. *The factorial analysis of human ability.* Boston: Houghton Mifflin.

Thorndike, E. L. 1924. The measurement of intelligence: Present status. *Psychological Review* 31:219–252.

Thurstone, L. L. 1938. Primary mental abilities. *Psychological Monographs,* no. 1.

Torgeson, J. K. 1978. Performance of reading disabled children on serial memory tasks: A selective review of recent research. *Reading Research Quarterly* 14:57–87.

Torgesen, J. K. 1980. Conceptual and educational implications of the use of efficient task strategies by learning disabled children. *Journal of Learning Disabilities* 13:19–26.

Toulmin, S. 1958. *The uses of argument.* Cambridge: Cambridge University Press.

Tulving, E., and Madigan, S. A. 1970. Memory and verbal learning. *Annual Review of Psychology* 21:437–484.

University of Chicago School of Mathematics Project. 1990. *Everyday mathematics.* Chicago.

Van Haneghan, J. P., Barron, L., Young, M. F., Williams, S. M., Vye, N. J., and Bransford, J. D. 1992. The Jasper series: An experiment with new ways to enhance mathematical thinking. In D. F. Halpern, ed., *Enhancing thinking skills in the sciences and mathematics,* 15–38. Hillsdale, NJ: Erlbaum.

VanLehn, K., and Brown, J. S. 1980. Planning nets: A representation for formalizing analogies and semantic models of procedural skills. In R. E. Snow, P. Federico, and W. Montague, eds., *Aptitude, learning and instruction* 2:95–137. Hillsdale, NJ: Erlbaum.

Voss, J., and Means, M. 1992. Invitations to thinking II: Upping the ante. Paper presented at the annual meeting of the Cognitive Studies for Educational Practice Program. Stanford, November.

Vygotsky, L. S. 1978. *Mind in society: The development of higher psychological processes.* J. Cole, V. John-Steiner, S. Scribner, and E. Souberman, eds. and trans. Cambridge: Harvard University Press.

Wagner, R. K., and Sternberg, R. J. 1985. Practical intelligence in real-world pursuits: The role of tacit knowledge. *Journal of Personality and Social Psychology* 49:436–458.

Weinstein, C., and Palmer, D. 1988. *Learning and study skills inventory.* Clearwater, FL: H. & H.

Weinstein, C. E., and Underwood, V. L. 1985. Learning strategies: The how of learning. In J. W. Segal, S. F. Chipman, and R. Glaser. *Thinking and learning skills.* Vol. 1, *Relating instruction to research,* 241–258. Hillsdale, NJ: Erlbaum.

Wertsch, J. V. 1991. *Voices of the mind: A sociocultural approach to mediated action.* Cambridge: Harvard University Press.

Whitehead, A. N. 1916. *The aims of education.* Address to the British Mathematical Society, Manchester, England.

Williams, S. M., Bransford, J. D., Vye, N. J., Goldman, S. R., and Carlson, K. 1992. Positive and negative effects of specific knowledge on mathematical problem solving. Paper presented at the annual meeting of the American Educational Research Association, San Francisco, April.

Williams, S. M., Bransford, J. D., Vye, N. J., Goldman, S. R., and Hmelo, C. E. 1993. Using an anchored computer simulation to facilitate qualitative reasoning in mathematics. Paper presented at the annual meeting of the American Educational Research Association, Atlanta, April.

Wineburg, S. S. 1991. Historical problem solving: A study of the cognitive processes used in the evaluation of documentary and pictorial evidence. *Journal of Educational Psychology* 83:73–87.

Winograd, P., and Gaskins, R. W. 1992. Metacognition: Matters of the mind, matters of the heart. In A. L. Costra, J. Bellanca, and R. Fogarty, eds. *If mind matters: A forward to the future* 1:225–238. Palatine, IL: Skylight.

Winograd, P., and Paris, S. G. 1988. A cognitive and motivational agenda for reading instruction. *Educational Leadership* 46:30–36.

Wittrock, M. C. 1986. Students' thought processes. In M. C. Wittrock, ed., *Handbook of research on teaching,* 3d ed., 297–314. New York: Macmillan.

Wixson, K. K., and Lipson, M. Y. 1991. Perspectives on reading disability research. In R. Barr, M. L. Kamil, P. Mosenthal, and P. D. Pearson, eds., *Handbook of reading research* 2:539–570. New York: Longman.

Wood, D., and Middleton, D. 1975. A study of assisted problem-solving. *British Journal of Psychology* 66:181–191.

Wong, B. Y. L. 1985. Self-questioning instructional research: A review. *Review of Educational Research* 55:227–268.

Wundt, W. 1980. Selected texts from the writing of Wilhelm Wundt. In R. W. Rieber, ed., *Wilhelm Wundt and the making of a scientific psychology.* New York: Plenum Press.

Yerkes, R. 1921. Psychological examining in the United States Army. *Mem. National Academy of Sciences* 15.

Zeitz, C. M. 1989. *Expert-novice differences in memory and analysis of literary and non-literary texts.* Technical Report 89-1, Department of Cognitive and Linguistic Sciences. August.

Zimmerman, B. J. 1989. A social-cognitive view of self-regulated academic learning. *Journal of Educational Psychology* 81: 329–229.

Zimmerman, B. J. 1990. Self-regulated learning and academic achievement: An overview. *Educational Psychologist* 25:3–17.

Index